CHILDREN AS CHANGE MAKERS

Unleashing Children's *Real* Philanthropic Power

Alison Body

First published in Great Britain in 2024 by

Policy Press, an imprint of
Bristol University Press
University of Bristol
1–9 Old Park Hill
Bristol
BS2 8BB
UK
t: +44 (0)117 374 6645
e: bup-info@bristol.ac.uk

Details of international sales and distribution partners are available at policy.bristoluniversitypress.co.uk

British Library Cataloguing in Publication Data
A catalogue record for this book is available from the British Library

ISBN 978-1-4473-6577-8 hardcover
ISBN 978-1-4473-6567-9 ePub
ISBN 978-1-4473-6568-6 ePdf

Cover design: Lyn Davies Design
Front cover image: Alamy/Tim Gainey
Bristol University Press and Policy Press use environmentally responsible print partners.
Printed and bound in Great Britain by CPI Group (UK) Ltd, Croydon, CR0 4YY

FSC
www.fsc.org
MIX
Paper | Supporting
responsible forestry
FSC® C013604

To my sons – Iden and Quinlan

May you always have the strength, wisdom, courage and conviction, to speak truth to power

Contents

List of case studies

About the author

Alison Body is Senior Lecturer in Philanthropic Studies and Social Policy at the Centre for Philanthropy, University of Kent. She started her career in 2001 working in children and youth charities, specialising in early intervention services and advocating for children's participation rights. Her experience includes leading a large children's charity, strategic development of the third sector, fundraising and volunteer management. In 2008, she joined Kent County Council as a Commissioner of Early Intervention Services. Driven by these experiences, she completed her PhD at the University of Kent in 2016, exploring the relationship between children's charities and the state. After working at Canterbury Christ Church University between 2015 and 2017 as a Faculty Director in the School of Childhood and Education Sciences, she joined the University of Kent staff team in January 2019.

She has written numerous research articles and reports exploring philanthropy and the third sector, particularly in relation to children, young people and education. In line with her interest in the intersection between the third sector and state, her publications cover topics such as youth participation, voluntary action in primary education, fundraising in schools, co-production of public services and most recently children's perceptions and experiences of charity and charitable giving. Her first book, *Children's Charities in Crisis: Early Intervention and the State* (Body, 2020), explored the impact of austerity on children's charities.

As a result of her passion about the natural world, she, along with her husband Tom, is one of the founding Directors of Led by the Wild CIC, a community conservation and environmental education organisation supporting children, young people and communities to positively and proactively engage in nature restoration, while reaping the health, wellbeing and educational benefits of the natural world. Led by the Wild supports hundreds of children, young people and individuals every year to explore, cultivate and celebrate their eco-citizenship.

Acknowledgements

To my colleagues at the University of Kent – thank you first to those at the Centre for Philanthropy: Emma Beeston, Beth Breeze, Rhodri Davies, Stephanie Haydon, Emily Lau, Lucy Lowthian, Claire Routley, Weinan Wang and Karl Wilding. A second thank you to colleagues from across the university I either worked with or alongside and who have influenced this journey, including Kate Bradley, Lindsey Cameron, Jack Cunliffe, Eddy Hogg, Eleanor Jupp, Jeremy Kendall, Derek Kirton, Kate Ludlow, Dawn Lyon, David Nettleingham, Carolyn Pedwell, Sweta Ranjan-Rankin and Iain Wilkinson to name but a few. Thank you all for the debate, the support, the challenge and the good humour. Your work, our discussions and our debates have helped shape my thinking and this book. I am proud to be part of such a team of people, each advocating for a better world.

To my colleagues beyond the walls of the University of Kent, those who inspire me daily: Jon Dean, Angela Eikenberry, Angela Ellis-Paine, Lee Jerome, Jayne Lacny, Rob Macmillan, Andy Mycock, Sevasti-Melissa Nolas, Andrew Peterson, James Rees, plus many, many more. Thank you for your voice, your scholarship and your friendship.

To my comrades from across the children and youth sector, not limited to but including Stella Baynes, Meg Henry, Ashley Hodges, Fozia Irfan, Isaac Jones, Bridget Kohner, Rania Marandos, Miranda McKearney, Keren Mitchell, Liz Moorse, Amy Neugebauer, Jo Rich and Louisa Searle. Thank you for sharing your skills and wisdom and making this work worthwhile. Thank you for doing amazing things to bring about change in the world and make it a better place. I am and remain forever grateful that you turn up and fight the good fight daily.

To my best of friends, Becky, Emily and Katy, and my co-directors and wonderful friends who help bring the ideas in this book into reality through our shared endeavour of Led by the Wild, Claire, Eric, Tom and Sara – you have all listened to me good-naturedly whittle on about this book for so long. Thank you for your patience, love and support!

To my parents Karen and Bob, there are few words which can express my gratitude for your neverending love and support – even if we do disagree about politics sometimes! I cherish your wisdom, your compassion, your kindness and your guidance.

To my husband Tom and our boys, Iden and Quinlan. You three are my absolute everything, thank you for all your wonderful support, cups of tea and welcome distractions. And more than anything, thank you for keeping me grounded and always feeling loved in a sometimes scary world.

And a very last thank you to my faithful, completely adored, home-office companions who have got me through writing this book – my wonderful, hairy lurchers, Holly and Lily. You have kept me company every single day, kept my feet warm and provided the one sure convincing reason to leave the desk for regular walks!

Introduction

In a world both fraught with challenges and rich in opportunities, which relies on the collective action of its citizens to positively progress, a group of powerful philanthropic actors who can help to achieve transformative change have been consistently overlooked: our children.

Philanthropy plays a fundamental role in civil society, with children and young people globally being one of the most common beneficiaries of philanthropic gifts. Yet children's voices are all too often absent from philanthropic conversations and decision making. We frequently ignore their role as current social actors and, importantly, as active members of the philanthropic ecosystem. Throughout the pages of this book, I argue why it is not only important that we start to take children's philanthropic engagement more seriously, but also that is vital if we are to achieve a more just, equitable society which works for all.

Philanthropy – 'the love of humankind', 'good will to others', 'voluntary action for social good' – why would anyone take issue with such a notion? Nonetheless, it is a concept which attracts a great deal of scrutiny, debate and indeed criticism, often associated with ideas of power, influence and privilege. I don't dismiss these criticisms; indeed, I think these debates within philanthropy are important, necessary and healthy. However, I worry that within this scrutiny and common focus on big philanthropy, we have lost sight of what to me is a more central, uniting and unifying debate: what does it mean to be philanthropic and why does this matter? In this book I present our philanthropic behaviours as acts of citizenship, showing the importance of our everyday participation in philanthropic decision making and linking this to social justice, acts of participation and democracy. I argue that our philanthropic actions should not be solely tied to the personal sphere, as is so often the case, but instead should be understood through a lens of participation and indeed collective action, alongside our moral obligation and responsibility to others as fellow citizens. In essence, our philanthropic self should be a central consideration of our citizenship. So, I have come to spend much of my time considering the act of philanthropy through this lens of citizenship, and something I have termed 'philanthropic citizenship'.

Embedded in ideas of compassion and active kindness, philanthropic citizenship is a dimension of citizenship behaviour associated with intentions and actions, such as volunteering, social action, charitable giving and activism, that aim to produce social and/or environmental benefit. I argue that a core principle of philanthropic citizenship learning moves beyond ideas of conventional and traditional charity, instead embracing a richer understanding of giving and voluntary action which includes a justice mentality, where individuals are encouraged to critically explore and engage with the wider issues which sit behind charity, and explore alternative responses, such as collective action, advocacy and campaigning (Body, 2024).

Therefore, in this book I turn a critical eye to the way in which we share power, on the constraints and confines we employ as we socialise children into the philanthropic ecosystems, and on the stories we tell them (and ourselves!) about what it means to be a good citizen. This book is about how we as a society, including civil society organisations, critically question our own modes of operation, systems and structures in order to support children unleash their real philanthropic power – *as they see fit, not as we determine.*

We can all enact our rights as philanthropic citizens and much of what I discuss in this book could probably be ascribed to wider society more generally. Nonetheless, I am particularly interested in how we socialise our children into what we consider 'good' philanthropic behaviours, teaching them to be charitable, to be advocates, to be allies, to help others and to take action when they see, feel or experience injustice. However, as I argue throughout this book, for too long philanthropic behaviours have largely been discussed within the private and personal sphere. Children are regularly taught to volunteer, to give and to fundraise, and even while some of the actions happen en masse, such as national fundraising campaigns, it is less frequent that they are taught to connect these personal actions to wider notions of collective action, advocacy, activism and social justice. Indeed, children's philanthropic behaviours are more often wrapped up in ideas of civic duty, service and virtue than they are connected to these more progressive, socially just oriented notions. In this book I seek to challenge this and present a model of children's philanthropic citizenship, rooted in real-life examples, and lived experiences that seeks to encourage children and young people to imagine new ways of being, and consider how these new ways of being may become a lived, shared reality.

I write this book primarily as an academic, former children's services commissioner and youth worker, drawing together years of research and experience of working with and for children and young people, and with those organisations working hard to support them. Nonetheless, like most of us, my professional self is never wholly separated from the rest of my identity. Therefore, I also write it as a mother who wants a fair, equitable, safe, just and sustainable world for her children, where they can practise their active citizenship within a just and compassionate, democratic society; as a school governor who strongly believes an education centred around social justice is vital in achieving this; and as director of a community conservation organisation passionate about engaging children in the ecological wonders our world has to offer, alongside the challenges it faces.

In short, this book is based on a simple premise – that a fair and just world requires an active and thriving civil society. Now while we may debate exactly what a thriving civil society looks like, the idea of this being a central facet of democracy remains a constant across democratic political spheres. Thus, I want to explore and question how our children and young people become engaged in this civil society as philanthropic actors, what opportunities are afforded to them and how messages about what it means to be an active philanthropic citizen are framed and presented.

The argument in this book

Traditional views of philanthropy are often separated between mere acts of charity and the pursuit of true social justice. This dichotomy places charity as something practised by the many, while reserving the label of 'philanthropist' for the privileged few. In this setup, the wealthy elite hold considerable sway in defining what justice entails, leaving most people – those who are most intimately familiar with injustice – to occupy the roles of everyday givers to and recipients of charity. In the following chapters, drawing on extensive research, I show how this is the world of philanthropy we inadvertently cultivate for our children, teaching them that philanthropic power resides with the select few rather than the collective voices of the masses. But what if we flipped the script? What if the power was vested in the voices of the many rather than the few, and philanthropy played a key role in making this shift happen?

While there is a lot to be celebrated across our extraordinary world, societies and communities, we are also facing unprecedented challenges, and it often feels like we are not moving quickly enough in the right direction. Our children are growing up facing unparalleled challenges from economies collapsing, infringements of human rights, increasing poverty, rising mental health issues and climate catastrophe. In the face of these challenges, I argue that it is vital that civil society, voluntary sector organisations and educators seek to empower, support and facilitate children and young people to have a voice and take action, as they see fit, in terms of how the world (both locally and globally) tackles these problems. This is by no means suggesting that we shift the responsibility for these issues onto their shoulders (they are our crosses to bear and we must bear them seriously), but we must also include children in the problem solving, as they are likely to be the ones who feel the greatest impacts of our actions – or indeed our inaction.

While there has been increasing discourse about philanthropy for justice, this book aims to highlight how we continue to cultivate children as philanthropic citizens within a framework that confines their actions to the realm of charity rather than justice. An exclusive emphasis on charity encourages our children to give and address social problems at an individualistic and reactive level, without delving into the historical and current factors that perpetuate oppressive circumstances for communities and individuals. Moreover, it reinforces the idea of rewarding benevolence, glossing over the deeply political aspects of conversations about injustice and inequality. This approach does little to challenge ongoing, persistent cycles of inequality and inequity. Our children are introduced to and conditioned within narrow definitions of philanthropic citizenship, which are bounded by notions of civic duty, virtue and service.

The ideas put forward in this book suggest a profound shift towards a framework of justice – one that actively involves children and young people not only in the practice of philanthropic actions as one way in which to address societal issues, but also in critically questioning the very nature of philanthropy itself. Throughout these pages, the aim is not to undermine the value of benevolence; indeed, the virtues that underlie charitable acts are crucial. Rather, the argument here is that teaching philanthropy solely as an act of benevolence falls short. It stifles children's voices and excludes them from the broader discourse about their own lived experiences. By supporting and engaging children in philanthropy within a framework of justice, we create room to challenge prevailing attitudes, beliefs, and policies – and we help them (and us) to create a fairer society for all.

Empowering children as philanthropic citizens should not confine them to the realm of benevolence alone. Instead, it should be a space where alongside expressing generosity and kindness, we can also support them to actively and critically question social divisions and institutional policies that propagate and sustain inequality.

Philanthropy as participation

In an era defined by mounting global challenges, philanthropy is commonly called upon as a powerful force for positive change, offering a potential beacon of hope in the face of entrenched injustice and escalating climate crises. However, philanthropy is widely debated, deeply contested and rarely straightforward (this will be explored in greater detail throughout this book), so defining what it is may be a tougher ask than we first thought. Nonetheless, what I will do, which may be helpful to you the reader, is to be clear about what I mean by 'philanthropy' in this book.

Robert Payton and Michael Moody have long defined philanthropy 'as voluntary action for the public good' (Payton and Moody, 2008). I largely subscribe to the breadth and looseness of this definition as it encompasses many things, including the voluntary giving of time, money, goods and connections. We often shorten this to time, talent, treasure and ties. Furthermore, it includes the idea of voluntary association, which is organised activity, without which most voluntary giving and service wouldn't occur or, even if it did occur, might well be ineffective. These activities will look different in different cultural contexts, different societies and different global contexts, but nonetheless almost everyone will have a connection to philanthropy in one way or another, be it through mutual aid in the community to benefiting from medical breakthroughs funded by philanthropic efforts. It is both a tangible and intangible web of activity which is embedded in all our lives, meshing communities together locally, regionally and globally.

Nonetheless, philanthropy itself is a contested concept (Daly, 2012) and can be seen by many as inherently problematic. While proponents of philanthropy promote its positive, transformative effects on society, with the ability to offer alternative solutions and ways of being outside or alongside the role of government (see Breeze, 2021), critics point out that many manifestations of it can be considered counterintuitive to democracy and social justice (see McGoey, 2015; Reich, 2018; Vallely, 2020). And while we may be tempted to dismiss these concerns as criticisms more related to what is referred to as 'big' philanthropy, where celebration and concerns are expressed as the uber-wealthy are able to wield power through philanthropic efforts, political theorist Emma Saunders-Hastings (2022) warns us that this is too simplistic a view. Central to Saunders-Hastings' argument is that philanthropy, in all shapes and forms, produces relational inequality through the creation of 'objectionably hierarchical social and political relationships' within which the donor is assumed to have better knowledge of recipients' needs and interests than the recipients themselves. She continues to argue that democracy is always a preferable way in which to address societal needs and that democracy is a system which respects individuals' status as equals, while philanthropy involves the wealthy and privileged exercising influence over social and political outcomes, normally in ways which are beneficial to them and/or their own worldview. In this book, I argue that the prevailing methods of socialising children as philanthropic citizens are heavily influenced by these market-oriented values. These values are rooted in conservative theories of poverty and need, framing philanthropy as a virtuous and benevolent endeavour. This perspective often attributes the causes of suffering to individual characteristics or cultural traits, promoting a top-down approach to addressing issues and prioritising the interests of donors, over the communities they seek to serve (Herro and Obeng-Odoom, 2019).

Thus, in this book I want to talk about how I would like to flip the focus and consider the everyday philanthropic actions by the rest of us, and particularly children and young people, and how these can become more aligned with democratic principles and collective action. I want to talk about children dropping a pound in a pot, volunteering to do a litter pick or leading a campaign for social change. And I want to talk about the decisions we make when we embody philanthropy as part of our citizenship, what type of citizenship are we embodying, and how we then behave towards others.

I want to talk about philanthropic actions as part of a collective responses to social inequality and unfairness, and as part of mobilising social change. Most importantly I want to talk about this from the viewpoint of children and young people.

For me, one of the most welcome books of recent years was Lucy Bernholz's *How We Give Now: A Philanthropic Guide for the Rest of Us* (2021). What I particularly liked about this book was, as the title suggests, the focus on the philanthropic behaviours by the rest us, not the rich, not the famous and not the 1 per cent. I leave those many debates of both criticism and defence to my many more worthy academic and professional peers within the field of philanthropic studies. Indeed, big philanthropy is interesting and important of course, as was highlighted earlier; nevertheless, it is also often imbued with power, inherently undemocratic, 'sways systems meant to serve – and be governed by – all people' (Bernholz, 2021: 5) and inaccessible to the vast majority of us, especially children and young people. Furthermore, these debates on big philanthropy both ignore how we come to learn our own giving and civic behaviours, and indeed ignore the giving behaviours of most of the global population – that is, the rest of us! Therefore, the focus in this book is on how children and young people interpret and practise their philanthropic behaviours in everyday life.

Bernholz's book focuses on philanthropy as an act of participation. This participation happens every single day, by pretty much every single one of us, including children and young people, in one way or another. It is not exclusive for the privileged and wealthy – it's something we can all participate in, regardless of wealth, privilege and background, as an expression about the world we want to see, what we value and what we view as our moral obligations to others. We can enact this participation through the giving of our time, talent, treasure and our ties, but what is the most powerful is when these everyday individual actions come together as collective action and collective voices – then they can change the world.

Philanthropic citizenship (I will expand on this notion in Chapter 1) is simply one expression of our citizenship, but for children and young people who are too commonly excluded from political and decision-making processes, it becomes a very important aspect of that citizenship, as it is one of their only modes of political expression. It is an expression of their voice, agency and power, which they can wield without waiting until they reach a certain age or are permitted to by adults (although, as I will explore throughout this book, all too often, adults control and indeed manipulate this arena). It is their way of articulating the type of world they want to imagine, and a space in which they can imagine different ways of being. Thus, what this book does do is attempt to consider how we as civil society can support children to wield their own philanthropic power as allies.

Overview of the book

In this book I draw together over ten years of academic research into children, young people and charities, and over 20 years of working with and on behalf of children and young people. While I mainly focus on England and the UK, I also draw on examples and learning from across the globe demonstrating the universality of these arguments, particularly within Western democracies. This book is divided into three core parts.

Part I, which includes Chapters 1 and 2, sets out the concept of philanthropic citizenship and positions this in wider debates on philanthropy, education, social justice, children's rights and contemporary political debates. In Chapter 1, I consider how children's philanthropic citizenship is framed in contemporary society. I argue that we need to shift our focus from a virtue orientated framing to one of justice. Chapter 2 considers some of the wider conversations which impact children's rights as philanthropic citizens, including the debate as to whether children are viewed as 'becoming' or 'being' citizens in their own rights, the rise of a character education agenda across Western democracies with its individualistic, neoliberal focus, and the narrowing of spaces for protest, advocacy and activism. Here I argue that these shifting landscapes are narrowing the spaces in which children can express their voice and collectively imagine new ways of being.

Part II, comprising Chapters 3–9, considers philanthropic citizenship in action. This is the main thrust of the whole book, discussing how individuals, institutions, communities and civil society organisations can both help and hinder children as change makers, both as current and future citizens. Throughout this part, I refer to examples to exemplify points. I have also invited various organisations to share their work here in the form of case studies, which sit in separate text boxes and provide examples of organisations trying to think differently in this space, actively helping children and young people to unleash their real philanthropic power.

Chapter 3 kicks off this part by considering the role of kindness and family within this conversation. Drawing on research and examples, such as the YouTube star MrBeast, while acknowledging kindness is important, here I argue that it should be the gateway to considering ideas of justice rather than as an end in itself. Chapters 4 and 5 both focus on children fundraising, with Chapter 4 arguing for a more children's rights-oriented approach to contemporary fundraising practices, and Chapter 5 considering the issue of how particular child fundraisers are exemplified as exceptional in the media and public discourses. Here I contend that when children conform to virtuous modes of philanthropy, which are characterised by unquestioned notions of the good citizen and civic duty, media and societal discourses celebrate them as current and future heroes. When children move outside these bounded notions of citizenship in their philanthropic actions, when they challenge the status quo, the narratives become much more complex and problematic.

Chapters 6 and 7 consider some of the more traditional and formal spaces wherein children learn 'how' to be philanthropic. Chapter 6 focuses on the role of schools, highlighting how most schools frame philanthropic giving as an act of benevolence, often taught in transactional, individualistic ways. Co-authored with Amy Neugebauer, CEO of The Giving Square based in the US, we consider how schools may be able to approach these ideas differently. Chapter 7 focuses on the role of uniformed groups, such as the Scouts. At this point I explore how conservative understandings of what it means to be a good citizen are exemplified and reinforced within this space, and both the potential strengths and issues with that, considering alternative approaches, such as the Woodcraft Folk. Chapters 8 and 9 move us into a different conversation by focusing more on children engaging in community organising, protesting and activism. In Chapter 8 I consider the role of the child as a political being, the role of organisations, such as Citizens UK in supporting children to campaign, children's role throughout history in leading change and children's rights to protest. Chapter 9 focuses on children's engagement in the environmental movement, and the wins, the setbacks and the narratives surrounding their agency as eco-citizens.

Part III concludes the book, considering the impact and possibilities, drawing on the discussed data and evidence in the previous parts and positioning this in the wider academic literature. Chapter 10 considers the ways in which we – meaning all of us who are part of the philanthropic ecosystem, from individuals in communities, charity leaders and philanthropic funders to researchers and practitioners – can share power and encourage a philanthropic ecosystem which is framed by justice, solidarity and collective action. Finally, the concluding Chapter 11 draws together the key arguments and considers what next in terms of helping to cultivate and empower a kinder and more compassionate world which recognises the importance of social and environmental justice, and collective action.

PART I

Concepts, theory and politics

1

Philanthropic citizenship: a new mindset

Introduction

In this chapter I argue that the prevalent political and educational narratives involving children and young people's philanthropic behaviours depict philanthropy as an embodiment of virtues and benevolence. While such approaches to philanthropy underscore individual habits and concern for others, they fall short in terms of enabling children to contemplate or deeply engage with the systemic challenges underpinning social issues. This constrains children's growth as philanthropic citizens. Consequently, in this chapter I advocate for an approach that embraces transformative, critically engaged, social justice-oriented philanthropy, which involves probing systemic issues and advocating for collective action.

Across the globe, children and young people frequently demonstrate various forms of philanthropic behaviour, both formal and informal, such as fundraising, contributing to food banks and participating in community clean-up efforts. Indeed, nonprofits long-term sustainability relies on the proactive engagement of younger participants (Gorczyca and Hartman, 2017). Apart from providing invaluable support to numerous deserving causes, the objective is to instil in children enduring 'habits' of giving and civic engagement that will persist throughout their lives. Unsurprisingly, families, schools and communities expend considerable effort to bolster the development of children's philanthropic behaviours as an integral part of their citizenship and civic participation (Body et al, 2020, 2022). We commonly refer to this as 'philanthropic citizenship', which is defined as 'a dimension of civic engagement associated with intentions and actions that intend to produce public benefit, for example, volunteering, social action, charitable giving, advocacy, and activism' (Body, 2024). While there is an extensive body of literature on philanthropy and civic engagement among adolescents and adults (Barrett and Pachi, 2019), it is widely acknowledged that there is a lack of substantive critical discourse and deliberation concerning the civic socialisation and philanthropic education of younger children (Body et al, 2020). Conversely, educational, social and psychological theory and research consistently emphasise middle childhood and the primary school years (covering those aged 4–11) as pivotal in shaping the development and normalisation of civic, social and political behaviours (Feinstein and Bynner, 2004; van Deth et al, 2011; Peterson, 2016).

This chapter, drawing on multidisciplinary literature from philanthropy, education, child development, psychology and philosophy, is structured as follows. First, I explore the research on how children's philanthropic behaviours are cultivated, emphasising middle childhood as pivotal for developing enduring prosocial behaviour. Next, I delve into the essence of philanthropy, drawing on philosophical foundations. Here I consider the role of 'moral content' (Schervish, 2014), 'moral virtues' (Martin, 1994) and 'moral creativity' (Nussbaum, 1998) in cultivating children's philanthropic citizenship. Through this lens I scrutinise dominant Western approaches to nurturing philanthropic citizens from a young age, critiquing their focus on character virtues, neoliberal models and benevolent orientation. Finally, I consider the possibilities of philanthropic citizenship through the lens of critical citizenship education in order to deliver a more nuanced, rights-oriented, activist approach to engaging children in philanthropy as current donors, beneficiaries and active social actors within the philanthropic ecosystem, practically considering some of the core components of philanthropic citizenship. The chapter concludes with a discussion arguing for a justice-oriented approach to philanthropic citizenship and considers what next for this important yet overlooked area of research and practice.

Cultivating children's philanthropic civic behaviours

In August 2020, six year-old Ayaan and Mikaeel, supported by their community, raised more than £100,000 for the Yemen crisis (*BBC News*, 2021b). The crisis, which resulted in tens of thousands of deaths, left an estimated 24 million people – equivalent to 80 per cent of the country's population – in need of humanitarian aid to survive. According to the United Nations International Children's Emergency Fund (UNICEF), the scale of this crisis was the largest in the world. Moved by this, the best friends from Redbridge, East London, set up a lemonade stand to raise funds because they wanted to help. In this story and countless others throughout this book, we witness the power, will and passion of children and young people as change makers, as proactive, powerful citizens within their own rights, wanting to make positive changes in the world. This is just one example of philanthropic action by children, and while impressive in scale, it is important to say from the outset that the 'size' of the impact is not the focus here; it is the intention by children to do something positive in the world, to make a change to help others and to put into action a sense of voluntary action for public good – in short, to be philanthropic (see Body, 2024).

I will start here by considering some of the established research on cultivating children's philanthropic behaviours. Understanding the intricate interplay of situational factors with children's socialisation is essential for comprehending the multifaceted mechanisms that influence philanthropic behaviours. For example, Silke et al (2018) highlight the significance of various factors such as parental giving, involvement with charities and exposure to media campaigns in shaping children's inclinations towards giving. Furthermore, peer attitudes and participation in charitable activities within school and community settings significantly influence children's attitudes towards giving (Agard, 2002; Adriani and Sonderegger, 2009; Leimgruber et al, 2012). Although increased parental giving behaviours do not always directly translate into higher levels of giving from children (Eisenberg-Berg, 1979; Ottoni-Wilhelm et al, 2017, 2013), there exists evidence of a correlation between parental and their adult children's giving behaviours (Wilhelm et al, 2008). Peer influence also plays a crucial role, as children often adjust their giving decisions due to peer pressure (Leimgruber et al, 2012; Wildeboer et al, 2017).

Additionally, several sociocognitive and socioemotional factors support the development and manifestation of prosocial and civic behaviours – behaviours aimed at assisting others. During the initial five years of childhood, characterised by rapid brain growth (OECD, 2019), learning and development are of paramount importance (Schleicher, 2019; Spiteri, 2020; UNICEF, 2020). Warneken and Tomasello's (2009) experimental study with children aged 14–18 months indicates that even at this young age, children display innate altruism, demonstrating a willingness to help others without expecting any rewards, driven by an intrinsic desire to assist them in achieving their goals. They suggest that 'children start out as rather indiscriminate altruists who become more selective as they grow older' (Warneken and Tomasello, 2009, p 466). Moreover, Wörle and Paulus (2018) conducted experiments exploring children's normative expectations regarding the fair distribution of resources, revealing that notions of philanthropy, such as charity and giving, are deeply ingrained norms in children as young as three to six years old. Older children, particularly those aged five to six, exhibit a heightened inclination towards ensuring a fair allocation of resources, showing a preference for aiding those perceived as less affluent within experimental settings.

An increasing number of psychologists have underscored the underlying role of emotions such as empathy, sympathy and guilt, and cognitive developments such as perspective taking in children's prosociality and civic engagement (Eisenberg-Berg, 1979; Eisenberg and Miller, 1987; Eisenberg et al, 2006; Sierksma et al, 2014). They each emphasise middle childhood (approximately between the ages of 6 and 11) as a critical period for the development of prosocial reasoning in children, during which children become more adept at understanding and evaluating the moral dimensions of social situations. Furthermore, studies suggest that without proactive engagement in civic learning, children can develop discriminatory and prejudiced worldviews from a young age (Ramsay, 2008; Oberman et al, 2012).

Psychological research and child development theories provide evidence that children's empathy, sympathy and perspective-taking skills begin to develop around the age of four and progress with encouragement, becoming more advanced during middle childhood (Weller and Lagattuta, 2013; Ongley et al, 2014). Numerous scholars have meticulously traced the trajectory of children's cognitive development, with Theory of Mind emerging as a pivotal cognitive capability. This involves understanding that other individuals possess distinct thoughts, beliefs, desires and intentions, which may differ from our own (Lecce et al, 2014). Throughout their schooling years, children progressively refine their Theory of Mind abilities, using them to navigate intricate social scenarios with greater sophistication. Empirical investigations support the notion that as children mature, their proficiency in discerning beliefs and perspectives amplifies, and they adeptly apply these skills across diverse contexts and scenarios (Lecce et al, 2014). Notably, their capacity extends to accurately assessing one person's beliefs regarding the intentions of others (Miller, 2009), as well as employing a greater frequency of mental state terminology to describe social behaviours (Meins et al, 2006). For instance, Paulus and Moore (2012) suggest that prosocial behaviours, such as comforting and helping, are evident early in life, and their frequency and complexity increase during the primary school years. Studies examining sharing tendencies indicate that while three to four and seven to eight year olds are willing to share items such as toys and food, the number of children who share and the quantity of resources they give increases with age and positive reinforcement (Fehr et al, 2008).

Within the educational context, research suggests that children are eager to engage in philanthropic and civic behaviours (Body et al, 2020; Lau and Body, 2021; Power and Smith, 2016). Such findings are consistent with UK-based studies involving young adolescents, including those at the upper end of primary school age, which indicate children's positive attitudes towards charity, with high expectations of charities and civic action to address social issues (CAF, 2013; Power and Taylor, 2018). Finally, several studies highlight the significant level of political and civic literacy in younger children (van Deth et al, 2011; Götzmann, 2015; Abendschön and Tausendpfund, 2017). Van Deth et al's (2011) panel study involving 700 children in Germany during their initial year of school (aged six to seven) also challenges the conventional notion that adolescence is the primary period for cultivating political and civic orientations. Their research reveals that these orientations take shape much earlier, as young children exhibit the ability to articulate political opinions and attitudes, showcasing fundamental political knowledge and orientations essential for active political engagement (van Deth et al, 2011). This underscores middle childhood as a pivotal phase for both civic and philanthropic education, necessitating increased academic and practical attention (Dias and Menezes, 2014).

A virtuous approach to philanthropy

Payton and Moody (2008) acknowledge that our understanding of philanthropy is often informally and haphazardly learned from family, church and tradition, resulting in a limited perspective. However, they argue that philanthropy should be taken seriously, urging a critical exploration of its problems, possibilities and opportunities. Additionally, they propose utilising philosophical thinking about virtues to comprehend philanthropy and its implications. Human nature demonstrates a range of virtues and vices, but shared language binds us in terms of recognising positive virtues, such as kindness, generosity, honesty and integrity. In Wright et al's (2020) work, virtues are defined as enduring, well-grounded character traits that are consistently expressed in a diverse array of situations, driven by appropriate motivations.

Schervish (2006, 2014) and Martin (1994) advocate for virtuous approaches to philanthropy rooted in Aristotle's philosophy. Schervish frames philanthropy within a 'moral citizenship of care' framework, emphasising the importance of caring for others in society. He views morality as an essential dimension of human interaction, highlighting that philanthropy should be supply-led, responding to the needs of others with empathy and concern. Schervish views morality in this light as 'an essential organic dimension of human interaction, in general, not something imposed from the outside and a way of thinking, feeling, and acting in the light of goals, desires, aspirations and purposes' (2014, p 390). Accordingly, Schervish presents the notion of the moral biography, which is the way in which individuals carry out agency. This agency is enacted through two elements. The first of these is the implementation of capacities, which are a collection of the resources we control, and include all forms of capital or wealth that individuals possess, such as status in society, skills and financial resources. Within children, such capacities may be their knowledge, their lived experiences or a utilisation of their rights as represented by the United Nations Convention on the Rights of the Child (UNCRC) (see Chapter 2). The second element is purpose, which is the resolve to which we apply these capacities. Nonetheless, while children may easily have this resolve (see Body et al, 2021), they are largely dependent on the adults within their sphere to be able to put this resolve into action. As Schervish summarises, 'philanthropy is the response to affective demand such that donors directly fulfil the needs of others simply because they are people in need' (2014, p 396).

Similarly, Martin (1994, 2012) combines this idea of care and capacities with action, viewing philanthropic actions as an act or activity, built on many widely recognised moral virtues, including generosity, compassion, courage, fairness, integrity and so on (Martin, 1994). In this sense, virtues are considered as traits of 'character', providing individuals with 'morally desirable ways of relating to people, practices, and communities' (Martin, 1994, p 5). Virtuous philanthropy aims to cultivate nurturing relationships and relies on these compassionate behaviours. Martin (1994) identifies a total of 30 philanthropic virtues, which he divides into two broad and overlapping categories: participation virtues and enabling virtues. Participation virtues, including benevolence, justice, reciprocity, enlightened cherishing and self-affirmation, centre on inspiring acts of generosity and giving. Enabling virtues provide the moral resources for effectively pursuing philanthropic actions – for example, respect for others, self-direction and moral leadership (1994, p 5). It is the combination of these virtues put into philanthropic action which, he argues, 'provides a forum for moral creativity, for putting our version of a good society into practice, and for fostering caring relationships that enrich individuals and communities alike' (1994, p 172). Therefore, Martin argues that giving is not just a matter of fulfilling a moral obligation, but can also be a source of personal fulfilment and happiness (Martin, 2012). According to him, giving can promote what he calls 'virtuous cycles' of happiness, where the act of giving leads to positive emotions and social connections, which in turn motivate further giving and enhance wellbeing. Giving children opportunities to develop these virtues is essential, as it fosters caring relationships and contributes to personal fulfilment and happiness.

Within both Schervish's and Martin's approaches, being a good philanthropic citizen is framed around a sense of individual virtues, care, moral obligations and benevolence. Indeed, it is difficult to argue with the concept of virtues per se, most people would agree that being kind, generous, compassionate, honest and so on are good things within democratic societies. However, *how* these actions are orientated matters. A benevolent orientation focuses on addressing need through sympathy, gifting time, money and/or efforts to those in need to alleviate suffering, and has less focus on questioning of structural and systemic factors that contribute towards inequality and equity, paying little attention to systemic change and policy reform (Louis et al, 2019). Therefore, a focus on individual virtues can suggest an apparent lack of concern for collective action in favour of individualistic actions, which risks overlooking systemic injustice and promoting paternalism (Power and Taylor, 2018). As Louis et al (2019, p 3) argue:

> when they come from a benevolence perspective (palliating the suffering of the needy), actors often give to individual victims without fixing root causes or systems that create suffering. When they come from an activism perspective (seeking to stand beside, and empower,

united attempts to change the system), actors often endure the suffering of present victims in a struggle to achieve future change.

This is not to suggest that benevolent and activist perspectives cannot not co-occur, but instead that benevolent respondents do not tend to engage in activism; however, those who come from an activist perspective engage in both benevolent and activist behaviours (such as political advocacy) (Louis et al, 2019).

Children's experiences of philanthropic action

Too often, benevolent perspectives alone, emphasising virtuous philanthropy, dominate the cultivation of children as philanthropic citizens. Throughout each of the chapters in Part II, I explore how different spaces and places help to cultivate children's philanthropic citizenship, primarily as an act of benevolence. For example, Chapter 6 delves into a survey of primary school teachers in England (Body et al, 2023), revealing a norm of charity and fundraising in educational spaces. Yet, this often takes an individualistic approach, lacking opportunities for collective action and discussion of issues of social justice. The emphasis is on monetary giving, with limited engagement in voluntary action or advocacy. Notably, children from more privileged backgrounds have greater access to philanthropic opportunities, potentially entrenching inequalities (Body et al, 2023). This perpetuates charity as a response to social need rather than encouraging critical examination of systemic injustices (Westheimer, 2015).

Chapters 4 and 5 explore some of my own research (Body et al, 2020) involving 150 children aged four to eight in England and their experiences of charity. The findings underscore the influence of market-oriented values, promoting giving for personal gain rather than ideals of equality and justice. Despite regular engagement in fundraising, only a small fraction of children are meaningfully informed about the causes they are asked to support, and even fewer have a say in which charities they support. This raises concerns about tokenistic giving and a lack of recognition of children's rights to participate in decisions affecting them, Imposing philanthropic decisions without critical engagement risks reducing philanthropy to a transactional process. This limits children's understanding to a narrow, funding-centric view rather than embracing the broader concept of social change advocated by nonprofits and philanthropic institutions (Body et al, 2022).

In summary, research underscores how benevolent perspectives in children's literature (see Chapter 3), education (see Chapter 6) and extracurricular activities (see Chapter 7) may inadvertently reinforce simplistic notions of philanthropy, marginalising communities and perpetuating problematic stereotypes. The prevalence of individualistic approaches to giving in schools, coupled with unequal access to philanthropic opportunities, may further entrench disparities. Additionally, the dominance of market-oriented values in children's charitable activities raises concerns about superficial giving and restricts their comprehension of philanthropy's broader capacity to drive social change.

Shifting the narrative

To move beyond virtuous philanthropy, there is a need to embrace more transformative approaches that address systemic issues and promote collective action. Encouraging children to question societal issues and participate in philanthropic activities with a focus on justice and equity can empower them to become critical and engaged citizens. When we view philanthropy as an embodied part of citizenship, we draw on wider notions of citizenship and society in our understanding of enacting philanthropy. Through this lens we can view giving as an act of participation in society, a way in which we can help shape the society we want, rather than simply respond to need (Bernholz, 2021).

The prominent philosopher Martha Nussbaum focuses on the idea of 'moral creativity' to respond to this challenge. In her book *Cultivating Humanity* she focuses on what type of citizen we need in the world to cultivate humanity where 'we recognise the worth of human life wherever it occurs and see ourselves as bound by human abilities and problems to people who lie at a great distance from us' (1998, p 9). She argues that there are three capacities which are essential to the cultivation of humanity: the capacity for critical reflection; the need for global perspectives; and the narrative imagination. These abilities need to be underpinned by knowledge and scientific understanding. In short, 'becoming an educated citizen means learning a lot of facts and reasoning. But it means something more. It means learning how to be a human being capable of love and imagination' (Nussbaum, 1998, p 14). This draws our attention towards the idea of a global citizenship lens in our understanding of philanthropy, which is underpinned by critical reflection and a sense of 'bounded humanity' which requires collective thought and action. Nussbaum argues that this kind of 'moral creativity' requires a combination of empathy, reason and imagination, and that it is essential for living a fulfilling and meaningful life. Cultivating moral creativity is good not only for individuals but also for society, as it can help to foster greater understanding, compassion and cooperation among people with different values and beliefs. However, Nussbaum also argues that the eradication of humanities and the arts from education means that students are losing 'the ability to think critically; the ability to transcend local loyalties and to approach world problems as a "citizen of the world"; and, finally, the ability to imagine sympathetically the predicament of another person' (Nussbaum, 2016, p 7).

Indeed, scholars, educators and practitioners worldwide increasingly encourage children and young people to adopt a critical lens in their citizenship – in England we often refer to this as 'critical thinking skills, while in France it is the 'critical spirit' (Johnson and Morris, 2010). Viewing philanthropy through a global and critical citizenship lens involves encouraging active roles both locally and globally in building more peaceful, sustainable, equal, tolerant and inclusive societies. This perspective requires us to examine thoughtfully the diverse ways in which all citizens live, understand societal divisions and strive for the common good (Nussbaum, 1998). Thus, under this definition of philanthropy, we adopt a positive, progressive idea of philanthropy. This is not to say that virtues are not important; indeed, they can be considered the building blocks on which moral creativity is established. Therefore, instead of viewing arguments of virtues and citizenship as binary divides, we can view this as a spectrum on which the cultivation of virtues allows us to put into action a sense of 'bounded humanity' (Nussbaum, 1998) wherein we utilise our moral creativity to transcend individualistic approaches and cultivate collective responses.

Such an approach lends itself to considering more radical or transformational forms of philanthropy, which seek to foster new economic institutions, and local, grassroots initiatives, which aim to tackle manifestations of imperialism, colonialism and poverty (Herro and Obeng-Odoom, 2019). This encourages a more critical perspective of the institutions of capitalism, such as banking, energy supply and the labour market, which are largely seen as reinforcing the privileged position of dominant groups in society. Instead, this perspective seeks to prioritise participatory approaches to philanthropic decision making, encouraging a reclaiming of the state and holding it to account. In short, it is about reshaping and reorienting the philanthropic ecosystem towards changing systems. I will return to this idea in Chapter 11 of this book.

A transformational approach to cultivating philanthropic citizenship

The concept of philanthropic citizenship is of course universal and can be applied to any age; nonetheless, here I specifically reflect on these ideas of cultivating philanthropic citizenship within childhood, highlighting five crucial components.

The first – and probably most obvious – component within our conceptualisation of philanthropic citizenship through a critical citizenship lens would be a simple act of participation: giving and doing. This generally means 'donating of one's resources without contracting to achieve a comparable economic compensation' (Martin, 1994, p 10). This means that philanthropic citizenship includes an act, such as advocacy, volunteering, social action, charitable giving and activism, which when we consider this from a children's rights perspective requires the active participation of children in the decision-making processes (Nolas, 2015; Body et al, 2022). In helping children to cultivate their philanthropic citizenship, they should be supported and made aware of all the ways in which we can philanthropically participate beyond simply the donation of money, including giving time, talent and voice. Thus, in order to cultivate this aspect of philanthropic citizenship, children should be encouraged to take responsible ethical action and reflect on this action, considering what is the most ethical and appropriate action, and when. This isn't to create a hierarchy of giving responses – for example, activism isn't always better than fundraising. For instance, in 2020 when there were devastating wildfires across Australia, my two sons organised a fundraiser to support wildlife organisations in that area. Effectively this was the only way they could realistically support the crisis. Yet they still also take part in the Fridays for Futures school strikes and various other protests to seek to defend nature. They understood and connected both these actions as supporting nature. Both responses are legitimate and both responses are required. It is the knowledge to access the whole suite of philanthropic responses available in our toolbox (see Chapter 3) which matters and being able to be part of a collective response to collective issues.

Therefore, our second crucial component highlights that even when the act of participation may be individual, it is important to then consider how we help children connect these acts to wider notions of collective action, as was explored earlier. This centres on the idea of creating 'communities of enquiry' (Fisher, 2008). Communities of enquiry can be defined as collaborative and inclusive groups where individuals engage in critical thinking, dialogue and exploration of ideas to deepen understanding and promote mutual learning. This is not to suggest that all participants should join in with a 'groupthink' approach; indeed, maintaining individual identities and ideas is important. Nonetheless, this approach seeks to counteract what Giroux describes as the neoliberal 'individualistic and competitive approaches to learning' (1997, p 109) and to promote to children and young people a 'larger moral ecology beyond their own individual concerns' (McLaughlin, 1992, p 243).

This helps us identify a third crucial component of philanthropic citizenship: empowerment, which is another important component of developing children's moral capabilities (Covell and Howe, 2001). This is about helping children to develop the disposition to be committed and motivated to help change society (Veugelers, 2007; Johnson and Morris, 2010), and to develop civic courage and responsibility for decisions taken. Indeed, empowerment relies on cultivating the skills, knowledge and values to imagine a better world and challenge the status quo. Empowerment can operate at various levels, ranging from the individual to the community and even broader societal and global levels. It is frequently employed to combat issues relating to inequality, discrimination and social injustice, empowering marginalised groups to advocate for their rights and wellbeing effectively.

Under this element, we must recognise that empowerment and collective action – our fourth crucial component – are deeply intertwined, as one often leads to the other. Collective action centres on the collaborative efforts of individuals or groups who unite to achieve shared objectives or address common concerns. This form of action thrives on the principle that by coming together, people can pool their resources, knowledge and efforts to create a more significant impact than they could achieve as individuals. Core elements of collective action encompass the identification of shared goals, organisation and coordination among participants, mobilisation of individuals for active participation, and engagement in advocacy and activism. Collective action assumes a variety of forms, ranging from grassroots movements and community organising to formal organisations and associations (see Chapter 8). It serves as a potent mechanism for generating social and political change, as it amplifies the voices and influence of individuals when they work collectively towards a common purpose. As I show in Chapters 8 and 9, empowered individuals and communities are more inclined to engage in effective collective action because they possess the knowledge, confidence and capabilities required to advocate for their, and others', rights and interests. Additionally, engaging in collective action can further empower children and young people, as they witness the tangible impact of their collaborative efforts and gain confidence in their capacity to effect change. These concepts occupy central positions within movements dedicated to advancing social justice, equality, and human rights, as they provide the means by which individuals and communities can actively participate in shaping the world around them for the better.

The final crucial component of philanthropic citizenship involves the intention to create social and/or environmental benefits. We can break this down into two key aspects. First, the act of intending to produce benefits requires critical thinking to identify the underlying problem that the action aims to address, analyse its root causes, and determine the most ethical and effective approach to tackle it (Suissa, 2015; Kisby, 2017; Jerome and Kisby, 2019). For example, this involves thoroughly examining the cause, actively involving the recipients as partners and co-producers in the response (Jefferess, 2008), and considering what would be an appropriate and ethical philanthropic response, even exploring whether other avenues, such as government support, might be more suitable. Thus, children's participation should be informed by what is the most appropriate response to that need and, indeed, children should be encouraged to consider what is the more appropriate vehicle in terms of attending to that need. Second, the act must be directed towards generating some form of environmental or social good (Payton and Moody, 2008). While the concept of 'good' can be subject to varying interpretations, in this context it generally refers to the intention to protect human and/or environmental rights (Martin, 1994). Therefore, proponents of philanthropic citizenship advocate for critical thinking within a framework of justice (Nussbaum, 1998; Westheimer, 2015; Simpson, 2017; Body et al, 2020). As Simpson (2017, p 90) explains, having a social justice mentality or mindset entails a commitment to equality, along with developed critical and independent thinking, which ultimately results in ethical action. Indeed, this requires us to equip children, as appropriate to their age and evolving competencies, with the knowledge of how to collectively impact systemic change and with the skills on how to use knowledge to influence power, and how our overall and wider behaviours influence society and injustice.

Conclusion

In this chapter, I explore how children and young people are socialised to give within Western democracies. Focusing on England as a case study, I trace how education emphasises a virtues-based approach to teaching philanthropy, highlighting benevolence, civic duty and individualistic traits. While accepting that virtues have an important role to play within the socialisation of children as philanthropic actors, I argue that such approaches maintain the status quo and do little to help engage children in challenging systems of inequality and inequity. Instead, I call for a more justice-oriented approach to cultivating children's philanthropic behaviours, focused on ideas of justice, activism and system change.

This is not to say that every act must be one of activism or justice – of course that's not the case. Sometimes we act in benevolence as benevolence is what is required, or we give in a moment without considerable thought simply because we were asked to do so. Nonetheless, the wider framing of our actions matters; it is the background to the tapestry of our philanthropic behaviours and provides the roadmap for when and how we conduct and guide our own philanthropic journeys. While virtuous approaches to philanthropy emphasise individual virtues and care for others, they do not allow or facilitate us to fully address systemic challenges underlying the huge range social issues we are currently facing from infringements of human rights, persistent poverty and climate catastrophe. Embracing transformative philanthropy involves questioning systemic issues and promoting collective action. Empowering children with the tools and knowledge to engage meaningfully in philanthropy can help support them both now and in the future as active and compassionate citizens, driving transformation and progress. As we move towards a more transformative philanthropic perspective, we can create a more just and equitable society for all.

2

Children as citizens: a fight for rights

Introduction

As a mum to two boys, I am concerned about what the future holds for my children. Indeed, as a citizen of the world, I am concerned about that future for *all* children. The existential threats of climate change are taking hold, though their seriousness appears to be continually largely ignored by many governments, human rights are being limited across many parts of the world, and war in Europe, rising tensions in the Middle East and conflicts across the globe all cause significant concern. But also, within that is a lot of hope, amazing people doing amazing things, many of which I will touch upon in this book. Nonetheless, in this chapter I want to focus on some of the challenges facing our children as citizens of the world, particularly the conceptualisation of childhood, children's rights and how we construct notions of good citizenship within civil society.

In the evolving landscape of childhood citizenship, children are often cast as future stakeholders rather than co-citizens. The UNCRC (1989) sparked a paradigm shift, challenging us all to reconsider the complex nature of children's citizenship – whether it is a right, a developmental milestone or a response to societal demands. Thus, the debate between 'being' and 'becoming' citizens unfolds: should children be acknowledged as fully enfranchised members of society or do their rights evolve with their cognitive and emotional growth? Advocates for 'being' champion children as integral citizens, while the 'becoming' perspective recognises maturation, calling for age-sensitive participation. I, along with others, argue that striking a nuanced balance is crucial, recognising children as citizens while accommodating their unique developmental needs. Nonetheless, despite international legal frameworks, critiques highlight children's exclusion from impactful decisions, a challenge exacerbated by the COVID-19 pandemic. Meanwhile, character education rises in prominence, emphasising virtues through community action, while critics caution against its potential to divert attention from structural inequalities.

Amid these discussions, a stark reality emerges – threats to civil liberties and the right to protest. Many governments, including my own here in England, propose legislation limiting these rights, creating a hostile climate towards activism. In this tumultuous landscape, children forge their identities as citizens, inheriting a discourse that both celebrates and undermines their rights. As stewards of their world, I suggest, it is our responsibility to empower them to claim their rightful place as active, empowered social actors.

Children as citizens

The concept of childhood citizenship is widely debated. It is constructed by a complex set of societal, political and cultural forces, which each evolve over time (Lister, 2008). This has led to various interpretations and reinterpretations of children's citizenship over time and place. Indeed, the concept of individuals as citizens can be tracked back as far as ancient Greece and Rome, where specific structures supported political and civic engagement, while others upheld exclusive, elitist and patriarchal civic participation norms (Coady, 2008). In these historical contexts, citizenship largely related to men who expressed their perspectives through political involvement. Political philosophers spanning Aristotle, Aquinas, Augustine, Marilius, Hobbs, Locke, Kant and more contemporary thinkers like Marshall have all contributed to shaping the understanding of citizenship (Coady, 2008). Scrutinising these philosophers' debates and definitions underscores the tension identified by Coady (2008) between the idea of citizenship as a rightful entitlement and the practical but constrained realities.

In more modern understandings of citizenship, which emerged in the early to mid-1900s, there has been growing recognition of individuals' civic freedoms and rights, such as freedom of speech, legal protections, property ownership, universal suffrage (men's and then later women's), and eventually social and welfare rights. Throughout this era, children were perceived not as equal or current citizens, but as *future* citizens in the making. More contemporary times have witnessed ongoing shifts in perspectives brought about by initiatives like the United Nations Convention on Rights of the Child (UNCRC) in 1989, as well as sociological discourse on identity, child and youth engagement concerns, and wellbeing issues. This led to a re-evaluation of child and youth citizenship, with some viewpoints regarding their citizenship as a right, while others view it as a developmental period. Thus, the discourse surrounding children's status within the framework of citizenship encompasses a debate and set of tensions between the concepts of children 'being' and 'becoming' citizens. This deliberation hinges on the fundamental question as to whether children should be construed as fully enfranchised citizens, like their adult counterparts ('being'), or whether their citizenship is characterised by an evolving process in which distinct rights and considerations are warranted ('becoming') (Roche, 1999).

Roche argued that it is imperative that adults recognise children as full members of society ('being'): 'the demand that children be included in citizenship is simply a request that children be seen as members of society too, with a legitimate and valuable voice and perspectives' (1999, p 479). This advocates for recognition that children inherently possess fundamental rights and, as such, should be accorded the status of full citizens. This perspective prioritises treating children with a required measure of dignity, equity and fairness. Furthermore, proponents of this paradigm argue that children merit equal entitlement to rights, as they function as indispensable constituents of the societal fabric and collective. It is an approach which converges with the principles of human rights, advancing the notion that rights ought to transcend age demarcations, advocating for the notion that children, notwithstanding their developmental stage, possess an agency that can be channelled towards meaningful contributions within their immediate contexts. Thus, adopting a children's rights perspective (see later on in the chapter) requires the participation of children in decision-making processes that impact their lives.

Proponents of the children as 'becoming' citizens perspective argue that children's intellectual, emotional and social maturation is an ongoing trajectory, which entails limitations in terms of their comprehension and exercise of rights. From this perspective, children are seen as lacking in skills, maturity, capacity and knowledge to independently navigate certain decisions. This viewpoint posits that children's rights should be progressively actualised in tandem with their evolving cognitive and emotional faculties. The argument is that specific rights, such as voting rights or legal responsibilities, should only be given to children when they are of an age to manage these appropriately. Advocates of the 'becoming' paradigm highlight the significance of safeguarding, protection and scaffolding for children as they navigate the complexities of becoming a full citizen. This approach contends that even while children are included in decisional proceedings, a safeguarding mechanism is imperative.

The middle ground, and the space in which I position the arguments within this book, advocates for age-sensitive participation. This more nuanced stance acknowledges the progressive evolution of children's capacities and supports their engagement in accordance with their developmental maturation. This discourse champions a recognition of children's rights as divergent from those of adults, reflective of children's distinctive needs and susceptibilities. The aspiration is to strike an equilibrium between embracing children as citizens while accommodating their distinct developmental attributes. This results in significant debate about whether children ought to be nurtured primarily as citizens in the making or be recognised as having voice and agency in the present. Indeed, the extent to which children's voices are recognised and integrated is the direct consequence of where we consider them to be on the 'being' versus 'becoming' axis. Within this book, I advocate for this middle ground, recognising children's rights as citizens of now, but also the need for adults to help scaffold, shape and cultivate their citizenship opportunities in a way which prioritises their emotional and physical wellbeing.

Children's rights

Ratified by the UK in 1991, the UNCRC sets out the human rights of every person under the age of 18. It was adopted by the UN General Assembly in 1989 and is the most widely adopted international human rights treaty in history. Most pertinent to our conceptualisation of philanthropic citizenship, I highlight the following articles:

- Article 12 (respect for the views of the child). Every child has the right to express their views, feelings and wishes in all matters affecting them, and to have their views considered and taken seriously. This right applies at all times, for example during immigration proceedings, housing decisions or the child's day-to-day home life.
- Article 13 (freedom of expression). Every child must be free to express their thoughts and opinions and to access all kinds of information, as long as it is within the law.
- Article 29 (the aims of education). Every child has the right to an education that nurtures holistic development, cultural awareness, and societal preparedness, and development of respect for the natural environment.
- Article 31 (cultural activities). Every child has the right to leisure, cultural engagement, and practicing one's faith, devoid of prejudice or bias.

Protective rights and autonomy rights interweave throughout the UNCRC. Each signatory pledges universal access to education, encompassing primary, secondary and tertiary levels, while upholding the dignity of students within educational settings (Article 28). Together these articles should, respectively, ensure that children's views are respected and that all children are given the freedom to express their views. Put simply, this is to be understood as a child's right to be consulted and listened to in matters that affect their life (Nolas, 2015). According to Freeman, Article 12 is particularly significant 'not only for what it says, but because it recognises the child as a full human being with integrity and personality and the ability to participate freely in society' (Freeman, 2000, p 37).

Jerome and Starkey (2021) explore children's rights education by adapting Friere's pedagogy to contemporary society. Friere's work is underpinned by two key concepts, which Jerome and Starkey argue are key to understanding children's rights education, first that 'education is a political act' and, second, 'this act consists of an exchange between educator and educated carrying within it emancipatory potential from a repressive order' (Butler,

2008, pp 304–305). They argue that in order to adopt a children's rights approach in education, children must be able to engage in tensions within their community, 'to wrestle with real problems' and 'connect individual experiences and concerns to broader social just principles' (Jerome and Starkey, 2021). These ideas are closely aligned with the conceptualisation of philanthropic citizenship I presented in Chapter 1, which seeks to move beyond a 'charity mentality' and instead embrace a 'social justice mentality' (Simpson, 2017).

Guiding the practical realisation of these rights are two pivotal General Comments: UN General Comment No. 12 (The child's right to be heard) and General Comment No. 7 (Implementing child rights in early childhood). General Comment No. 12 emphasises the importance of children's participation as a substantive dialogue rather than tokenistic gesture, where children's ideas and concerns bear ethical significance in policy and programme development. This active engagement spans beyond mere moments to encompass an ongoing collaborative approach in diverse spheres of children's lives. Notably, the past few decades have given rise to several models of children's participation, each imparting a unique perspective on the landscape (for example, Arnstein, 1969; Hart, 1992; Fajerman, 2001; Sheir, 2001). Arnstein's 'ladder of citizen participation' has stood as both a common and a contentious model, sparking adaptations and divergences. For instance, Hart (1992) reshaped Arnstein's model into a progressive process, reflecting the varying degrees of power wielded by children and adults. In essence, participation is envisaged as contextual, relational and site-specific, where the engagement between children, youth and the participatory framework evolves to cater to their unique needs.

However, the acknowledgement of children's rights versus the reality of how these rights are enacted remains a constant source of debate. Indeed, the UK and other nations have been criticised for their lack of attention to implementing children's rights. As the Committee on the Rights of the Child commented in 2001: 'Children do not lose their human rights by virtue of passing through the school gates.' This was followed by further criticism in 2002, when the Committee documented its concern that 'in education, school children are not systematically consulted in matters that affect them' (United Nations General Assembly, 2002, p 7). It recommended that the UK government should 'take further steps to promote, facilitate and monitor systematic, meaningful and effective participation of all groups of children in society, including in school, for example, through school councils' (p 7). While there has been acknowledged progress on children's participation rights (Nolas, 2015), there is much more work to be done and the COVID-19 pandemic only exacerbated existing inequalities (Cuevas-Parra, 2021). The extent to which other countries have implemented children's rights also varies. At one end of the spectrum, countries like Sweden, Norway and Iceland have sought to establish robust legal frameworks. In contrast, countries grappling with political instability or deeply entrenched cultural practices face more difficulties. Technological advancements have also played a pivotal role, allowing children to voice their concerns and viewpoints to global audiences.

While governments may not always be quick to act on children's rights, the collective responsibility for safeguarding and advancing children's rights rest not only with governments but with the global society as a whole. Philanthropic actors have an important role to play here, both advocating for and modelling children's rights as a priority. Indeed, the importance of this role is exemplified by the case studies throughout this book and particularly in Chapters 8 and 9, as well as those discussed in more depth in Chapter 4. Conversely many argue contemporary fundraising practices with children do not adhere to children's rights as enshrined in the UNCRC (see Chapter 4). Therefore, while many philanthropic actors have done well to propel children's rights forwards, too often other parts of the philanthropic ecosystem can hold these rights back and act as a barrier.

The rise of character education versus citizenship

Within the UK (and beyond) sociologists, educationists and social policy scholars have long been concerned with how we raise the good citizen, with volunteering and giving being seen as important factors. This approach has been reflected in English education policy over successive governments, from Labour's focus on the social and emotional learning (1997–2010) to the Conservative government's (2010–2024) focus on character education, which concentrated on the development of an individual child's virtues, resilience and grit (Jerome and Kisby, 2019, 2020). Particularly enthused about character education, Nicky Morgan (Education Secretary 2014–2016) dedicated over £14.5 million to character education initiatives (Marshall et al, 2017). Building on this, Damian Hinds (Secretary of State for Education 2018–2019) set out the quality benchmarks for Ofsted to begin to monitor schools on their character education from September 2019, which was implemented by Gavin Williamson (Secretary of State for Education 2019–2021), a mantle picked up by Nadhim Zahawi (Secretary of State for Education 2021–2022), who continued a scrutiny of character and moral education, with a particular emphasis on political impartiality. Following a rapid succession of three education secretaries in a matter of months, Gillian Keegan (Secretary of State for Education 2022–2024) continued this focus stating at the Church of England National Education Conference: 'Your [Church of England] schools are more likely to be good or outstanding than those without a religious character.' Indeed, among subsequent education secretaries across the last decade, 'there is manifestly a high degree of elite social reproduction through a dominant system of independent and/or selective education which inculcates the structures and values of an essentially Christian ethos, focusing on moral/character education' (Hilton, 2022). Meanwhile, critics of the character education programmes have attacked them for taking an approach which 'seeks to fix the kids' rather than teach children to question wider structural inequalities or root causes to social problems (for example, Holden and Minty, 2011; Suissa, 2015; Kisby, 2017; Allen and Bull, 2018; Bates, 2019; Jerome and Kisby, 2019), branding the approach as 'unclear, redundant, old-fashioned, essentially religious, paternalistic, anti-democratic, anti-intellectual, conservative, individualistic and relative' (Jerome and Kisby, 2020, p 1).

Nonetheless, service learning, volunteering and community action have remained consistent pillars of the character education agenda, under the auspices of good citizenship. This fits well with the 'responsibilisation' agenda of recent and successive governments (Clarke, 2005; Allsop et al, 2018), where citizens are expected to take increasing personal responsibility for their own educational, health and welfare needs, with significantly increased expectation of communities to address societal challenges. Such thinking ties in neatly with the Labour's (1997–2010) promotion of the Third Way, followed by the Conservative's promotion of the Big Society (Body, 2020). The ideological narrative of the Big Society, coupled with the political reality of austerity and public sector cuts, has put increasing focus back on charity and voluntary action as an alternative (Mohan and Breeze, 2016). While the language of the Big Society has dropped away from the Conservative narrative, the focus on neighbourhoods, communities and local social action did not, and remained an important feature of their policy. This was encapsulated perfectly in the Civil Society Strategy 2018, through an intent focus on neighbourhoods and volunteering (HM Government, 2018). In this strategy, particular attention is paid to research from the Jubilee Centre at Birmingham (Arthur et al, 2017), which states that 'research suggests that if children are involved in action for the benefit of others before the age of 10, they are twice as likely to sustain it throughout their lifetime as young people who only start at age 16 to 18' (HM Government, 2018, p 31).

Relating to this, several conversations have emerged regarding children's civic behaviours, under a variety of conceptual frameworks from discussions about kindness, civic virtues, service learning, citizenship, character, prosociality and moral education (Westheimer, 2015). Each of these concepts is widely contested. As noted earlier, while a popular theme with the current Conservative governments, character education has come under significant criticism for being too narrow and instrumental (for example, Suissa, 2015; Jerome and Kisby, 2019, 2020), while citizenship comes under scrutiny for being too wide and all-encompassing

Table 2.1: Citizen types

	The personally responsible citizen	The participatory citizen	The justice-oriented citizen
Description	Acts responsibly in his/her community. Obeys rules and follows laws. Recycles, gives to charity, gives blood and so on. Volunteers to 'lend a hand' in crisis.	Active member of community organisations and/or improvement efforts. Organises community efforts to care for those in need, promote economic development or clean up the environment. Knows how government agencies work. Knows strategies for accomplishing collective tasks.	Critically assesses social, political and economic structures to see beyond surface causes. Seeks out and addresses areas of injustice. Knows about democratic social movements and how to effect systemic change.
Sample action	Gives to a food bank.	Helps to organise a food collection.	Explores why people are hungry and acts to solve the root causes.
Core assumption	To solve problems and improve society, citizens must have good character; they must be honest, responsible and law-abiding members of the community.	To solve social problems and improve society, citizens must actively participate and take leadership positions within established systems and community structures.	To solve social problems and improve society, citizens must question, debate and change established systems and structures when they reproduce patterns of injustice over time.

Source: Adapted from Westheimer and Kahne (2004)

(Kisby, 2017). Westheimer (2015) identifies, through extensive research in the US (Westheimer and Kahne, 2004), three 'types' of citizenship promoted by educational programmes: the personally responsible, the participatory and the socially just (see Table 2.1). The personally responsible, epitomised in character education, works on the assumption that in order to solve problems in society citizens must be responsible, law-abiding and honest, and must possess identified 'civic virtues' such as integrity, grit, resilience and kindness. The participatory programme is epitomised through service-learning programmes, where individuals are encouraged to actively participate in their community within the current community structures. Socially just programmes would ideally include active participatory and personally responsible learning, while simultaneously developing the knowledge and capabilities to critically question the established systems, critically assess social, political and economic structures, and address the root causes of problems through seeking structural change to find solutions to societal issues like food poverty (Westheimer, 2015, p 39).

Westheimer (2015) argues – and, based on my own research, I agree – that school programmes hoping to develop the personally responsible citizen often fail in increasing children's participation in local and national civic life. Equally, Westheimer's qualitative and quantitative data show that programmes that emphasise participatory citizenship do not necessarily develop children's skills to critique the root causes of social problems. Furthermore, programmes which focus on critiquing the root causes of social problems, without participatory involvement, are unlikely to increase civic engagement. Therefore, it is a combination of participatory and justice-oriented programmes that is most likely to support active civic engagement.

In short, when policy makers, educators, voluntary sector organisations and communities pursue ideas of philanthropic citizenship, they do so in many ways and to many different ends. The pedagogical approaches towards and the framing of philanthropic citizenship has real consequences for the type of giving activities and engagement we encourage and the type of society we imagine, and therefore requires further scrutiny (Holden and Minty, 2011).

The curtailing of activism and civil liberties

Over the past decade, we have witnessed increasing dissent in Western societies, as many governments seemingly become progressively anti-activism and anti-democratic. For example, if we look at the UK government (2010–2024), over recent years we can see a sweep of reforms which are anti-activism, a stance which is argued as anti-democratic. Of course, these policies have evolved over the years and successive governments, but actions by the Conservative government (2010–2024) and its policies and stance on activism can be viewed as undermining democratic values.

Let's start by considering legislation the UK government has introduced seeking to limit the right to protest and freedom of assembly. For example, the Police, Crime, Sentencing and Courts Bill proposed in 2021 included measures that could grant police more powers to restrict protests, potentially undermining the ability of activists to voice their concerns and exercise their democratic right to peaceful assembly. Despite much protest and objection from civil society actors, the government's Police, Crime, Sentencing and Courts ('Policing') Act came into effect in April 2022. The Act made wide-ranging changes across the criminal justice system in areas such as police powers, judicial procedures and offender rehabilitation. It also potentially has a serious impact on human rights, particularly the right to protest. Most of the public order provisions in the Act, which affect the right to protest, came into force on 28 June 2022. In 2023, the government then introduced the Public Order Act.

As Adam Ramsay spelt out in an article in *Open Democracy*, the new anti-protest legislation launched on 15 June 2023 has been branded unlawful.

Prior to this, law enforcement had the authority to curtail or halt a protest if there was a risk of causing 'serious public disorder, significant property damage, or prolonged disruption to the community's normal functioning'. Modifications to the UK Public Order Act now empower the police to impede or terminate a protest if they believe it has the potential to create 'more than minor disruption to the community's routines'. They have the authority to apprehend anyone participating in a protest or even those who encourage others to join. Additionally, officers are now obligated to consider the 'accumulated disruption' resulting from various protests, even if these events are orchestrated by distinct groups and revolve around different issues. Furthermore, the term 'community' has been redefined to encompass all those impacted by a protest, not solely individuals residing or working in the vicinity where the protest occurs (Ramsay, 2023). In response, human rights organisation Liberty started legal action against the Home Secretary Suella Braverman (2022–2023), with Katy Watts, a lawyer at Liberty, stating:

> 'This is yet another power grab from the Government, as well as the latest in a long line of attacks on our right to protest, making it harder for the public to stand up for what they believe in. The wording of the Government's new law is so vague that anything deemed "more than a minor" disturbance could have restrictions imposed upon it. In essence, this gives the police almost unlimited powers to stop any protest the Government doesn't agree with.' (Liberty, 2023)

In addition, the UK's former Conservative government's response to certain peaceful activist movements, such as climate change protests and anti-austerity movements, has involved police interventions, arrests and legal actions that could be seen as attempts to suppress dissent. For example, during the climate change protests organised by Extinction Rebellion, there were instances of police intervention, arrests and measures that could be perceived as attempts to suppress the movement. Some activists claimed that such actions were aimed at deterring participation and silencing voices advocating for urgent climate action. Indeed, between 2020 and 2023, more than 100 individuals who engaged in nonviolent climate-related protests have faced imprisonment (University of Bristol, 2023).

And it is not just critics from within the UK who are concerned about the threats to civic freedom. In March 2023, the UK was downgraded within the scope of an annual global index gauging civic freedoms by Civicus. This reclassification is attributed to the government's progressively authoritative pursuit of enacting stringent and punitive legislation aimed at curtailing public demonstrations (Butler, 2023). As Butler (2023) articulated in *The Guardian*, Civicus constitutes a collaborative effort encompassing more than 20 civil society organisations of global reach. The Civicus Monitor is an observatory dedicated to monitoring the democratic and civic vitality of 197 nations worldwide. This consortium functions to deliver an annual assessment detailing the relative vitality of civil society on a global scale. The classification scheme delineates countries into distinct categories: 'open', 'narrowed', 'obstructed', 'repressed' or 'closed'. Notably, the UK's classification has undergone a transition from 'narrowed' to 'obstructed'. Consequently, it finds itself in the company of nations such as Poland, South Africa and Hungary, which share similar designations within this context (Butler, 2023).

Like Ramsay (2023), Civicus' 2023 annual report draws upon several instances of regulatory measures that have been introduced or are under consideration. The ongoing parliamentary deliberations concerning the Public Order Bill are highlighted, as this legislation aims to suppress what are termed as 'guerrilla-style' protests. The report also raises concern regarding perceived endeavours by the UK government to erode human rights principles. Furthermore, it underscores the government's adversarial stance towards charitable organisations and advocates who actively challenge or vocalise opposition against its policies pertaining to areas such as climate change, anti-racism and the rights of refugees and asylum seekers (Butler, 2023). Overall, the trend of resistance to peaceful protests and nonviolent activism within the UK remains a concern. However, it is also evident from this report that it is not only the right to protest in the UK which is under attack. Similar actions to repress protests in Australia have also taken place, while in Sri Lanka, protests sparked by economic anger led to the president launching a violent crackdown characterised by detentions and torture, with a similar response to protests occurring in Kazakhstan. And the world watched in horror as women-led mass protests in Iran led to indiscriminate killings by the state (Civicus, 2023).

In August 2023, a report entitled *Defending Our Democratic Space: A Call to Action* was released by the Sheila McKechnie Foundation and Civil Exchange. This report highlights how many people feel their voices aren't being heard and that their concerns are being ignored by those in charge. The authors of the report suggest that this is deliberate and that the then current and past governments have intentionally made it harder for regular people to have a say in important decisions. They have done this by weakening the things that usually let people speak up and hold leaders accountable, like charities, groups that run campaigns, and other parts of civil society that work for the public's benefit. The outcome, according to the report's authors, is a noticeable decline in the quality of services, policies and legislation, coupled with a reduction in transparency, accountability and trust in the government. Certain political figures and ministers, the report contends, have positioned entities, such as charities, campaigners, members of the judiciary, legal professionals and sections of the media as obstructions to democratic processes rather than as integral components thereof. The report also encourages everyone to take action. It points out that even though groups working for the public are being targeted, they have a special ability to see the bigger picture. They can bring together a wide group of people who care about these issues, not just the ones directly involved. The report highlights that just waiting and hoping that the problems will go away isn't enough. Some big things, like the influence of powerful businesses and the impact of social media, will still be there regardless of who is in charge. So, they end with a strong request to politicians from all sides. It asks them to listen to what people want and to promise to support and fix the space where everyone can take part in making decisions. This way, they can make sure that democracy works well and meets the changing needs of the people. As the report concludes: 'If you join up the dots between the various things that are happening, you have what amounts to a very serious threat to democracy itself' (Sheila McKechnie Foundation and Civil Exchange, 2023).

This means that our children and young people are not only growing up in an environment where they have fewer rights in terms of protesting and engaging in nonviolent activism than generations before them, but also within a period of time which problematises and purposefully frames peaceful activists as unhinged, radical and dangerous extremists. As our children grow, we and they must find ways in the present and the future to navigate these complex debates and ensure they are continued to be allowed a voice.

The nursery of democracy

When we consider the challenges facing children's philanthropic citizenship, we are then left to consider how engagement in civil society and philanthropic endeavours can help children, and wider society, overcome the barriers they face. I largely covered this in Chapter 1 on the discussion on philanthropic citizenship, and I will return to this argument in Part III of this book when I consider 'what next?', but in the meantime I want to briefly draw attention to Alexis de Tocqueville (1835), the famous French political thinker and historian, who observed American society in the early 19th century and documented his observations in his seminal work *Democracy in America*. One of Tocqueville's key insights was the importance of what he called the 'associational spirit' in American society. The associational spirit refers to the propensity of Americans to come together voluntarily to form various associations, clubs and organisations aimed at addressing common interests, concerns and goals. Tocqueville was struck by the widespread presence of these voluntary associations, which he saw as a unique feature of American democracy. He also recognised that these associations played a crucial role in shaping American civic life and contributed significantly to the vitality of American democracy. He believed that this spirit of association was a counterbalance to the potential dangers of individualism and isolation. By joining together in associations, citizens were able to work collectively towards shared objectives, fostering a sense of community and civic engagement.

Tocqueville's work is highly relevant to understanding children's philanthropic citizenship. According to him, common sense tells us that good people create a good society; therefore, it is equally true that a good society creates good people. For him, participation in democracies and civic associations through our voluntary actions had cognitive, emotional and political benefits. Participants develop decision-making skills and knowledge on how society works; they develop a sense of fellow feeling for one another, taking other's views into account; and they learn how to make real changes as a collective, which benefit all rather than just the elite. We can immediately draw the similarities between this and the approach here to philanthropic citizenship, where these behaviours are viewed as a way of life rather than a set of discreet actions.

Tocqueville's insight on the associational spirit is highly relevant to children's philanthropic behaviours and their understanding of social justice for several reasons. Firstly, as I will outline throughout this book, children's philanthropic citizenship develops via learning through active participation. Children who engage in philanthropic activities, such as volunteering or participating in community service projects, are actively participating in associations focused on social good. Through these experiences, children learn the value of collective action and cooperation in addressing societal challenges. Furthermore, engaging in philanthropy, from helping behaviours to activism, allows children to develop empathy for others and a sense of solidarity and allyship with those in need. They witness firsthand the positive impact their actions can have on individuals and communities, reinforcing the idea that working together can make a difference.

Cultivating philanthropic citizenship encourages civic responsibility. Through engaging in philanthropic activities, children learn that they have a role to play in the wellbeing of their communities. They understand that they are not passive recipients of societal benefits, but active participants with a responsibility to contribute positively. This promotes a sense of belonging within a group or association, whether this is a school community, community organisation or family initiative, fostering a sense of belonging and connection. This aligns with Tocqueville's observation that associations help combat the potential isolation of individuals in a democratic society. Therefore, they develop a long-term commitment to social justice through early exposure to such ideas, potentially instilling a lifelong commitment to advocating for fairness, equity and social change.

In short, considering the challenges raised in this chapter, philanthropic activities potentially provide a space to empower children by allowing them to actively participate in making positive contributions to their communities.

This sense of agency can translate into a deeper understanding of their role in a democratic society. Indeed, Tocqueville's insight into the associational spirit highlights the significance of collective action and voluntary associations in democratic societies. When applied to children's philanthropic behaviours and understanding of social justice, it emphasises the transformative potential of early engagement in activities that promote the common good and foster a sense of civic responsibility.

Conclusion

In this chapter I have sought to take a broad tour of some of the debates impacting children's rights as citizens, highlighting some of the challenges and opportunities. Navigating the complex arguments concerning the 'being' and 'becoming' dichotomy, I find a middle ground, advocating for an age-sensitive participation that honours the unique developmental trajectories of children. This balanced approach seeks to draw together children's evolving capacities with their rights as citizens.

The exploration of children's rights and the challenges they face in exercising those rights, particularly in the context of civic engagement, highlights a critical juncture in modern society. The UNCRC serves as a cornerstone for safeguarding and promoting the rights of individuals under the age of 18. Articles such as 12, 13, 29 and 31 underscore the importance of respecting children's views, providing freedom of expression, ensuring quality education and allowing for cultural engagement without bias. However, despite the legal framework in place, there remains a significant gap between policy and practice. The UK, like many other countries, has been criticised for not fully implementing children's rights, particularly in educational settings. I will return to this theme throughout the rest of the book, but particularly in Chapters 4 and 8. The need for genuine, substantive participation rather than tokenistic gestures is underscored by General Comment No. 12, which emphasises the ethical significance of children's ideas and concerns in policy development.

However, the rise of debates between character education and citizenship discourses further complicates the landscape. While character education emphasises personal responsibility and virtue, citizenship education encourages active participation within established systems, and justice-oriented citizenship encourages challenging these systems and structures when they are viewed to perpetuate injustice and inequality. Striking a balance between these approaches and fostering socially just citizenship, which critically questions and seeks systemic change, is crucial for a well-rounded civic education. Yet, as we examine the current sociopolitical climate, there is a concerning trend of governments, including that of the UK, enacting legislation that restricts the right to protest and freedom of assembly. The Police, Crime, Sentencing and Courts Act has caused many to raise significant concerns about the erosion of democratic values and the potential suppression of dissenting voices. This shift towards anti-activism policies across many Western democracies poses a serious threat to democratic principles and civic freedoms. It becomes a duty for all of us to call for a recommitment to democratic principles, emphasising the need for open dialogue and inclusivity in decision-making processes, and protecting these spaces for our children and young people.

It is this context I argue that Alexis de Tocqueville's insights on the associational spirit are particularly relevant. The spirit of association, as observed in early 19th-century America, provided a counterbalance to individualism and isolation, fostering a sense of community and civic engagement. This concept resonates with the notion of philanthropic citizenship, emphasising active participation in associations focused on social good. Ultimately, the cultivation of philanthropic citizenship among children holds the potential to empower them as active contributors to their communities and beyond. Through philanthropic activities, children can learn the value of collective action, empathy for others, and their role in shaping a democratic society. This sense of agency can lead to a deeper understanding of civic responsibility and a lifelong commitment to social justice. Nonetheless, a justice-oriented approach to philanthropy means we must also encourage children to question the institution of philanthropy itself and many of the philanthropic institutions within this ecosystem, a discussion I will return to in Part III of this book.

In conclusion, the challenges facing children's civic engagement underscore the critical need for genuine implementation of their rights and the preservation of democratic spaces. Nurturing philanthropic citizenship provides a pathway to empower children as active, responsible members of society, ultimately contributing to the broader goals of democracy and social justice.

PART II

Philanthropic citizenship in action

3

The foundations of philanthropic citizenship: the conversation starters

Introduction

According to Martin (1994), kindness is an act of benevolence along with compassion, generosity and love, and is a foundational concept of philanthropic behaviours. Therefore, it seems to be a good place to begin our conversation on children's philanthropic citizenship in action. Indeed, like many parents, carers and educators, I have constantly encouraged and told my children to 'be kind'. But rarely have I sat back and thought what this really means: be kind to whom, why and to what ends?

Kindness itself is a concept that collectively still matters, which is universally valued (Hanel et al, 2020). As Martin (1994) argues, kindness seeks to further the wellbeing of other people. Indeed, the world is awash with people, organisations and even governments telling us to 'be kind'. It has become a popular hashtag on social media platforms such as X (formerly Twitter) and has multiple books published from gurus to academics, on the merits of kindness. We have World Kindness Day, a global 24-hour celebration dedicated to paying it forward and focusing on the good. We are encouraged to perform acts of kindness, such as giving blood, helping a neighbour or volunteering in the community. It even has the international festival 'Kindfest' dedicated in its honour each year. In these spaces we are constantly being reminded of research which consistently tells us that kindness is overall good for society's wellbeing (Curry et al, 2018), for fostering connections and communication across differences. Kindness matters.

Nonetheless, as I will explore in this chapter, there is a darker side to kindness, one which can silent the voices of the marginalised and disguise privilege behind a veneer of good acts rather than justice (Inayatullah and Blaney, 2012). It is in danger of becoming a concept which denies individual experiences and structural injustice, with the simple motto of 'be kind'. It has been boxed up and marketed as a saleable virtue, merchandised across the planet as the neoliberal world has been quick to commodify, individualise and package up this concept. Indeed, the irony of fast fashion, which we know causes huge harm both environmentally and in vulnerable communities, producing t-shirts and merchandise embezzled with this motto, never escapes me. Furthermore, concepts of kindness play into gendered notions of care and stereotypes concerning who should be kind and indeed who requires our kindness. As a result, it can take away individuals' agency, setting the giver of kindness and the recipient at opposite ends of the scale.

Therefore, in this chapter, I begin by focusing on the role of kindness as a foundational concept of philanthropic citizenship, as a 'conversation starter' for our discussions, examining the role of key influences in this space, such as YouTube star MrBeast, the family and the role of storytelling.

Encouraging kindness in the early years

My interest in how children's philanthropic citizenship started with a project I began in 2018, exploring children's conceptualisation of charity, kindness and giving. Working with a team of researchers, who were all training to work with young children, we engaged over 150 children aged four to eight in the study, which explored what kindness and charity meant to them (Body et al, 2019). Throughout this study, children returned to the central idea of kindness as being at the heart of how we should behave towards others. Indeed, children often saw charity as a set of behaviours, closely associated with being kind, for example:

'Charity means being kind to people and animals.' (Boy, 6)

'Being kind to homeless people.' (Girl, 8)

'Being good or doing something good for others.' (Boy, 8)

'I think it is about being good and helping.' (Boy, 4)

'Being kind to children who haven't got anyone to play with.' (Girl, 7)

Extensive research highlights the profound impact of early socialisation on a child's capacity for kindness – fostering a sense of fellow feeling that encompasses empathy, sympathy, and genuine concern (Roughley and Schramme, 2018, p 3). This influence permeates both familial and educational environments (Eisenberg et al, 2015; Sierksma et al, 2014). Parents, alongside educators (Berliner and Masterson, 2015), play pivotal roles in shaping a child's inclination towards empathetic contemplation of others, thereby paving the way for prosocial conduct (Dahl and Brownell, 2019). Indeed, while it's commonly assumed that teaching empathy automatically translates into more caring actions, studies like that of Berliner and Masterson (2015) challenge this notion. The journey from empathy to genuine prosocial behaviour is a nuanced one, requiring a blend of both emotional and cognitive responses (Gibbs, 2019). To truly empathise, a child must not only recognise and accurately label specific emotions, but also differentiate between their own feelings and those of others, all while deciphering potential underlying causes.

Research shows that children as young as 18 months old can already display concern and subsequent prosocial behaviour through affective perspective taking (Vaish et al, 2009), such as offering solace to distressed individuals and lending a helping hand to those in need (for example, Warneken and Tomasello, 2008). Even at just 24 months old, children exhibit empathetic responses that can culminate in acts of kindness. A study by McHarg et al (2019) observed tender, caring gestures from children towards a distressed 'baby'. This early display of social competence might suggest that socialisation plays a less significant role in their development. However, when parents in the same study engaged with their child's empathetic curiosity about the 'baby', it significantly heightened the likelihood of the child demonstrating caring behaviours. This underscores the pivotal role of parental socialisation in nurturing empathy in young children (Zahn-Waxler et al, 2018; Dahl and Brownell, 2019).

The environments that facilitate this development encompass both the home and more formal settings, such as school or community groups (Eisenberg, 1983), where an adult, be it a parent or educator, assists children in identifying and articulating various emotions (Berliner and Masterson, 2015), engaging them in contemplation and discourse about empathy. These practices position the child as an active participant in their own empathetic development and subsequent enactment of prosocial behaviours (Dahl and Brownell, 2019). In everyday life, children are further exposed to prosocial acts through various means, including adults and peers modelling, instructing or rewarding such behaviours (Eisenberg, 1983). Notably, the practice of rewarding prosocial behaviour can present challenges. Given the early emergence of positive behaviours like helping and sharing even before formal socialisation begins, Warneken and Tomasello (2008) argue that the motivation for such action is intrinsic. From this, they go on to present data which suggests substituting this intrinsic drive with an external incentive could eventually override its initial internal origin, potentially yielding the opposite effect – meaning that to externally reward prosocial behaviours, such as giving, we may override the initial, natural altruistic tendency.

Indeed, I remember a scenario with my youngest son. He had just started school and was struggling to settle, displaying several behaviours the school found 'unsocial'. He was given a jar, and every time he was good or kind, he got to put a marble in the jar. When the jar was full, he won a prize. My goodness, it took a long time for him to fill up that jar! But when he did, he was delighted on two counts: first, he 'won' some art supplies which he was pleased with and, second, he was absolutely convinced he now never needed to 'be good' again, as the job was done – the jar had been filled. Given he was later in his school life diagnosed as neuro-diverse, I now have very mixed feelings about this amusing anecdote, but it served as an important reminder to me then about the importance of intrinsic and extrinsic motivations!

Thus, it is also important to acknowledge that prosocial behaviour, by its very definition (Grusec et al, 2002), is not always entirely selfless, as it can be motivated by selfish considerations ('pseudo-altruism'; see Eisenberg, 1983). In this vein, it is posited that empathy does not invariably lead to altruistic action and may even steer away from it (Feigin et al, 2014; Berliner and Masterson, 2015). The roots of altruism lie in a desire for interaction and cooperation with others (Dahl and Brownell, 2019); therefore, children may initially engage in helping behaviours out of a desire for involvement or because they perceive such behaviour as a societal norm (Feigin et al, 2014). Dahl and Brownell (2019) illustrate this with the example of a young child initially assisting with tidying up from a perspective of participation. The subsequent praise from an adult serves as positive reinforcement, leading to a repetition of the behaviour. Dahl and Brownell (2019) contend that, in this scenario, the impetus originates from the child, suggesting that the impact of adults on prosocial behaviour may be limited in children who are more passive when opportunities for social interactions arise.

These early experiences play a pivotal role in the further advancement of empathy and prosocial behaviour, all of which directly impact on a child's philanthropic citizenship. Sociopsychology aids in comprehending how children first develop as social beings and subsequently engage in altruistic acts towards others (Feigin et al, 2014). This sheds light on how dispositional traits in children can positively influence their giving behaviours. Research underscores that children are inclined to give too and assist others from a very young age, even in situations where there is no personal gain and when the recipient is a stranger (Warneken and Tomasello, 2008; Wildeboer et al, 2017). In essence, parents and educators should lean more on this intrinsic motivation and the natural course of its development, reinforcing feelings of autonomy and competence, rather than resorting to material incentives and rewards, which can have adverse effects. I explore this idea further in Chapter 4. However, simply encouraging our children to 'be kind' can be equally problematic, as I will discuss in the following section.

The problem with kindness and social justice

There are few people who I think would argue with the notion of the importance of kindness. Nonetheless, as a standalone virtue, an end unto itself kindness can both help and hinder justice.

Kindness is the quality of being friendly, generous and considerate. It involves acts of compassion, empathy and benevolence towards others. It is most often enacted on an individual level, where one person shows care and concern for another. It's about creating positive and supportive interpersonal relationships. Acts of kindness are typically driven by a desire to alleviate suffering or promote wellbeing. It's often about making others feel valued and appreciated, and tends to have an immediate and direct impact on individuals, often resulting in positive emotions and improved wellbeing. Forester (2021) argues that to genuinely express kindness, we must: (1) acknowledge another person's vulnerability, loss or suffering; (2) understand the underlying factors contributing to their vulnerability; (3) identify how we can actively alleviate or mitigate that vulnerability to effect positive change; and (4) crucially, cultivate the motivation to take action and make a tangible difference. Nonetheless, Scott and Seglow (2007) argue the importance of the motivation of the kindness, suggesting forced altruism or kindness, which may not recognise the first three parts of Forester's argument, and skip straight to part (4), may well have the opposite effect from that intended, causing more harm than help for recipients.

Social justice, on the other hand, is the concept of promoting fairness, equality and equity in society. It addresses systemic issues of injustice, discrimination and inequality. Efforts to promote social justice aim to address broader social, economic and political structures that perpetuate inequality. It seeks to create systemic change for marginalised and oppressed groups. Advocates of social justice are motivated by a desire to rectify historical and ongoing injustices. It often involves challenging and changing policies, laws and institutions, working for longlasting, systemic change. It focuses on reshaping societal norms and structures to create a more equitable and just society. There are of course several important points of connection between the two. Both are grounded in compassion and empathy seeking to recognise the inherent worth and dignity of all individuals. Indeed, both concepts often involve advocating for those who are marginalised, oppressed or disadvantaged in some way, and both promote inclusivity, where everyone is treated with respect and dignity.

Nonetheless, each is also in tension with one another. Kindness often operates on an individual level, while social justice focuses on systemic change. Balancing these approaches can be complex, as individual kindness may not be sufficient to address deep-seated systemic issues. Social justice requires confronting systems and institutions that perpetuate inequality, which may involve challenging established norms and potentially causing discomfort or conflict. And each requires a different sense of prioritisation and resources. Kindness often involves immediate, direct assistance to individuals in need – ideas we commonly associate with charity rather than philanthropy. Whereas social justice efforts may require allocating resources in ways that address broader, systemic issues, which might not always prioritise immediate relief to those in acute need.

The notable drawback of the kindness agenda is that acts of kindness run the risk of becoming selective, almost transactional and ultimately fleeting gestures directed at individuals we consider deserving of our attention in any given moment. Moreover, these acts often appear to serve our own interests more than benefiting the recipients. The sense of satisfaction we derive from showing kindness doesn't quite match the degree of relief from hardship or misfortune experienced by the person on the receiving end. Research even supports the idea that being kind has positive effects on our health, but the impact on those receiving our kindness may not be as pronounced (Ciocarlan et al, 2023). The real crux of the issue here is the sense of collective social responsibility and solidarity which is not really encouraged under the blanket of kindness. This is not just a set of actions to perform, but a way of existing and being which, while it may be motivated by kindness and compassion, requires a depth which is beyond both these ideas. It is about connectiveness to one another, through which we generate a shared sense of values and collaboration. Our sense of justice is acting on that shared value inclusively, prioritising the wellbeing of all as mutually valued.

As explored in previous chapters, under an agenda of responsibilisation and character, since the 1980s, an ideology of individualism, self-efficacy and purported meritocracy has guided the worldviews of many. Kindness fits within this framework, offering occasional moments of performative compassion amid what could otherwise be seen as an unrelenting focus on individual needs and goals, which we celebrate often ostentatiously. Let me illustrate my point here. It is a kind act to give food to the foodbank, it is a collective act to organise a food collection for the food bank, and it is a socially just act of collective responsibility to campaign for the right of food to all and to vote in a way which helps the most vulnerable in society.

Kindness can also be seen as a veneer of affability, manifested through the polite treatment of others. Indeed, society, families, communities and schools often tell children to choose kindness and to 'manage' or suppress their emotions, closing down their rights to be angry, and to express that anger, when something is unjust (Galligan and Miller, 2022). For example, I distinctly remember being teased as a child for wearing hand-me-down clothes. A teacher encouraging the other child to 'be kind' as the response to their bullying, and me to 'be kind' in moving on was never going to suffice in that situation – it needed a direct, specific response which challenged the other individual's stance and micro-aggression, and fixed the harm caused. Instead, the whole scenario was wrapped up in the veneer of kindness, not justice. I remember feeling my voice had been quashed, and the next day, I remember putting on those clothes again with a sense of embarrassment and, indeed, shame. Taking a neutral stance on difficult issues, rather than encouraging democratic thinking and indeed allowing children to express their anger, can limit civic participation (Ross and Vinson, 2013). Philanthropy, charitable giving and social justice are, and indeed should be, contentious, debated topics (Morvaridi, 2015). Recognising children as social actors and current citizens means it is important that they too are provided with the opportunity to critically explore these challenges and debates around how we enact our philanthropic citizenship (Weinberg and Flinders, 2018). Justice requires us to seek to rectify imbalances in resources, power, and privilege in ways that arise from a place of awareness and moral conviction, but equally kindness is an important step in the road towards justice. Kindness alone will not allow us to solve injustice; nonetheless, it is a good place to start the conversation!

The commodification of kindness: Beast Philanthropy

'So many people are conditioned to think giving money to charity is a burden or a sacrifice. But when people realize helping is enjoyable and beautiful, that will change the way they think about giving', Darren Margolias is quoted as saying in the Rolling Stone Magazine, as Margolias emphasises how the YouTube star MrBeast simply wants 'to school the next generation' in the 'benefits of unconditional giving' (Dickson, 2022).

Recent years have borne witness to a commodification of kindness, a process by which acts of kindness or expressions of empathy are turned into commodities or products that can be bought, sold or otherwise exchanged within a market or economic system. This can take various forms, and it often involves the packaging and selling of goods or services that are associated with notions of kindness, empathy or altruism. When it comes to our children's lives, this is probably nowhere more evident than in the digital content produced for them daily, by millions of online content providers. There is a growing interest in exploring the role of digital communities in children's philanthropic and civic learning. However, this area of research is still in its early stages, especially when it comes to younger children. Emerging research has shown that when children engage with platforms that have civic content, they are more likely to become involved in civic activities within their own communities (Lamarra et al, 2019). Indeed, studies in Scotland have examined children's digital literacies. One finding was that when children interacted with different characters online, they were able to consider and discuss different perspectives and viewpoints (Martzoukou, 2020).

YouTube as a platform has grown significantly in prominence over the past decade and one of the most prominent spaces in which children interact with online personalities. While this has come with both opportunities and threats, one of the most prominent personas who occupy the limelight is the character of MrBeast. MrBeast, aka Jimmy Donaldson, has become one of the most successful YouTube content creators, making him a multimillionaire and influencing hundreds of thousands of children around the planet. While much of MrBeast's content is elaborate challenges and dares undertaken by the public or his friends, my interest here is in MrBeast the philanthropist, under the guise of his YouTube channel and brand Beast Philanthropy.

I think my two sons were somewhat surprised when I sat down with them in the summer of 2023 and asked how I could view this channel, as in truth

I had no idea how to access this content. We sat for many hours watching MrBeast rescue paralysed dogs in Thailand, rebuild an orphanage in South Africa, pay for children's surgery in the Philippines, give out prosthetic limbs, give out clothing across the world and help 1,000 blind people see for the first time, to give just a few examples. Watching these videos generates income and thus the content becomes self-sustaining, with the charitable work funding itself off the voyeurism of the watcher. Indeed, the MrBeast model of philanthropy wholly relies upon entertaining as many people as possible and then using the subsequent advertisement revenue, brand deals and merchandise sales to fund future philanthropic ventures, alongside growing the MrBeast brand, leading to increased revenue for the for-profit side of the venture.

I'll admit that I watched with a sense of uncomfortable fascination. Alongside these extraordinary acts of giving are other MrBeast content platforms which demonstrate an equally extraordinary, shameless waste of wealth and exuberance, where MrBeast is seen to blow up cars worth more than a million pounds, handing out iPhones to children on Halloween, gift tens of thousands of pounds to unsuspecting followers or perform outlandish stunts which show a reckless abandonment of money and wealth. As Wade (2023) points out, this was most glaringly evident in a video that cost $3.5 million to produce and has garnered over 360 million views. In it, MrBeast re-enacted scenes from the Netflix series *Squid Game*, featuring 456 participants vying for a prize of $456,000. Unlike the series, the elimination of contestants luckily didn't culminate in their gruesome demise. However, what was also missing was any acknowledgement of the irony, considering *Squid Game*'s blunt critique of how economic inequality allows vulnerable individuals to be exploited for the amusement of the wealthy (Wade, 2023). While for an entertainment gameshow this may seem crass but ethically OK, once the same approach is applied to charity, it does become more questionable. This is the content my children, and hundreds of thousands like them, see on a daily basis – what does this unfettered, performative content teach them about philanthropy and helping others?

First, let's acknowledge the model works, well for Donaldson at least. Donaldson is the most popular YouTuber on the planet with over 130 million subscribers. His YouTube videos were watched by over 600 million people in just a three-month period. The influence he wields is staggering to say the least. MrBeast's form of philanthropy is one of spectacle and spectacular, seeking to attract large audiences. As both my children pointed out to me, MrBeast is doing good. Because of him, thousands of animals are in a safe home, orphaned children in South Africa have a safe home to live in, children in the Philippines can walk, 1,000 blind people can now see – it is undeniable that some positive outcomes have occurred thanks to

MrBeast's philanthropic efforts, which would not have happened without his investment. Nonetheless, this does not give him a 'free pass' as a philanthropic actor (Davies, 2023) – what he does, why and how, has lasting consequences for how children and young people experience philanthropy and thus warrants further discussion.

Indeed, numerous commentators have offered thoughtful reflections on whether Beast Philanthropy is ultimately 'good' or 'bad' for philanthropy. Davies (2023) argues that, while acknowledging issues, there is good in MrBeast's mode of philanthropic giving – he is modelling an idea that if you are wealthy, you have a responsibility to give, and is bringing philanthropy into the mainstream and making each of us more aware of the issues. Indeed, while MrBeast's campaign to cure 1,000 people's blindness attracted significant criticism for 'charity porn', supporters lamented the virtues of bringing this issue into popular public discourse (*BBC Newsbeat*, 2023). Nonetheless, do we require more awareness raising and the stark inequalities prevalent in global society?

Wade (2023) argues that the underlying business model of Beast Philanthropy capitalises on the fine line of everyday life to elicit emotional reactions from regular people, many of whom are just one small step away from ruin. This approach not only distorts our motivations for helping others, but it also inevitably introduces biases in determining which people, places and causes are deemed 'deserving'. Ultimately, is the message we are sending our children 'why bother giving if it doesn't translate into compelling content?' (Wade, 2023). Davies (2023) offers similar reflections, raising concerns that this model can:

> give the impression that philanthropy is all about wealthy lone saviours swooping in and spraying money around to recipients that they have personally chosen; instead of acknowledging that most philanthropy is about the fairly considered distribution of resources through a range of expert non-profits who do their best to ensure that those resources get to the areas of greatest need ... a generation of younger people who grow up watching these videos will end up with a very warped view of philanthropy.

Furthermore, various concerns arise from the way in which these practices tie wealth creation to charitable activities, presenting them as the 'solution' to societal problems, as Nickel and Eikenberry note: 'Philanthropy reflected in, distributed by, and used in the service of capitalism can only be the voice of capitalism and the complete destruction of imagination of alternatives' (2009, p 986).

Miller and Hogg (2023) extend this argument by highlighting that MrBeast explicitly positions his own wealth and influence – generated through

YouTube views – as the remedy for social issues. Indeed, Donaldson himself points to the fact that he seeks to take a neutral stance in order to maintain his ratings: '"I don't want to alienate Republicans and Democrats", he says. "I like having it where everyone can support [my] charity ... it would be very silly of me to alienate basically half of America"' (cited in Dickson, 2022).

This limits teaching children about philanthropy's true potential for transformation, and moves the focus away from justice-oriented models of philanthropy – the type of approaches which are more likely to address social inequalities (Davies, 2023; Miller and Hogg, 2023; Wade, 2023)

It is obviously commendable and admirable for that MrBeast seeks to give away his entire wealth and is already having a huge impact on the communities on which he bestows his fortune. According to an interview in *Rolling Stone*, Donaldson states that the MrBeast Philanthropy channel contributes 100 per cent of its revenue to a warehouse that operates mobile food donations throughout eastern North Carolina and reportedly delivered 1,000,563 meals by the end of 2021. Nonetheless, it does raise significant questions about the nature of philanthropy and how children come to interpret their own philanthropic power. Through the MrBeast videos, children are repeatedly told they are being philanthropic simply as a consumer of content – through them 'liking' the videos. Children are not being encouraged to engage more systematically in the injustice which informs the need for the charity or, indeed, explore their own agency and voice.

This type of content is unlikely to abate anytime soon. In a world where many controversial influencers continue to garner attention, I would much rather my children watch and engage with MrBeast and Beast Philanthropy. Nonetheless, we should remain cautious if this is the only space in which our children learn about their philanthropic power, as it is passive, limited, reinforces ideas of saviourism, individualistic, capitalist-content driven, commodifies suffering and emotion, and largely performative, with little hope of challenging wider injustices, but like our discussion on kindness previously, it is perhaps not the worse place (I write this between somewhat gritted teeth) to begin a critically considered conversation.

Family matters

On a personal note, the profound impact my parents had on shaping both the child I once was and the adult I have become cannot be overstated. Spanning over 40 years, my parents dedicated themselves to fostering vulnerable children, whether for short-term or long-term care. Growing up amid a diverse array of brothers and sisters, each with unique life experiences, very much shaped my perspective on justice, equality and opportunities. This went far beyond the idea of giving money; it was about understanding people, connections, relationships and allyship. Likewise, the civic engagement opportunities children experience when they are young profoundly shape their values as adults.

While the family is widely acknowledged for moulding our civic values, the intricate relationship between civil society and the family often escapes attention, with both entities erroneously linked to opposing political ideologies. Existing literature tends to associate civil society with a left-leaning orientation, while the family is typically aligned with the right (Power et al, 2018). This dichotomy has fostered the misconception that the family operates outside the realm of civil society, and some even contend that strong family ties may impede a healthy public sphere. Challenging this notion, Muddiman et al (2020) position the family as a gateway to civil society activities and a site of civil society engagement in itself. Indeed, research underscores the pivotal role families play in shaping children's philanthropic experiences and attitudes (Ottoni-Wilhelm et al, 2017, 2023; Body et al, 2020; Muddiman et al, 2020). Notably, approximately only a quarter of children openly discuss voluntary action as a family matter, revealing a communication gap regarding these values (Body et al, 2020). Furthermore, studies highlight that relationships with mothers and grandparents significantly influence young people's civic participation, underscoring the family's importance in fostering engagement in civil society (Muddiman et al, 2020).

The exploration of children's involvement in volunteering activities, particularly during their primary school years, remains a largely uncharted territory within the academic landscape. This gap arises not only from a lack of comprehensive data but also from a prevailing tendency to view children predominantly through the lens of familial units rather than recognising them as autonomous individuals (Sarre and Tarling, 2010). Despite these challenges, existing data uncover significant contributions made by children in the UK's volunteering landscape, contributions that often go unnoticed due to age-related considerations. In this intricate web of influence, gender and ethnicity emerge as pivotal factors shaping children's formal volunteering activities (Sarre and Tarling, 2010). The influence of family dynamics on children's civic involvement adds further complexity to the narrative. From shared meals to occasional disagreements, family life plays a pivotal role in moulding the civic attitudes of the younger generation. This complex process of socialisation extends to the transmission of religious beliefs and gender norms, creating a dynamic interplay between family engagement, civil society and civic values (Muddiman et al, 2020).

Moreover, a study conducted in California sheds light on the profound impact of parental attitudes and behaviours on children's civic participation (White, 2021). Children raised in environments where parents prioritise community responsibility are more likely to embrace volunteering, driven by their parents' humanitarian-egalitarian values and active civic engagement.

The intricate links extend beyond values to encompass parental levels of social trust, civic efficacy and participation, all of which are commonly reflected in their children's civic inclinations (White and Mistry, 2016). In the context of the UK, family volunteering opportunities emerge as transformative gateways for children to enter the space of civic participation. However, data suggest potential barriers for families with children aged five to ten engaging in family-based volunteering, thereby revealing nuanced challenges that must be addressed in order to foster a culture of civic engagement from a young age (Kamerade, 2022). Furthermore, family involvement, encompassing discussions about charity and philanthropy, positively correlates with children engaging in charitable activities (Ottoni-Wilhelm et al, 2017). Moreover, modelling sharing behaviours and positive parenting foster children's empathy and generosity (Ben-Ner et al, 2017; Duong and Bradshaw, 2017). While friends also play a significant role, with 29 per cent of young people expressing a willingness to participate in social action if they could do it with their friends (Brasta et al, 2019), friendships may even exert a stronger impact on young people's civic engagement than family (Šerek and Umemura, 2015).

When it comes to philanthropic behaviour, few stories highlight the importance of encouraging children's endeavours as effectively as the story of Eve Alderman and her dad, Ian. 'Never under-estimate the difference you made and the lives you touched' – these are the words inscribed on a keyring gifted to Eve Alderman as she and her father, both of whom are autistic, undertook the huge challenge of hiking from John O'Groats to Land's End in 2022. Raising awareness, funds and support for autism, and supported by mother and wife Sarah, they continue to trek the length and breadth of the British Isles, hiking all of Scotland's great trails in 2023, 1,900 miles, across 29 different trails. All of this is captured and documented through beautifully honest blog posts on social media and YouTube videos through their platform 'Our Spectrum Adventures'.

In the majority of these daily posts, Ian, the author of these blogs, captures the importance of the ecosystem which surrounds children's philanthropic efforts. The kindness of strangers is a constant and driving force of the pair's success and is continuously recognised throughout their journey. Given that in Chapter 5 I focus on the media only really recognising exceptionalism through exceptional means, these everyday acts of kindness remind us of the ecosystem of support in communities which surrounds children's philanthropic efforts. Indeed, Eve and Ian's efforts are consistently recognised through gifts of accommodation, food, gifts and supporting fundraising efforts by people who are strangers to the pair, but simply wish to encourage them on their pilgrimage to raise funds and awareness of autism. In this sense, here again we see kindness as a gateway to increasing philanthropic citizenship, as a space that adults, both family and strangers, use to help encourage and empower children as philanthropic citizens.

Promoting civic learning among children requires active engagement with parents, caregivers and the family unit. This holistic approach has the potential to significantly strengthen efforts to cultivate civic and philanthropic engagement in the next generation. It is why innovative projects, such as Family Volunteering Club, which is featured as a case study here, provide such important examples of the role of civil society in supporting and promoting children's engagement in civic life, where children are encouraged to engage in acts of kindness and then to use this as a space to begin to explore the more critical aspects of cause-related issues in which the children and families are engaged.

Case study 1: Family Volunteering Club

My son was 18 months old and though I was loving being a parent, I knew I'd neglected my 'old self' for a long time and had been thinking a lot about how to 'find her' again.

Doing stuff in the community has always been important to me. Before having my son, I volunteered for many years with two different amazing charities in London, both supporting homeless communities in the city. I learnt so much from the people I met, and it was positive for me in many ways to have the opportunity to be part of these incredible communities. But now I had a small person in tow – it wasn't appropriate to go back to these specific places and I was searching for where I could take him along, but was met with lots of brick walls. So I decided to do it myself!

With excitement and some trepidation, in autumn 2019 I created a small pilot programme of child-friendly volunteering sessions with a range of causes in my local area in south London – and we were inundated. It was such a joy, and I knew this was the start of something much bigger. Fast forward a few years, having grown the programme locally, completed our first pilot in Stevenage, and gained charitable status as a registered Charitable Incorporated Organisation and established itself in the sector as a pioneering, accessible and inclusive programme which has the potential to transform opportunities for families to participate in community regularly and easily, we are now on an ambitious and exciting journey to have national impact.

While Family Volunteering Club (FVC) was initially about making it easier for parents and carers to give their time, energy and ideas to local causes (which it also still is), actually, the bigger impact we are seeing now is in helping to nurture the next generation of global citizens. We are doing this through creating programmes of locally run, regular, fun, impactful, child-friendly volunteering sessions. From gardening in community spaces to helping at food banks – we create opportunities for children and their grown-ups to connect with and support local causes. We want to make civic participation as easy and part and parcel of family life as, for example, going to a swimming or football lesson.

Children are empowered to learn about – in an age-appropriate way – important societal issues, and the role that they can play in making positive change. FVC helps them feel pride in and connection with their local area, as well as being somewhere to have fun, meet new people, build confidence and learn new skills. Meanwhile, adults have the opportunity to give their ideas, time and energy to local causes that matter to them, while having fun with their child.

Importantly, we don't want children just to learn about these societal injustices, but we want them to begin to question why they exist, and this is embedded into the structure of our sessions. Feedback from recent sessions shows that 79% of attendees were engaging with the partner charity/community group for the first time. 57% reported they and their child had learned something new with the remaining 43% saying that as well as learning something new, a conversation about the cause/societal issue with their child had been stimulated and they felt motivated to learn even more about it after the session.

Some words of feedback for why participants enjoy Family Volunteering Club:

- 'It was great! Love my son helping "the real world" and learning to help others so young.'
- 'It was so brilliant, I loved getting to know one of our local charities and feel really inspired to do more volunteering with my daughter in the future. Thank you!'

Maddy Mills, CEO, Family Volunteering Club

Storytelling and the moral imagination

Growing up, my children loved their bedtime stories. Some years back, knowing my interest in children and charity I was gifted the book *The Giving Tree*. Admittedly I'd heard of the book, but had very little knowledge about the story and was expecting a lovely tale of friendship, reciprocity and kindness. Let's just say the story didn't quite meet my expectations!

If like I was, you are unfamiliar with the story, it is about a boy who loves a tree. As the boy grows, he visits the tree frequently. He takes the tree's apples, which he proceeds to sell for profit. He then takes the tree's branches and builds a house, eventually cutting the tree down to build a boat and sails away. The tree is reduced to a stump and has nothing left to give, but 'luckily' still provides a seat for the boy, who is now an old man. My two boys, and indeed myself, were far from impressed by this story – instead of the heartwarming tale I was expecting, we saw it as a story of greed, exploitation, selfishness and self-sacrifice. We had a good conversation about this book, thinking about what it meant to give, what it meant to take, greed, selfishness and selflessness – it was certainly a 'teachable moment' which stayed with them.

Storytelling is an important way for children to learn about being kind and helpful to others (Kidd and Castano, 2013; Aksoy and Baran, 2020). Unsurprisingly, many studies have shown that stories can inspire children to be kind and considerate (Larsen et al, 2018). Indeed, multiple scholars suggest that storytelling can encourage kindness and empathy in children (Peterson, 2016; Kidd, 2020). However, they have the power to do more than this. The prominent philosopher Martha Nussbaum (1998) suggests that stories can teach children important values and start conversations about fairness and justice. Nonetheless, not all stories have the same effect on children's behaviour (Narvaez, 2002). For example, children are more likely to be inspired by characters who are ordinary and relatable, rather than those who are extraordinary, such as superheroes, or hard to relate to, such as anamorphic figures (Han et al, 2017). Interestingly, research suggests that reading stories about real people can make children more giving and helpful, while stories with imaginary characters (like talking animals) may not have the same effect (Larsen et al, 2018).

However, even though our society is becoming more diverse, it's still hard to find children's books that feature characters from different backgrounds in terms of gender, race and privilege (Hamilton et al, 2006; Koss, 2015). Nussbaum (1998) studied how stories can help children become good citizens who care about others and the world. She believes that stories help children imagine what it's like to be in someone else's shoes, which is important for being compassionate and understanding others' needs. As children grow up with these values, they develop their own sense of compassion. Nussbaum (1998) also says that we need to start teaching children about being good citizens early on. Stories can help children see that life isn't always fair, and they can emotionally connect with the importance of helping others (Nussbaum, 1998, p 93). So, storytelling and literature play a big role in teaching children about being good to others and responsible citizens.

To understand this further, my colleague, Jayne Lacny and I decided to examine modern children's picture books with a focus on how those books portray philanthropic citizenship (see Body and Lacny, 2022). We wanted not only to explore the representation of this concept, but also to identify books that did it well and understand why. Through this process, we looked at over 500 children's picture books and closely examined 104 that portrayed philanthropic acts in a meaningful way. What we found was that even from this earliest exposure in literature, these stories reinforce the idea of philanthropy as a benevolent act. The analysis revealed a prevalent portrayal of voluntary action as individual, private and focused on virtues like kindness and generosity, neglecting broader societal implications. These stories often feature a single benevolent hero saving the poor or helpless, perpetuating a simplistic view of philanthropy. However, more worryingly these narratives sideline beneficiary voices, reducing them simply to recipients of charity and neglecting to consider their own agency. This portrayal not only limits philanthropy to acts of benevolence by the privileged but also diminishes the voices of the communities it aims to support, reinforcing inequity and inequality. Additionally, we found that these stories were fraught with problematic portrayals of gender, race and power within philanthropy, too often perpetuating ideas of White saviourism, colonialism and paternalism (Jefferess, 2008; Vallery, 2020).

Stories to cultivate philanthropic citizenship

Disappointed with prevailing trends in children's literature, Jayne and I set out on a quest to uncover books that not only celebrate diversity but also challenge conventional ideas of personal responsibility. Our goal was to find literature that delves into the intricate connections between voluntary action, philanthropy and larger societal forces such as economics and politics. Despite not always making the top 500 children's books list, we discovered a wealth of options that go beyond merely narrating stories of charity; these books spotlight competent children actively engaging in ethical actions, shifting the narrative from kindness to one of solidarity and allyship.

Our focus on books promoting philanthropic citizenship highlighted a common thread across children's literature – a central character's active involvement driven by critical inquiry within broader political and social frameworks (Nussbaum, 1998; Westheimer, 2015; Simpson, 2017; Body et al, 2020). Take *Follow the Moon Home: A Tale of One Idea, Twenty Kids, and a Hundred Sea Turtles* by Cousteau and Hopkinson (2016) as an example. The protagonist, Vivienne, identifies a problem affecting sea turtles due to light pollution on the beach. Through meticulous planning and collective action, she successfully leads a campaign to protect the turtles. The book not only underscores environmental conservation but also emphasises collaboration, community involvement and the impact young individuals can have on the world. It encourages children to engage in research, critical thinking and active participation. Authored by environmental leader Philippe Cousteau, *Follow the Moon Home* inspires change by challenging the conventional notion of children as mere participants in environmental initiatives. Cousteau's call to action in a letter at the end of the book to 'young activists' exemplifies how social activism can be cultivated within schools and communities, emphasising children's potential as critical thinkers and problem solvers (Cousteau and Hopkinson, 2016, pp 38–39).

Similar trends emerge in books like *Greta and the Giants* (Tucker and Persico, 2019), drawing inspiration from environmental activist Greta Thunberg. The story intertwines critical thinking with collective action, urging readers to engage in climate protests, adopt eco-friendly practices and advocate for positive changes. Political engagement is further emphasised in books like *Sofia Valdez, Future Prez* (Beaty, 2019) and *The Day War Came* (Davies, 2018), linking the narrative to wider social and political actions. Notably, several of these books are directly linked to real charities, exposing children to the broader structures surrounding voluntary action and charitable organisations. For instance, *Beatrice's Goat* (McBrie, 2001) is supported by Hillary Clinton and endorses the work of Heifer International. *The Day War Came* (Davies, 2018) is endorsed by Amnesty International, and *Greta and the Giants* (Tucker and Persico, 2019) donates a percentage of sales to Greenpeace. In a departure from the typical donor-centric philanthropic narrative, some of these books shift the perspective to the beneficiary, providing agency and discussing the needs that drive philanthropic acts. Examples like *Beatrice's Goat*, *The Day War Came*, *Boxes for Katj* (Fleming, 2003) and *Dear Earth …From Your Friends in Room 5* challenge traditional donor-centric approaches, favouring community-centric ones and empowering children's voices.

While these books don't form an exhaustive list, they serve as examples of literature representing human possibilities for children's philanthropic citizenship. These stories offer tangible examples of diverse characters engaging in voluntary action for social good within a framework of social and environmental justice. Literature, though not a sole transformative force, provides an essential starting point for framing children's acts of giving in a justice-oriented framework (Nussbaum, 1998). Moreover, literature isn't the only medium through which children can engage in active, justice-oriented citizenship. Research highlights the importance of music, filmmaking and other forms of art in promoting youth activism (Williams et al, 2020; Yeom et al, 2020; Redwood et al, 2022; Howard, 2023). However, if we aim to nurture children's philanthropic citizenship, it's crucial to consider what we teach them about philanthropy through the literature we share. We must also counter dominant narratives that often promote gendered and racial stereotypes, framing giving as an individual act disconnected from wider social and political structures. Through thoughtful selection and discussion, literature can serve as a powerful tool in shaping children's understanding of philanthropy and inspiring them to become active, justice-oriented citizens, as demonstrated by the following case study from EmpathyLab.

Case study 2: EmpathyLab

EmpathyLab is a charitable social enterprise specialising in using reading and stories to build children's empathy awareness and skills. Our work is based on scientific research showing that empathy is a learnable skill, and that reading builds our real life empathy.

Our mission is to raise an empathy-educated generation, and we place a big emphasis on empowering children to challenge prejudice and division, to develop an understanding of social justice and to take positive action to inject more empathy into their homes, schools and communities.

The case study schools highlighted here use tools we have created in response to input from educators and psychologists. They include an annual Read for Empathy collection of 60 titles, Empathy Day every June and an in-depth schools programme.

Moorlands Primary Academy, Teacher, Jon Biddle: My Year 6 class focused on refugees. We spent time reading books, such as Morris Gleitzman's *Boy Overboard* and Elizabeth Laird's *Welcome to Nowhere*, plus non-fiction including Michael Rosen's *Who Are Refugees and Migrants?* As part of the research, we had speakers from Amnesty International and refugees from the local charity Great Yarmouth Refugee Outreach Support.

The impact on the children was striking. It was the first thing that they spoke to their parents about at the end of the day and they immediately wanted to have a class meeting to think of ways that they could help. Several talked about how when they had seen stories about refugees on the news, they didn't really pay attention before, but felt they now would.

Each pupil wrote a letter to a child refugee as part of Amnesty's Write for Rights campaign, and the school organised a refugee sleepover to give pupils a small insight into the experiences of refugees

The focus on empathy throughout the year, powerful books, and first-hand accounts about life as a refugee combined to give children a unique experience and caused a genuine shift in their attitudes. Before getting involved with EmpathyLab, we might have just tried to raise some money (perhaps more akin to sympathy than empathy). The Amnesty letters were undoubtedly the most powerful pieces of written work my students have produced. Year 6 students have since been involved with planning lessons about refugees for other year groups, which has created a real sense of cooperation and teamwork among the class.

- 'I used to think refugees were different from us. Now I don't.' Chantelle, Year 6
- 'It was some of my favourite work that we've ever done. We're learning about the real world and we're all part of it. Like, everyone, not just us and the people we know.' Ahmed, Year 6

Miranda McKearney and Sarah Mears, EmpathyLab

From kindness to allyship and solidarity

Kindness, allyship and solidarity are related concepts, but they have distinct meanings and applications, particularly in the context of social justice and intergroup relations. As discussed, kindness refers to the quality or act of being friendly, considerate, compassionate and generous towards others. It involves showing empathy and goodwill, often through small acts of care or support – indeed, how many times have we heard our children be encouraged to undertake small acts of kindness? Nonetheless, it is considered a universal value that can be applied in various situations and to people of all backgrounds, regardless of their social identities or affiliations, most often motivated by a general desire to promote wellbeing, comfort and positivity – for example, holding open the door for someone, helping a neighbour or comforting someone who is upset.

On the other hand, allyship involves actively supporting and advocating for members of marginalised or disadvantaged groups. It requires recognising and challenging systemic injustices, and using one's privilege to amplify the voices and concerns of marginalised individuals or communities. It tends to be utilised in specific situations where there are power imbalances or systemic discrimination, and typically occurs within the context of social justice movements, where allies work alongside marginalised groups to fight for equality and justice. It is driven by a commitment to dismantling oppressive systems and promoting equity. It involves taking intentional actions to challenge and change the status quo – for example, attending protests for racial equality, advocating for policies that support LGBTQ+ rights and/or actively listening to and amplifying the voices of marginalised individuals. Alternatively, solidarity occurs when individuals or groups support and advocate for one another, particularly in the face of shared challenges or systemic injustices, again often rising within social justice movements. It is driven by a commitment to dismantling oppressive systems, promoting equity and supporting marginalised or disadvantaged groups, and involves taking intentional actions to challenge and change the status quo grounded in a sense of shared identity or common cause.

Connection is at the heart of both solidarity and allyship. Solidarity, by its nature, implies a shared identity and a direct connection to a common experience or cause. Those who stand in solidarity forge deep emotional ties, uniting in purpose and understanding, often through shared struggles or shared identities. On the other hand, allyship involves supporting a cause or community without necessarily sharing the same identity or direct personal experience. It's a connection built on empathy, understanding and a commitment to dismantling systemic injustices. In terms of involvement, the distinctions between solidarity and allyship become clearer. Those in solidarity may not only express empathy but also directly experience the challenges faced by the group they support. Their connection is visceral, rooted in a shared lived experience that propels them to join the struggle for change. Conversely, allies, while undoubtedly supportive, do not necessarily share the same lived experiences or face the same systemic challenges as the communities they support. Their involvement is driven by a commitment to justice and equality rather than a firsthand understanding of the marginalised group's struggles.

Action is a defining aspect of both concepts. Solidarity often manifests through collective action, where individuals join forces, pooling their efforts and resources towards a shared goal. The unity inherent in solidarity leads to a powerful collective impact, as those connected by a shared identity work together for common objectives. In contrast, allyship places a spotlight on individual actions taken by those outside a marginalised group to support and uplift that group. Allies use their positions of privilege and influence to advocate for change, amplifying the voices of those facing discrimination. In essence, while solidarity and allyship share common ground in terms of support and collaboration, they differ in the nature of their connection and involvement. Solidarity is often rooted in a shared identity and collective experience, a deep connection that arises from shared challenges. Allyship, on the other hand, involves individuals from outside a marginalised group actively working to support and advocate for that group, recognising the importance of using privilege to effect positive change. Both concepts, with their unique strengths, play crucial roles in fostering social change and addressing systemic inequalities in a collaborative and impactful manner.

In the realm of children's philanthropic citizenship, the concepts of kindness, allyship and solidarity serve as foundational pillars for cultivating empathetic, socially conscious individuals who stand in allyship and/or solidarity with others. As our children learn to navigate the complexities of social justice and intergroup relations, they are encouraged not only to practise kindness through small acts of care and support but also to actively engage in allyship by advocating for marginalised groups and challenging systemic injustices. However, this learning does not happen by accident; it requires key, purposeful approaches, where children are encouraged and supported to develop a deep sense of connection and empathy, forging bonds of solidarity with those facing adversity. Whether through collective action grounded in shared experiences or individual acts driven by a commitment to justice, children can emerge as allies standing shoulder to shoulder with marginalised communities, fostering a more inclusive and equitable society for all, as outlined in the following case study, which is focused on the innovative, grassroots Agents of Change programme, developed by staff and pupils at St Lawrence Church of England Primary School.

Case study 3: St Lawrence School – Agents of Change

Agents of Change is a grassroots project aimed at providing children with the knowledge, understanding and skills to help inform positive change in themselves, their community, nationally and internationally. It aims at helping them foster an awareness of the legal and governmental framework in which they live, and develop the skills required to engage with them. It is designed to develop children's voice, talents and confidence in the impact they can have as global citizens.

Importantly, Agents of Change is equitable and neither the age, developmental stage, socioeconomic status or familial input of children are determining factors in their achievements. Staff within schools are trained to be inclusive and flexible with their guidance and encouragement, helping children to flourish in a bespoke manner at an appropriate pace.

All participating children are given a poster with 40 citizenship-based challenges, a passport with information that outlines related skills and inspiration for each idea. Children earn a stamp in their passport for every project completed. When children have completed seven projects, they can choose a badge (of which there are seven to collect) or will be given a certificate (depending on the package a school has purchased). We recommend that the badges and certificates are given during half-termly assemblies to maximise peer encouragement and celebration.

Children can work autonomously on projects or use the support of their friends, family or school. As much or as little guidance can be provided but the heart of individual projects centre around the child's personal beliefs and passions. Initiatives worked on in school can range from class or whole school projects. Pedagogically, Agents of Change can be used within a class topic and incorporate all subjects; for example, looking scientifically at the effect of plastics, extending vocabulary with persuasive language and letter writing, and developing art skills with posters. It can thus both enrich and invigorate the curriculum and be woven into as much of it as schools choose.

By August 2023, and since the beginning of Agents of Change in 2021, children at St Lawrence Church of England Primary in Rowhedge, Essex (the founding school) have completed over 2,500 projects. These incorporate individually led ideas, as well as class and whole school initiatives. They have received video encouragement from celebrities, and letters of encouragement from David Attenborough, the Prince and Princess of Wales, and many more. They have organised village litter picks inspired by Surfers Against Sewage, bought five acres of rainforest, created poetry about anti-racism, written stories about gender identity, and art about the environment. They have helped neighbours in need, learned to cook their favourite meal, donated coats and blankets to vulnerable members of their community, and spread positive messages to themselves, each other and globally.

The children are powerful advocates, one eight-year-old said: 'Agents of Change has changed me on the inside – I love being kind, it feels so special when I make someone else smile.' Another commented: 'Every school should make children like us, everyone should be an Agent of Change, it's the best thing I've learnt in school.'

By modelling the values of Courage, Community and Compassion everybody is enabled to be an Agent of Change in their own learning journey, and those of others by encouraging everyone to; Be Yourself, Investigate, Express Yourself, Brighten Today, Look Beyond, Shout Out Loud and Make Some Waves. At St Lawrence, staff and Governors are passionate that all children learn to be active citizens so that they become the change makers now and in the future.

St Lawrence Primary School, Agents of Change

Conclusion

In this book, I am concerned with how we help children shift from notions of kindness to that of collective approaches which embrace allyship and solidarity. While kindness provides a good starting point, if we wish to promote a more equitable and just society, it cannot be the end in itself. The case studies of Family Volunteering Club, EmpathyLab and St Lawrence School's Agents of Change programme illustrate a range of important attempts of encouraging this sense of connection and action. These grassroots initiatives empower children with the knowledge, skills and understanding to catalyse positive change not only within themselves but also in their community, nationally and even internationally. Each of the programmes goes beyond age, developmental stage, socioeconomic status or familial background, ensuring that every child can excel at their own pace.

Therefore, in this chapter, I assert kindness as an important foundational element of philanthropy, but caution against its potential drawbacks and limitations. While globally celebrated, kindness risks becoming a commodified virtue, especially in the digital age, where performative acts may mask systemic issues and silence marginalised voices. The case of MrBeast and Beast Philanthropy exemplifies this tension, highlighting ethical concerns over the commodification of kindness and the need for a more critical approach to philanthropy education. This tension between kindness and social justice is evident, with the former operating individually and privately, while the latter demands collective, systemic change. Furthermore, I argue that supporting children to shift from kindness to solidarity and allyship is crucial for fostering active, justice-oriented citizens. The family plays a fundamental role in shaping civic attitudes. Additionally, the analysis of children's literature underscores the importance of reshaping children's narratives to promote solidarity and allyship. Literature serves as a powerful tool in framing children's understanding of philanthropy within a justice-oriented framework, encouraging critical thinking and collective action.

In summary, in this chapter I have argued that as we seek to foster philanthropic citizenship in children, we must be conscious of the narratives we share, challenging stereotypes and reframing giving as an integral part of a broader social and political fabric. Ultimately, the interplay between kindness, social justice and philanthropy serves as a multifaceted lens through which we can navigate the complexities of supporting children to engage as compassionate and justice-oriented citizens. Balancing individual acts of kindness with systemic change and recognising the integral role of the 'conversation starters' in this process pave the way towards more inclusive and equitable conversations.

4

Starting young: giving and social action

Introduction

I'm not sure how it works in other households, but I feel my two sons are constantly asking me for money to give to one charity cause or another, through their school and community activities. I'm always happy to support; however, less common is their ability to give me a detailed description of what cause that money is for, and why or how the fundraising activity will benefit the cause. Sound familiar?

Children have increasingly been drawn into the world of fundraising as donors and are recognised as a valuable source of income for charities, as they contribute funds (normally those of their parents or carers) to partake in activities, such as school dress-up days, sponsored walks and bake sales. Drawing on extensive research on child-focused fundraising and the ethical dimensions of nurturing philanthropic citizenship, in this chapter I scrutinise the involvement of children as donors in national fundraising campaigns like Comic Relief, Kids Heart Challenge and Daffodil Day. Despite the widespread participation, questions arise about the meaningfulness of children's engagement and their status as legitimate donors. I critically explore the framing and ethics surrounding children's often passive participation in fundraising, raising a dual dilemma: first, such activity overlooks children's rights as active citizens, denying their agency in decisions affecting them – a fundamental principle of the UNCRC; second, it embodies tokenistic engagement, reducing giving to a transactional act, failing to meet the needs of children as donors or to appropriately and ethically consider the needs and rights of the beneficiaries.

I then explore the broader role of fundraising in fostering children's philanthropic citizenship. I argue that large-scale fundraising methods targeting children in schools and communities often hinder the development of sustained philanthropic commitment. This commitment should encompass both giving and critical reflection on the societal structures driving charitable efforts. This potentially stands in contrast to organisations primarily focused on transactional fundraising for financial gain, presenting complex ethical considerations. In dissecting the ethical dimensions of child-centric fundraising, I call for a re-evaluation of current practices. I advocate for an approach that not only empowers children as active participants in giving but also encourages them to critically engage with the broader social issues underlying these initiatives. By doing so, I hope to pave the way towards a more informed, engaged and ethically grounded generation of philanthropic citizens.

Big fundraising goes global

Do you remember your first experience of giving to charity? I remember mine clearly. I had to wear dots to school. I was so excited as I finally got to show off my favourite pink polka dot dress. It was originally my sister's, but as the youngest of four children, I inevitably ended up with hand-me-down clothes, not that it mattered, I loved it. I remember I had to pay 50p. I walked proudly into school, clasping that 50p so tightly in my palm – I can still remember the feel of it there. But for the life of me I cannot remember what charity it was for or even why we were raising money.

Large-scale charitable campaigns frequently involve schools as intermediaries, exemplified by initiatives like Kids Heart Challenge in the US or BBC Children in Need in the UK, where over 17,000 schools with three million children contribute to BBC Children in Need annually, yielding around £5 million (BBC Children in Need, 2023). Children participate in a wide range of activities, raising funds, which are all intended to contribute to good and worthy causes. Other examples of these charity fundraising campaigns in the UK are 'Sport Relief' and 'Red Nose Day', both of which are organised by Comic Relief, which is the working name of Charity Projects, an operating British charity. As of March 2023, the UK-based Comic Relief's Red Nose Day charity raised over £35.3 million for 2023. The main fundraising event for Comic Relief is an event called Red Nose Day, which usually takes place in mid-March – this event focuses on a celebrity and comedy spectacular, underpinned by the simple notion of making people laugh while raising money.

The triumph of these fundraising campaigns has ignited a global phenomenon. Charity Projects, which oversees the Comic Relief and Sport Relief campaigns in the UK, has even gone international, sharing branding and content with charitable organisations worldwide, allowing them to replicate the successful model. This has propelled Red Nose Day into a worldwide fundraising brand, adapting slightly across Western nations, yet largely adhering to a common structure, of celebrities taking on spectacular, fun, comedic and/or heroic challenges.

In the US, Red Nose Day has transformed into an annual fundraising event, dedicated to breaking the cycle of child poverty and 'aiming to secure a bright future for all children'. It celebrates its mission to unite people in laughter and joy, all the while generating funds and awareness to guarantee the safety, health, education and empowerment of children both in the US and abroad. Since its inception in 2015, Red Nose Day USA has raised an impressive $324 million and claims to have made a positive impact on the lives of more than 32 million American children and countless others worldwide. Like its British counterpart, children in the US are encouraged to don the iconic red nose and unleash their creativity through activities like the 'sell a joke' initiative. Across the ocean in Australia, Red Nose Day is focused on promoting awareness and supporting research relating to sudden infant death syndrome and other causes of infant mortality. Red Nose Day Australia claims that its fundraising efforts over three decades have led to an astounding 80 per cent reduction in sudden infant deaths. As for Finland, the annual Nose Day campaign (Nenäpäivä) orchestrated by the Nose Day Foundation takes centre stage. A month-long extravaganza culminates in the grand *Nose Day Show*, broadcast by Yle, Finland's national public service broadcasting company. This campaign directs its support to children in developing nations across Africa, Asia, the Middle East and South America, rallying behind nine charitable organisations. Since its inaugural event in 2007, the Nose Day Foundation has amassed more than €30 million to uplift the lives of children in the world's most impoverished communities.

Nevertheless, while the phenomena of Red Nose Days roll out internationally, within the UK the annual amount raised by the charity continues to fall. Indeed, the amount raised by this charity peaked in 2011 at £108.4 million, with the amount raised decreasing in the events since then to £35.3 million in 2023, suggesting that the British public may be falling out love with these large-scale events. I now briefly explore why that may be.

Celebrity and saviourism

Critics have long scrutinised the approach of large-scale national campaigns, citing concerns over White saviourism (Holbert and Waymer, 2022) and celebrity-centred spectacles (Lim and Moufahim, 2017). Here in the UK, MP David Lammy's criticism of Stacey Dooley's involvement in a Comic Relief expedition in 2020 highlighted the perpetuation of stereotypes, prompting the organisation to stop sending celebrities like Ed Sheeran to African nations for promotional filming. Instead, Comic Relief now aims to spotlight everyday life narratives within African nations to combat archaic notions associated with White saviours. Nonetheless, scholars also note that these campaigns often prioritise the spectacle of celebrity challenges over the charitable causes they support, oversimplifying issues and potentially skewing public perceptions, like the issues discussed with Beast Philanthropy (Lim and Moufahim, 2017). The media portrays celebrities' involvement as entertainment spectacles, overshadowing the charitable purposes they endorse and marginalising grassroots efforts. While these campaigns do raise significant funds and awareness, critics emphasise the need for a balance between influence and authenticity, transparency and long-term impact (Meister, 2019).

Schools disengaging

Alongside these issues and often as a response to concerns raised, there has been increasing criticism of schools being co-opted as intermediaries to these fundraising efforts, especially as we experience a global economic crisis. My colleagues and I conducted research in the UK (I will expand further on this in Chapter 6) and found that the cost-of-living crisis has led to a reluctance among many schools to partake in such fundraising initiatives (Body et al, 2023). Indeed, within state primary schools, a notable 66 per cent of teachers identify the economic circumstances of families as a substantial hindrance to children's active involvement in fundraising days, even raising concerns that some children purposefully don't attend school on fundraising days as they cannot afford to participate (despite the schools making contributions voluntary). A further 21 per cent stated that many of their students were recipients of charitable aid, such as foodbanks, and therefore by asking them to donate to support others in poverty, teachers felt undermined and trivialised the children's own lived experiences and 'otherise' them within the classroom as a beneficiary in need of saving. Our research revealed growing apprehension among primary school staff about enlisting children in fundraising asks:

'We have also found that a lot of our families are now financially very vulnerable so through our work on poverty proofing we have reduced our requests to parents for money.'

'We have been less comfortable asking those already struggling to find money for others. We ask for 5p now rather than 50p.'

'Some of our families struggle financially themselves so are unable to make donations. We are moving away from asking for donations as part of our poverty proofing agenda, so no child feels left out.'

Simultaneously, a substantial concern emerges from teachers regarding the way in which notions of charity are discussed within these fundraising days. Several educators express apprehensions about framing charity, benevolence and justice within these discussions, for example:

'There is something very uncomfortable about how we teach charity. It risks teaching children to pity others, and though empathy is a good thing, it seems we teach these ideas more in a way which positions wealthier children as superior to poorer children – by saying here, have our hand-outs but we do nothing to try and change the situation.'

'We have tried to move away from charitable giving towards social action. So, for example on Children in Need Day we ran a Day of Social Justice in School and tried to help the children to understand that although charity helps, social justice can change things so that charity is no longer needed.'

Indeed, whereas almost all schools participated in fundraising days like Comic Relief in the early 2010s when the campaign was at its peak, by 2023, according to Teacher Tapp data (an online survey platform which surveys over 8,000 teachers daily) less than half of schools participated. Similarly, fundraising income for Children in Need from schools has fallen consecutively for the past five years. While the cost-of-living crisis is undoubtedly having some impact on this, having researched extensively on this topic with schools, I suggest that something more is going on, where schools are carefully thinking about charity days as part of poverty proofing. Schools are also increasingly focusing on child-led social action events leading to wider diversity in activities, which from a perspective of children's long-term philanthropic citizenship is potentially a good thing. Nonetheless, as I will explore in Chapter 6, fundraising remains the dominant way in which children engage in active citizenship within school, and therefore this needs to be explored further.

Representation of children

Throughout these campaigns, significant concern is raised in terms of how children themselves are represented in national and international fundraising appeals. To date, fundraising literature largely focuses on the positive side of fundraising, with the main aim of raising the level of donations given (Bhati, 2021). There is very little which concentrates on the negative side of fundraising, such as contributing to negative discourses and the representations of different groups in society. Indeed, there have been various studies which have sought to discover how children can be used (and yes, I purposefully choose the word 'used' here) to illicit maximum levels of donations.

Children are a particularly popular cause among donors (Body and Breeze, 2016; Chapman et al, 2020). For example, research has concentrated on examining the impact of expressing negative emotions, such as children expressing fear or sadness, on the empathy of donors towards those children (Fisher and Ma, 2014). This revealed that participants experienced a sense of distress upon encountering images of suffering children, leading to a likely increased intention to give. Nonetheless, the study also suggests that using images of highly attractive children might negatively impact empathy and actual helping behaviours from prospective donors or volunteers. Instead, charities could benefit from selecting children of average or lower attractiveness when portraying need, especially when the need is not immediate or obvious (Fisher and Ma, 2014). While the authors caution charities to maintain high ethical standards when using images of children, the perceived (un)attractiveness of the child emerged as the most influential factor influencing a donor's decision to contribute. Similarly, a study by Small and Verrochi (2009) demonstrated that potential contributors are more inclined to contribute when presented with advertisements depicting a child with a sad expression. Likewise, an experiment conducted by Chang and Lee (2009) exploring the impact of framing child poverty messages suggests that presenting a charitable message in a negative frame is more persuasive to donors than its positive counterpart. And as Holland argues, the use of fundraising images of children from non-Western nations present an 'image of a ragged child who is not ashamed to plead' (Holland, 2004, p 148).

There are many that would argue this portrayal taps into the viewers' emotions, fostering a sense of urgency and compassion, ultimately influencing their willingness to support these children (Allred and Amos, 2018). Nonetheless, Bhati and Eikenberry's research with children in India highlighted how children wished to be portrayed as 'happy and in a "good light", telling the whole story about their lives' (Bhati and Eikenberry, 2016, p 31). As they argue in their research, most fundraising images used by charities depicted children in a manner designed to evoke sympathy from potential donors. These images often featured children seated or standing in soiled clothing, engaging in activities like eating food. Virtually all the pictures conveyed children as subjects of compassion or sorrow. Thus, charities approach children as commodities, orchestrating scenarios where they would 'dance or play' before the camera to capture more compelling photographs and craft narratives for donors (Hutnyk, 2004). It is apparent that these charities structure their campaigns based on what is marketable, simplifying the intricacies of a societal issue into a sentiment of pity, thus offering a narrow perspective on complex issues (Bhati and Eikenberry, 2016). Furthermore, while this debate has gripped charities for some time, overall little has changed. Indeed, Bhati (2021) argues that fundraising recipients are depicted in ways that reinforce stereotypical views and inadvertently perpetuate colonial narratives of 'othering'. This is achieved through a disproportionate focus on single mothers, infants and girls, with minimal portrayal of men and families. Furthermore, while there is a growing deliberate emphasis on presenting positive representations, images still portray children as imploring and shy, and perpetuate a sense of servitude. Such an approach further reinforces ideas of saviourism, wherein children are denied the right to their own voices, being politically silent and reliant on others.

In summary, while mass fundraising campaigns have brought in important funds for causes, the way in which they have done this continues to be brought into question, both in terms of how communities and children are represented in these campaigns and the modes in which children are encouraged to participate.

A question of ethics

At the heart of this chapter is a focus on the intricacies of fundraising with children. While these global campaigns undoubtedly generate critical funds for pressing causes, there exists a dual narrative. On the one hand, these endeavours instil a commendable sense of charity and generosity in the young participants, a quality that is to be lauded. Yet, research consistently echoes reservations about the transactional nature of children's involvement in these mass appeals, potentially eroding their long-term societal impact. In a study I conducted with colleagues in the UK in 2020, encompassing 150 children aged four to eight, we discovered an enthusiastic response to these fundraising initiatives (Body et al, 2020). However, a striking majority of children displayed a limited awareness of the underlying causes, with fewer than 20 per cent of the children being aware what cause the fundraising appeal represented and fewer than 8 per cent of the children participating in any form of decision making concerning their support for a particular cause. For these children, the fundraising campaigns were enchanting spectacles, a perception that inadvertently trivialised the causes they represented. They associated charity predominantly with the gratification of donning a funny costume or the exploits of a celebrity engaging in heroic endeavours like sponsored bike rides or runs. This underscores the challenge of capturing teachable moments about the essence of these causes. It is not a plea to strip fundraising of its vibrancy and engagement; rather, it is a call for it to be imbued with meaning, ensuring it remains faithful to the issues it seeks to address. Indeed, if we return to Westheimer's (2015) example of the foodbank, if we only teach to give to the foodbank, without questioning why it exists, we simply normalise food poverty and charity as the response, rather than teach question why food poverty even exists.

Scholars before me have raised similar concerns. As exemplified in the case of Comic Relief, critics have questioned the perpetuation of White saviourism and racial and cultural stereotyping, narratives that often shape a child's perception of global populations. Power and Taylor's study of 10–14 year olds unveiled a potential pitfall in schools emphasising charities as the panacea for social issues, potentially eclipsing alternative remedies and inadvertently hindering societal equity. The evidence further suggests that certain fundraising activities, such as non-uniform or dress-up days, may disproportionately impact families grappling with poverty, thereby highlighting underlying inequalities. At the core of these deliberations lies a profound ethical question: what defines ethical fundraising practices when children are involved? The UK Institute of Fundraising offers a foundational definition, characterising fundraising as the act of mobilising resources, including financial means, to support an organisation's endeavours. This role is indispensable, as charities hinge on more than just goodwill. However, the role and impact of charitable fundraising campaigns is greater than this; it shapes children's experiences, understandings and perceptions of the world, especially when such narratives are reinforced through literature and through YouTube content creators such as MrBeast, as we saw in Chapter 3. Therefore, in scrutinising the ethical norms that govern fundraising with children, I turn towards a critical consideration of children's rights within fundraising discourse.

The UNCRC, a landmark international human rights treaty ratified by the UK in 1991 (see Chapter 2), constitutes a pivotal framework. Article 12 of the UNCRC underscores a child's entitlement to voice their opinions and have them taken into account, while Article 13 underscores their right to express thoughts within legal bounds. These provisions emphasise a child's right to be consulted and recognised in decisions affecting their lives. This discourse on children's rights extends beyond viewing children as mere recipients and extends to how education on these rights can pave the way towards a democratised understanding of human rights. Notably, children's rights education, as embraced by UNICEF's Private Fundraising and Partnership Division, advocates for children to learn about their rights as right holders. This framework threads learning into the fabric of children's lives and emphasises fundraising campaigns as a conduit for understanding these rights. It's within this framework that we find space for children to steer charitable efforts, engage critically with causes and shape outcomes.

In 2021, my colleagues and I conducted a study examining the relationship between fundraising ethics and children's rights. In short, we found that beyond the function of safeguarding, fundraising ethics paid very little attention to children's rights (see Body et al, 2021). From a normative ethics perspective, fundraising ethics is guided by consequentialism, deontology or virtue ethics. Consequentialism prioritises actions yielding the best outcomes, deontology centres on acts aligned with established norms, and virtue ethics consider the individual's character. These theories, when applied to fundraising, set out conditions that define ethical fundraising practices (MacQuillin, 2023). These conditions revolve around the protection of public trust, servicing the donor's needs, the service of philanthropy, and rights–balancing fundraising ethics. However, when we examine current large-scale fundraising campaign practices with children through these lenses, it becomes evident that the child's position as enshrined in the UNCRC is frequently overlooked. This brings us face to face with two significant challenges. The first revolves around the recognition of children as donors and the ethical oversight that ensues. Often, children are marginalised as donors, particularly in school-led fundraising efforts, leading to an insufficient ethical consideration of their rights. This neglect runs counter to the UNCRC, which mandates a child's active participation in decisions that affect them. As highlighted, my own research in the UK indicates that children often lack awareness of the beneficiaries of their donations and exert limited influence over where their contributions are directed (Body et al, 2020, 2021, 2023). This presents a twofold issue: first, large-scale school fundraising campaigns often neglect the active engagement of children as capable participants with the right to influence decisions that concern them; and, second, this often results in passive tokenistic participation where children engage superficially, rather than being involved in meaningful decision making or assuming any role of power as the donor.

The second challenge grapples with the ethical responsibility of fundraisers and fundraising organisations to nurture children's long-term philanthropic citizenship. This conception is guided by a children's rights pedagogy informed by educational philosophers like Biesta, Friere, Lipman and Dewey, advocating for education as a space of moral reasoning, democratic inquiry and critical examination, serving equity and social justice. Integrating this philosophy into classroom dynamics encourages critical discourse on charity, prosociality and giving, cultivating a child's inclination towards philanthropic action and nurturing a sense of social justice. Charitable acts often offer an initial, first-step platform to contemplate these notions, yet without meaningful engagement, the opportunity remains untapped. Encouraging deliberation around charity's underlying causes, beneficiaries and structural inequalities aligns with the children's rights education framework and reinforces social justice and equality values. This approach empowers children not only to contribute but also to critically address broader societal issues. This stance challenges the mainstream presentation of charities as the sole solution to social problems and underscores the need for comprehensive approaches, including government intervention. It also places a responsibility on fundraisers and fundraising organisations to consider how children's engagement can, and should, be more meaningful.

Pursuing a children's rights approach to fundraising

In terms of ethical fundraising, MacQuillin (2021) highlights a crucial balance: the duty of fundraisers to advocate for beneficiaries, while respecting the rights of donors, leading to a mutually beneficial outcome that avoids harm to either party. This perspective extends to fundraising within schools from a children's rights standpoint, involving both the rights of fundraisers to seek support for beneficiaries and the pertinent rights of donors. A deeper exploration reveals that this 'support' entails more than financial contributions. Fundraisers bear an ethical obligation to actively engage children in a 'moral justification for moral intervention', cultivating an understanding of social justice and fostering meaningful involvement in giving (Rosso, 1991, p 4; Simpson, 2017; see also Chapter 1). Nonetheless, in fundraising campaigns targeted at children, appropriately engaging information to help children critically engage in the cause remains rare. A children's rights approach to engaging children as donors offers exciting opportunities for children to explore real issues and real responses, and opens up the spaces where children can meaningfully engage in conversations about charity, giving and beyond, extending into conversations about what this means for our wider citizenship (Body et al, 2020). For example, the co-construction of fundraising activities between organisations, schools and children provides a real opportunity for exciting curricula development in citizenship education.

As many of these large-scale fundraising campaigns take place in schools, where children have the right to meaningful and democratic citizenship education, the lessons taught hold lasting consequences for their future as engaged citizens (Covell and Howe, 2001). Ethical fundraising in primary (and indeed all) schools should encompass not only engaging children in charitable causes but also facilitating critical discussions on why these causes exist and exploring diverse approaches to address them. Teachers must be equipped with the necessary support and time to foster these discussions (Horgan et al, 2017). To ensure ethical fundraising from a children's rights perspective, we need collaborative processes involving fundraising organisations, education institutions, communities and children. In short, as an important part of the philanthropic ecosystem and in service to long-term philanthropy, fundraisers and fundraising organisations have an ethical responsibility to support schools and communities in adopting a children's rights approach, providing resources to facilitate understanding of diverse communities and needs, considering issues of inequality, and transparently explaining their decision-making processes. Simultaneously, philanthropic funders, schools, communities and children's groups must involve children as co-decision makers, encouraging them to consider ethical aspects of philanthropy and explore various giving mechanisms beyond monetary donations.

The great news is that there are several fundraising organisations who are already considering these challenges and counter challenges, providing information about the cause for schools to present in assemblies and to explore in class, and taking steps to consider children and young people's agency in giving decisions, such as SuperKind. SuperKind adopts an approach which seeks to educate, inspire and empower. As I will discuss in the following chapter, shifting a focus to child-led engagement in charitable causes enables children to make a meaningful impact on causes that matter to them. It isn't just about raising funds; it nurtures vital life skills like effective advocacy, communication, leadership and critical curiosity. It also allows and facilitates children to consider alternative responses to social issues which move beyond fundraising, including advocacy and social action.

Case study 4: SuperKind

We know that with the right tools, children can do amazing things. Yet when it comes to social action in schools, young people's contributions are often overlooked, reducing social action to merely the act of putting a coin in a fundraising bucket. In response, SuperKind was created to empower children to lead the way along every step of their fundraising journey – from choosing the cause that they'd like to support, to setting up their own fundraising page and collecting donations.

SuperKind is the world's only cross-charity fundraising platform safe for children under 13. On SuperKind, children and their schools can meaningfully, safely, and efficiently raise money for over 30,000 charities and good causes.

SuperKind replaces old-school paper fundraising forms. It means there is no money for children to collect, to leave in their bags and for teachers to count. It means that family and friends who live far away can still donate. And it means that all donations are eligible for Gift Aid, growing fundraising totals by up to 25 per cent. There are no costs to using SuperKind and we are a social enterprise ourselves. The fundraising platform is custom-built just for young people. It's designed to be easy to use independently by children as young as 7 and it's loaded with fun features – such as the ability to customise fundraising pages and earn badges.

SuperKind is unique among fundraising platforms in that it can be safely used by children under 13. Our whole platform is built with children's data and privacy front of mind. For example, parental approval is built into the system, and photos & videos are password protected by default. This differs from other platforms where anyone on the internet can view the fundraiser's name, school and see what they look like.

We believe that children can change the world. Sometimes they just need the tools. SuperKind's core ethos is that children should have maximum agency over their engagement with social action and fundraising. Our fundraising platform is designed to put all the ownership, power (and fun!) into the hands of young fundraisers.

Keren Mitchell, founder of SuperKind and father of four

The philanthropic toolbox

Like all of us, children have a diverse array of potential methods to engage with causes they are passionate about, of which giving money is one important way, but not the only way. They can raise awareness through educational campaigns and social media, organise fundraisers like bake sales or charity runs, volunteer their time for activities such as park or beach clean-ups, collaborate with local charities, and create artwork or music to highlight their cause. They can participate in letter-writing campaigns, join or start clubs, organise events like charity walks, engage in social entrepreneurship, advocate for policy changes, participate in or lead protests, conduct research, collaborate with others and leverage technology to spread awareness – the list is endless.

However, the critical point to emphasise here is that there is no singular, prescriptive approach when it comes to encouraging children to engage with social and environmental causes they care deeply about. Causes, by their very nature, are complex and multifaceted, requiring a nuanced response that reflects this complexity. What I am proposing here is that by limiting children engagement to monetary contributions or engaging in large-scale fundraising campaigns, we are not allowing them to recognise the other ways they can support a cause. Stopping at donating money hinders children's ability to connect the issue they wish to support and the root causes which result in this issue. Furthermore, a focus on money is often inaccessible to many children and young people living in circumstances of economic hardship.

It would be so much more impactful if we equipped our children with a comprehensive understanding of the diverse tools at their disposal. They should be empowered to mobilise their treasure, time, ties, trust and/or talents in the most effective and appropriate manner to address the specific needs they are passionate about. It is not merely the action itself that holds significance, but rather the foundational perspective from which we approach that action. When we orient our response through the lens of justice, it becomes evident that donating money alone may fall short of what is needed to drive substantive change. Justice requires a broader exploration of systemic issues, advocating for policy reform and addressing root causes rather than merely alleviating symptoms. This perspective compels us to seek out solutions that are both sustainable and transformative, recognising that a more comprehensive and thoughtful approach is necessary to truly make a lasting impact.

It is important to make it clear that this argument about going beyond donating money and fundraising is not meant to ignore all the positive ways in which children participate in raising much needed funds for charity; it is about proposing that this is seen as just *one* of many ways of supporting a cause rather than the only or indeed dominant one. Most charities rely on the generosity of individuals, including children and families to provide much-needed support in communities. But to teach children that donating money is their only choice of response, as is so often the case, bounds children's engagement in charity in a neoliberal and individualised discourse. It maintains the status quo rather than seeking to change systems.

This reminds us of the 'Parable of the River' in which in a riverside village, a villager saves a baby from the river. More babies keep coming, and the villagers form rescue teams. They work tirelessly, but the number of babies keeps growing. They save many, but not all. The priest blesses their efforts and life goes on … but no one seeks to question why the babies are ending up in the river. This parable is often used to distinguish the difference between charity and philanthropy – simply put, charity pulls the babies out of the river, philanthropic, justice-oriented action should aim to move up the river, and to try and stop the babies being thrown into the water. Similarly, we must encourage our children to both be prepared to pull the babies out of the river, but also question how the babies end up in the river and how they can stop them ending up there.

Therefore, it is not only important that we help instil in our children a sense of empathy and a desire to act, but also the critical thinking skills to assess the most effective means of engagement. By fostering a holistic understanding of how to effect change, we empower them to be agents of progress in a way that aligns with their unique capacities and circumstances. This approach, grounded in justice and tailored to the complexities of each cause, holds the potential to yield far-reaching and enduring results.

Engaging children in social action

Exploring this philanthropic toolbox further, in recent years, there has been a growing emphasis on empowering children and young people through what is coined as 'high-quality social action' – where young individuals actively take part in activities benefiting others and effecting positive social change for both their communities and themselves (Ockenden and Stuart, 2014). The launch of the *#iwill* campaign in 2013, backed by Step Up to Serve and enjoying cross-party support, demonstrated a noteworthy government commitment to boost social action among those aged 10–20, aspiring to a 50 per cent surge by 2020 (Ofsted, 2016). This commitment found additional backing from the Jubilee Centre for Character and Virtue's research, suggesting that early involvement in youth social action significantly enhances the likelihood of an enduring dedication to service (Arthur et al, 2017). Rigorous studies, such as those conducted by Kirkman et al (2016) utilising randomised controlled trials, reveal that participation in social action initiatives not only helps the developments of essential life skills but also sparks a heightened interest in future volunteering compared to those who haven't participated.

Beyond the statistics, facilitating children in making decisions, taking action and reflecting on their social change efforts, all under the supportive guidance of adults, has demonstrated positive outcomes for youth engaged in social action projects (Torres-Harding et al, 2018). Adding to this, the Royal Society of Arts' (RSA) *Citizens of Now* report (Tejani and Breeze, 2021) offers a detailed account of a three-year project involving primary schools in the West Midlands, showcasing the direct benefits for children. These benefits range from refining leadership, teamwork and problem-solving skills to instilling a profound sense of social responsibility and civic self-efficacy. Furthermore, engagement in social action has been linked to positive academic attainment, with meta-analyses suggesting substantial gains in academic achievement through the development of social and emotional skills (Durlak et al, 2011). Recognising the role of uniformed groups and community engagement activities as instrumental in cultivating children's civic engagement (Birdwell et al, 2013; Tyler-Rubenstein et al, 2016), studies also underscore the positive effects of involving children as agents of change in their communities, fostering civic engagement and awareness (Nicotera, 2008; Percy-Smith and Burns, 2012), while Fitzgerald's (2021) study in Ireland underscores the significance of social bonding and the development of positive interpersonal skills as prerequisites for children's active participation in collective social action. In essence, the evolving landscape of children's engagement in social action not only shapes their individual development but also contributes to the fabric of a more civically responsible and engaged society, igniting a flame of positive change from an early age. However, as will be explored further in Chapter 6, despite the evident positive impacts, significant disparities exist in access to social action projects. Deprived areas face considerable challenges, highlighting a socioeconomic gap in engagement (Tejani and Breeze, 2021). Additionally, overall levels of engagement, particularly for younger children, remain low (Body et al, 2024).

While the academic literature on children's civic learning journeys in the UK is still unfolding, various civil society organisations, including the RSA, the Linking Network, People United, Young Citizens and Association for Citizenship Teaching (ACT), play a pivotal role in promoting civic learning in schools and communities. Evaluations of these programmes reveal diverse impacts, ranging from enhancing interpersonal relationships between children from different backgrounds (the Linking Network [Cameron, 2020]) to increasing empathy and motivations to help others through participatory arts projects (People United, 2017). First Give, outlined in the following case study, offers a good example of combining ideas of charity, fundraising and social action in child-led activities.

Case study 5: First Give with Trinity Academy Doncaster (children aged 11–12)

Since 2014, First Give has been working in partnership with schools to inspire and empower children and young people to take action to make a positive change in society. Our core programme is designed to empower all classes in an entire school year group.

A combination of lessons delivered by teachers, plus facilitated workshops delivered by First Give, help build understanding of the issues facing the local community, alongside the confidence and skills to take action in support of local charities they choose to support. At the conclusion of the programme, students advocate for their chosen charity to win a First Give grant of £1,000, supplementing any support already given to the charities.

At schools across the country, children regularly take part in fundraising activities, but the First Give programme structure goes a step further, providing them with agency to choose the issues that matter most to them. Children are given the space to discuss, research and learn about social issues affecting their community, meeting with representatives from local charities. The agency they are given to lead on social action projects alongside the critical exploration of the issues they choose to address are two of the most critical elements of the programme.

As an example, Year seven students at Trinity Academy Doncaster researched a range of social issues that affected their local community. One class chose to research issues of poverty and deprivation across north Doncaster. They particularly learnt about the explosion of foodbanks over the last few years.

With the support of their tutor Ms Parish, the children invited representatives from a small, volunteer-led charity, the Thorne and Moorends Community Foodbank to come into school. When the charity suggested that they might want to make a special visit to volunteer for a morning, the answer was a resounding 'Yes!'.

Students were split up into groups on arrival and given a range of jobs to do. One group made hot drinks for visitors to the foodbank, while another group were tasked with packing up bags to be handed out.

Ms Parish told us 'The best thing about First Give and volunteering at the foodbank was the development of students' compassion. There were lots of inspired and emotional young people after the visit, and their biggest question was "Please can we do this every Thursday?" Some students have even spoken about helping out during the school holidays.'

When children are given the opportunity to connect with the issues that matter to them, and to take action to tackle these issues at a young age, they are more likely to develop a habit of generosity and service.

The students told us: 'Completing the First Give programme allowed us to learn about our local community and its needs. It made us reflect on the world around us and inspired us to want to continue to make a positive change.'

Louisa Searle and Isaac Jones, First Give

Considering social action as part of the philanthropic toolbox, it is crucial that children are not just participants in social action, but are actively taught to link their efforts to the broader concepts of collective action and social justice. The evolving landscape of youth engagement in social action, as highlighted by initiatives like the *#iwill* campaign and research from the Jubilee Centre, demonstrates that early involvement cultivates a lasting commitment to service. However, the true power lies in connecting these individual endeavours to larger societal issues. By instilling an understanding of collective action and social justice, children not only learn the value of their contribution on a personal level, but also begin grasp the systemic challenges and inequalities that necessitate collective efforts (I will explore this further in Chapter 9). This broader perspective not only fosters a sense of civic responsibility and civic empowerment, but also equips them with the critical thinking skills to question and challenge societal norms, ensuring that their social action endeavours can potentially become a force for transformative change, addressing root causes rather than merely alleviating symptoms. This holistic approach not only shapes engaged and responsible citizens, but also lays the foundation for a more just and equitable society.

Conclusion

In this chapter I argue that the discourse surrounding fundraising with children exposes a complex interplay of ethical considerations, societal dynamics and educational imperatives. While large-scale fundraising campaigns undeniably generate vital resources for charitable causes, they also engender critical questions regarding the meaningful engagement of children as donors and the ethical responsibility of fundraisers and fundraising organisations. Drawing from extensive research and ethical frameworks, in this chapter I underscore the imperative of adopting a children's rights approach to fundraising with children. At its core, such an approach entails recognising children as active agents with the capacity for meaningful participation and decision making in philanthropic endeavours. I advocate for fostering critical inquiry, empathy and a nuanced understanding of social justice issues among children, thereby nurturing a generation of philanthropic citizens equipped to address systemic inequities and effect transformative change, both in the present and for years to come. Moreover, I call for collaborative efforts among fundraising organisations, educational institutions, communities and children themselves to uphold ethical fundraising practices rooted in respect for children's rights, transparent decision-making processes, and the cultivation of informed and engaged citizenship. By embracing a children's rights approach to engaging children as donors, we not only ensure the integrity and efficacy of philanthropic efforts but also empower children to become active contributors to a more just and equitable society, thus realising the true, long-term potential of philanthropy as a force for positive social transformation.

I argue that the philanthropic toolbox available to children should be rich and varied, encompassing a wide range of methods beyond traditional donating of funds. From raising awareness through educational campaigns to engaging in social entrepreneurship, children have the capacity to leverage their time, talents and resources in diverse ways to address the causes they are passionate about. However, it is crucial to emphasise that there is no one-size-fits-all approach to encouraging children's engagement with social and environmental issues. Causes are multifaceted and complex, demanding nuanced responses that often go beyond monetary contributions. By limiting children's involvement to giving money alone, we risk overlooking the myriad of ways they can make a meaningful impact and connect with the root causes of the issues they seek to address. We normalise the idea of charity as the response the social norms, negating to consider other responses, such as governmental and policy change.

Moreover, a focus solely on donating money is inaccessible to many children living in circumstances of economic hardship, further underscoring the importance of embracing alternative forms of engagement. By equipping children with a comprehensive understanding of the diverse tools at their disposal, we empower them to mobilise their resources in the most effective and appropriate manner, fostering a sense of agency and responsibility, whatever their background or situation. Fundamentally, it is not just the action itself that holds significance, but also the foundational perspective from which we approach that action. By orienting our response through the lens of justice, we recognise the need for a broader exploration of systemic issues and advocacy for policy reform. This perspective compels all of us to seek out solutions that are both sustainable and transformative, acknowledging that lasting change requires addressing root causes rather than merely alleviating symptoms.

While donating funds remains an important aspect of philanthropy, it should be viewed as just one of many ways of supporting a cause rather than the dominant one. Encouraging children to explore diverse avenues of engagement fosters a more inclusive and equitable discourse around charity and social action, challenging market-oriented and individualised narratives that perpetuate the status quo. Ultimately, by instilling in children a sense of empathy, critical thinking and a commitment to social justice, we empower them to become agents of progress in a way that aligns with their unique capacities and circumstances. This holistic approach not only shapes engaged and responsible citizens but also lays the foundations for a more just and equitable society, where collective action and social justice are central tenets of philanthropy.

5

Heroism and exceptionalism: young fundraisers

Introduction

I have had a long-term interest in child fundraisers. I am not talking about children who become the object of a fundraising campaign, often due to health or medical reasons, or sponsorship of children from afar. Both are worthy topics of our attention. Nonetheless, the focus I wish to settle on here, building on the previous chapter in which I critique the problem of elevating giving of money as the only tool in children's philanthropic toolbox, is children who seek to raise funds independently, though almost always facilitated by family, friends or organisations, such as schools or charities.

To date, this topic has been, almost bizarrely, overlooked by scholars, practitioners and policy makers. A widespread literature search on the topic reveals a significant gap in the literature and understanding. A limited amount of literature discusses how to encourage children to be givers in the fundraising world, but there is almost nothing on the child 'doers'. Nonetheless, children play a vital role in leading fundraising campaigns for causes they are passionate about. This is widely celebrated by schools, families and the media.

For instance, in response to the Ukraine crisis, Save the Children highlighted the remarkable surge in contributions from children following the onset of the conflict (Hill, 2022), with each young fundraiser generating an average of £1,400, tripling the previous benchmark of £400. Mapping out these examples in an article in *The Guardian* newspaper, the creativity of child-led fundraising activities is clear (Hill, 2022). Evie and Rowan Lewis, aged 13 and 11, from Ilminster in Somerset raised £2,568 for Save the Children's Ukraine campaign by shaving their heads. Ella and Leo Ketley, aged nine and five, walked 43 miles, the same length of journey undertaken by many Ukrainian families seeking refuge in Poland, raising £1,859. Similarly, eight-year-old Zachary Clare did a 10-mile walk for the charity, raising a further £500. And seven-year-old Veda Plotkin and her three-year-old sibling sold hot chocolate and homemade cookies to passers-by from their doorstep in Haringey, North London, raising £256.

Collectively, these narratives converge to really show the power children can have when harnessed with purpose and directed towards action. Nonetheless, there has been little critique of these activities within society, how charities support and promote them, and how we, as a society, respond. Therefore, in this chapter I take a look at young fundraisers.

Child-led fundraising

While popular in practice, child-led fundraising remains a much-neglected conversation within fundraising and philanthropic literature. Like most aspects of philanthropy and giving, it is a form of fundraising which has multiple positive and negative aspects. Our evaluation of its 'goodness' depends on various factors, including the context, the intentions behind the fundraising, the support provided to the children, and the potential outcomes. I briefly summarise some of the main points here and then look to some real examples, where I explore these ideas in greater depth.

Most people view child-led fundraising as a good thing. It can be empowering for children, their families and their communities. It can foster a sense of agency, responsibility and critical engagement with social issues, and help children practise practical skills such as communication, teamwork, and leadership (Body, 2024). As was discussed in Chapter 1, direct, participative and critical engagement in these issues can also raise awareness about important causes among children, their families and their communities, encouraging empathy and compassion from a young age. Furthermore, fundraising efforts led by children can strengthen community bonds, encourage collaboration and promote a culture of giving, and children can learn about financial responsibility, budgeting and the value of philanthropy through hands-on fundraising experiences.

In 2018 I led a research project exploring children's views on charity (Body et al, 2019). A total of 150 children aged four to eight were engaged in a six- to ten-week project, working one to one or in a small group with members of the research team. The research project was split into two distinct sections. The first part of this project aimed to explore children's current knowledge and understanding of the concept of charity and charitable giving. Researchers worked in partnership with children to understand and explore their views and experiences. Researchers were tasked with listening to the child and supporting them to explore more widely, their areas of interest and their preferred giving decisions. The second part of the project aimed to then explore what children's preferences were in terms of charitable giving. To do this, researchers carried out an imaginary based scenario of having £100 to give away to any charity, or charities, of the child's choosing. Researchers explored with the child why they wanted to give to those charities and what had helped shape their decision. The first and second parts of this project were planned in the initial development of this research. However, interestingly as the research process developed, a third part of the project emerged. Over one third of the children, inspired by the project, chose to undertake charitable activities, fundraising, giving and advocacy of their own volition. This phase of the project completely emerged from the children themselves, inspired by their co-researching journey and supporting causes of their own choice.

Through this lens, philanthropic citizenship can be viewed as both a practice and an embodied response to injustice rather than a single, one-off facilitated action. Building on the engagement in the first two parts of this research project, children then proactively participated in multiple acts of charity, such as preparing donation boxes or fundraising for charities they had researched, but from a starting point which embraced a clear understanding of the cause, why it mattered and a connection to ideas of justice. The children engaged in critical thinking and debate on the issues of philanthropy and social justice, and then chose their charity and led on fundraising, as a response to an identified need (Body et al, 2020).

What also became clear through our research activities is that children initially and unsurprisingly made giving choices based on what they knew, which normally was limited to the major, well-marketed charities, representing causes such as homelessness, cancer research and animals. However, after being given the opportunity to research and explore different charities, most children re-evaluated their decisions on how they would give money. When children's giving decisions were compared before and after spending time exploring the topic, the findings showed children's decision making changed from choosing common charities they knew, those we may consider the big, major, well-marketed charities, to being more cause-oriented. Here they started looking at the cause they cared about and then looked at the charities that addressed that cause rather than the other way round. For example, one child undertook a co-researching project which led to her exploring donating clothes abroad. She was shocked that clothes donated are often resold to communities abroad rather than donated, or indeed end up as waste in rubbish dumps or littering beaches. She found a charity which only sought to send clothes that would suit the specific community's needs, after having identified the needs by working in partnership with that community. She then worked with friends and family to develop a specific parcel to respond to these needs directly, which included small women's clothing, children's clothing, shoes, underwear and maternity clothing.

Many of the children in our research project reflected and changed their giving decisions by the end of the project to donate to the less popular causes, such as supporting young carers, childhood illnesses and international aid charities, after they had completed research on the topic. Homelessness and tackling human suffering remained a strong theme among the children. Nonetheless, empowered by careful exploration of charities and cause areas that appealed to the children, this giving differed from the type of giving discussed in the first part of the project, before they had been engaged in researching the causes they cared about. Here we saw children taking a more critically conscious approach in their giving decisions, and they were more likely to choose causes closer to their own experiences, but importantly rooted in a social justice discourse. Having been on a 'research journey', many children, even in the younger years, also shifted their position from a transactional relationship, such as "I got a sticker because I gave food for the harvest festival" (Boy, 5), to one which embraced this reflection on inequality. For example:

'It is very important we help people who don't have homes, if they don't have a home, they could get cold and hungry, and even die.' (Boy, 5)

'If you are not kind to everyone, and I mean everyone, not just the people you like, then you are not kind.' (Girl, 6)

'I want to give money to them because they're for people who do not have homes and it's not fair because we get a warm house and they have to sleep in the cold on the street.' (Boy, 7)

These children began to form firm orientations in their views on giving, with a heightened awareness of the issues of equality and engaged in discussing the ways in which charities should work and how people should give in the future. We found this to be the most exciting part of this research. While it was not initially structured as part of the research process, the children leading on and critically engaging in their own giving decisions gave rise to several important and critical conversations between the researchers and children, including discussions about homelessness, poverty, climate change and inequalities in education. Here, we see a real power in child-led fundraising, not to tell children where or what to give, but giving them the tools and support to ask and explore giving decisions themselves, as well as the reasons behind the cause areas, empowering them as change makers (Body et al, 2019).

Thus, child-led fundraising stands as an underappreciated facet within philanthropic discourse, embodying both positive and negative implications contingent upon contextual factors, intentions and support structures. Through empirical exploration with children, it becomes evident that such endeavours empower children, fostering agency, empathy and critical engagement with social issues. Moreover, by embracing a reflective and research-driven approach, children transition from transactional giving to a nuanced understanding rooted in social justice principles. This transformative journey not only amplifies the impact of their philanthropic endeavours but also instils a profound sense of responsibility and compassion, positioning children as catalysts for meaningful change in their communities and beyond.

Media representation of young fundraisers

Having considered the benefits in engaging children as fundraisers and critically engaged in responding to causes, we now focus on media representation of young fundraisers. There are potentially two dominant media narratives surrounding children and fundraising. The first of these was discussed briefly in Chapter 4, wherein children are presented as passive and without agency, in need of saving. The second narrative surrounding children and fundraising is one of heroism and exceptionalism, a framing which is reserved for a very small group of young fundraisers. This narrative almost sits solely within discourses on social media, newspapers and charities' own media communications. Children as fundraisers themselves, as agents of change, are barely even acknowledged within academic and practice-based literature, let alone critiqued, theorised or discussed. The silence on this issue from practice and research speaks volumes of the priority children are given within this space. And while this may be unintentional, the consequences are potentially severe, as I will outline in the following sections, reproducing narratives of the ideal good citizen, bounded in notions of duty, service and compliance, while validating notions of adult superiority and marginalising children from political discussions (Alexander et al, 2022; Jones et al, 2023).

A focus on exceptionalism

I consider discourse as the collectively shared expressions, understandings, behaviours and modes of existence that shape or generate particular perspectives and contemplations of the world. This encompasses how we perceive ourselves and others as individuals. Media discourses of childhood are shaped by cultural, historical, social and political context (Prout and James, 1997). As discussed in Chapter 2, dominant discourses for childhood tend to focus on childhood innocence, passivity and naivety, reproducing adult authority and normative values (Crawley, 2011; Garlen, 2019). There is very little space to understand children as politically engaged, as agentic or as decision makers (this will be explored further in Chapter 8).

Furthermore, media research extensively documents the phenomenon where negative news garners more attention than positive news. News outlets frequently prioritise stories revolving around crime, deviant behaviour and misconduct, particularly emphasising the actions of young individuals. Upon scrutinising content and engaging in workshops with children and young people, Gordon et al (2015) suggest that it became evident that the news coverage predominantly leaned towards pessimism, featuring very few stories about the accomplishments or constructive contributions made by young people in their communities (Mejias and Banaji, 2018). It was apparent that children and young people believed they only garnered positive coverage when their achievements reached exceptional heights, which were unobtainable by most. They put forward the notion that an infusion of 'more positive narratives', celebrating collective endeavours, could profoundly influence how adults perceive them and subsequently impact the behaviour of children and young individuals (Gordon et al, 2015).

Likewise, the plotline of young fundraisers positions a minority of children as exceptional heroes. I argue that most often, these heroes are young, White, privileged children who are more commonly positioned as virtuous by diverting from their own pursuits to help others, through activities which most often focus on outdoor and adventurous pursuits. Indeed, children have achieved remarkable feats, such as five-year-old Ollie Sainthouse, who completed a 200-mile coast-to-coast walk in August 2023, raising more than £10,000 for Great North Air Ambulance (*BBC News*, 2023); seven-year-old Frankie McMillan from West Cumbria, the youngest ever British person to conquer Greece's Mount Olympus in September 2023, raising over £2,300 for Wasdale Mountain Rescue; or Jack Adams, who raised more than £3,500 from litter picking, walking and climbing challenges, including walking the 102-mile Cotswold Way and climbing 11 mountains in 10 days in Snowdonia.

Each of these children have achieved amazing things – that is undeniable; nonetheless, a media focus on exceptionalism suggests that the activity is removed from other children, that it is unusual and unobtainable by most children and youth. However, in fact, hundreds of thousands, if not millions of children undertake fundraising and voluntary action every single week, collectively raising large amounts, contributing valuable volunteer time or simply handing over their pennies. Yet these stories are rarely mentioned or recognised more widely, or indeed drawn together as stories of collective endeavours to illuminate what children are passionate about, to infuse these much-needed 'more positive narratives' (Gordon et al, 2025). This lack of focus on the collective action of children – for example, the countless children regularly raising funds for food poverty or homelessness – from both the media and indeed charities themselves undermines children's agentic role as fundraisers – or indeed, as change makers (Spyrou, 2020). These children are effectively seeking to take a stand on an issue which matters to them, in a manner which is open to them, as they are excluded from all formal political processes such as voting. It depoliticises the narrative, instead focusing on the virtuous nature of a few exceptional children rather than the issues children more widely seek to resolve – for example, the story of Alfie, the star of the story headlined 'Kind-hearted Wrexham boy's fundraisers for foodbanks now open', who sells off his football memorabilia to raise money for the foodbank (*The Leader*, 2023), or Travis, who dreams of being 'famous for helping people' and fundraises tirelessly to run his own foodbank. The focus in each of these stories is on the moral character virtues of the child, not the issue they are concerned about: food poverty. That part of the narrative is shut down.

Mejias and Banaji's (2018) thematic analyses of media messages and policy documents concerning young people found that the limited positive portrayals of young individuals can be grouped into four clear representative categories: altruistic; civically or politically engaged; heroic or brave; and capable and resilient. These depictions also reinforce a rigid set of moral standards linked to the actions of young people in the civic realm. In researching this subject myself, I spent days scouring media, social media and fundraising platforms to research children's positive engagement in the world of fundraising and civic engagement, focusing on particular children who received specific attention and were framed as 'exceptional' by the media. I reviewed children who had been awarded New Year Honours, nominees and awardees for the Pride of Britain over the past few years and the JustGiving awards, and time and time again, the same children came up, most of whom were White, male and typically from relatively privileged backgrounds. To explore this point further, I then took all these remarkable young people's names and ran them through a Nexis search engine, which searches a database of news and media articles. From the small sample of 30 children I was looking at, consistently, stories of the 26 children who were visibly White were shared up to two or three times more (achieving on average 1,236 hits) than the four children who were from ethnic minorities (achieving on average 466 hits). Nonetheless, regardless of ethnicity, all stories were told in a performative manner which conformed to ideas of the individualised, responsible citizen, without consideration of the broader context. This risks two outcomes: first, we continue to unjustly relegate stories from ethnic minorities, and females, to the sidelines, depoliticising their voices; and, second, we continue to promote servitude and kindness over action. Kindness and service should be celebrated of course, but when we only celebrate the private act of kindness we risk, as Westheimer (2015) argues, and returning to our parable of the river, 'teaching children to rescue, cloth and feed babies, but not to seek ways to prevent them ending up there in the first place'. The risk here is that we celebrate civility and docility. We showcase the individualised virtues rather than considering collective solutions to social problems. Indeed, there is a notable and uncomfortable trend in the celebration of exceptional child fundraisers. In short, fundraising successes which achieve viral levels of celebration are most commonly White, privileged boys, undertaking adventurous or entrepreneurial activity.

Another exceptional example of philanthropic action can be seen in the inspiring actions of Max Woosey, who spent over three years sleeping in a tent to raise money and awareness of cancer and life-limiting illnesses. While the dedication and passion of Max was and should be celebrated, I also argue that his story became co-opted into media and mainstream framings of the ideal good young citizen. Max fitted much of the narrative that I have just discussed – son of a Royal Marine, a scout, rugby-loving, privately educated, well-spoken, articulate boy from north Devon in the UK, Max gained significant attention for his remarkable charitable efforts, character and resilience. He embarked on this unique adventure in 2020 to raise money for the North Devon Hospice, a local charity that provides support to people with life-limiting illnesses. Like Captain Tom Moore's fundraising efforts which went viral, Max's endeavour captured the hearts and imagination of people far and wide. Despite the challenges of weather, discomfort and the commitment required, Max persevered in his tent, raising funds for the hospice while also drawing attention to the charity's vital work, raising over £750,000. His story garnered media coverage and his determination inspired many to donate to the cause. Cementing this as an example of 'true Britishness', Max met the then Prime Minister Boris Johnson and was awarded the Blue Peter badge, the Point of Light Award, a Young Citizen of the Year Award by the Rotary Club of Braunton, the Melvin Jones Fellowship – one of highest awards a person can receive in recognition of their service to the community – from Lions International, an Unsung Hero Award from chief scout Bear Grylls, a Pride of Britain (Spirit of Adventure) and the British Empire Medal – one of the youngest people ever to receive this award. He embodied symbolic goodness, and this was further recognised by his invitation to attend King Charles III's coronation in May 2023.

I am not in any way seeking to criticise Max, or indeed any other young fundraisers – they are truly admirable in their intentions and perseverance to help others. Instead, I seek to problematise the seemingly growing issue that all too often, children are co-opted into a media and political ideological narrative that suits those in power; my argument is with that, not the children seeking to do good. Thus, I critique the systems and structures surrounding these children and young people which seek to promote what the ideal good philanthropic citizen is. Indeed, Max Woosey himself points to this disproportionate attention to his campaign and uses this to draw attention to the power of children:

> 'Before my neighbour died of cancer, he gave me a tent and told me to "have an adventure" ... The North Devon Hospice took such good care of him, I wanted to do something to say thank you to them ... It is crazy that it has got so much attention, but I hope it makes people see that children are capable of a lot more than people think.' (*BBC News*, 2023a)

In many ways this phenomenon mirrors that of Captain Sir Tom Moore, a British Army officer who gained international recognition and admiration for his remarkable fundraising efforts during the COVID-19 pandemic. In the weeks leading up to his 100th birthday in April 2020, Captain Tom set out to complete 100 laps of his garden with the goal of raising £1,000 for the National Health Service (NHS) Charities Together. He aimed to complete the laps before his 100th birthday on 30 April. As news of his endeavour spread, Captain Tom's fundraising campaign captured the public's imagination. Donations poured in from all over the world and his campaign quickly gained momentum. As his 100th birthday approached, Captain Tom not only reached his initial goal, but far exceeded it. He became a national hero and a symbol of unity during a time when the world was grappling with the challenges of the pandemic. By the time his fundraising campaign concluded, Captain Tom had raised over £32 million (later surpassing £39 million with Gift Aid) for the NHS Charities Together. In recognition of his extraordinary efforts, he was knighted by Queen Elizabeth II in a special ceremony held at Windsor Castle on 17 July 2020. While the Captain Tom Moore legacy was later shrouded in controversy, his fundraising success during the latter years of his life remains phenomenal.

But like Max Woosey, what was it that made Captain Tom Moore's efforts stand out to achieve such fundraising success? While timing was important as we faced a global health crisis, it was also about character. Tom Moore's character deeply resonated with the British public. Adorned in his meticulously decorated military attire, he embodied resilience and fortitude. He was viewed as resourceful and determined, wholeheartedly dedicating himself to raising funds for an important cause. He was unoffensive and unchallenging, and the symbol of a sense of bygone British values. As the *Yorkshire Post* stated, echoing many other outlets: '[His] wisdom stems from this national hero's own military service in India and Burma when he lost his comrades in the name of freedom. This was – and remains – the greatest generation' (Richmond, 2020). But what about the countless others who performed heroic and even everyday acts during this time – who do we celebrate and why?

In terms of representations of child fundraisers, this requires further research, attention and scrutiny. I argue that all too often, through these narratives, ideas of the heroic youth are bounded by inflexible conceptualisations of active citizenship (Mejias and Banaji, 2018), confined by civic duty and service – where children's engagement was not positioned as political or engaging with institutions. As Mejias and Banaji contend, 'young people are essentially 'backed into a corner' by the inflexibility of such ideological scholarly, policy and media discourses regarding their civic possibilities' (2018, p 1728).

'Utilising' exceptionalism

Charities are buying into these same narratives of exceptionalism to achieve fundraising success. Indeed, Max Woosey's fundraising success was quickly co-opted by other fundraising campaigns. For instance, in July 2021, Max became the face of the fundraising campaign by a children's charity to raise funds for vulnerable children across the UK. Invited to meet the Prime Minister to promote the campaign, and indeed camp out at Number 10 Downing Street, the charity released a press release celebrating the event. The statement is accompanied by a picture of Max with the then Prime Minister Boris Johnson, drinking tea in the garden in front of a tent, and accompanied by a statement from the former Prime Minister saying:

'Today I met Max who has done an absolutely stellar job of raising money for some very worthy causes by sleeping outside for over a year now. Max has inspired young people all over the country and I support his efforts today to raise money for the children who need it most.' (*BBC News*, 2021b)

In my book *Children's Charities in Crisis* (Body, 2020), I tracked a decade of radical change in policy and funding in children's early intervention services across England, fronted by the Conservative government, demonstrating the damage to children's support services due to policy shifts, alongside huge funding cuts and, most importantly, the impact of these cuts on vulnerable children themselves. Indeed, many children's charities also raised such concerns and continue to do so as I write this book. Nonetheless, in this example, we see a fundraising campaign, fronted by a young person, being supported by a prime minister of a government who, time and time again, led on decisions which curtailed support for the very 'children who need it the most' (Barnardos, 2022b). In demonstrating this support, Johnson was drawing on the symbolic power of charity (Dean, 2020), and Max's fundraising efforts, to positively reflect on himself and his political party. It was a political performance, which was, perhaps unwittingly, supported by the charity, perpetuating the idea that the government was supporting vulnerable children. Here Johnson was celebrating individual generosity, while simultaneously underinvesting in children's services. As Dean (2020) put it, the Prime Minister was basking in the 'good glow' of the young fundraiser's efforts. While the uncomfortable underlying narrative was – children are in vital need of support, in the absence of governmental support, a child has been recruited to ask other children to fundraise to plug the gaps. I cannot help but question what this teaches our children about the role of charity in society and, indeed, how we value children themselves. I watched the media closely, expecting some sense of outrage at the audacity of a prime minister stating this while simultaneously holding the purse strings so tightly shut for vulnerable children's services – but little came; instead, the focus was almost wholly on the heroic exceptionalism of the young fundraiser, with headlines such as the following:

'I'm 11 and pitched a tent by No 10 – then Dilyn came to say hello'
(*The Independent*, 20 July 2021)

'Max Woosey: Devon camping challenge boy pitches tent at No 10'
(*BBC News*, 9 July 2021)

'Marathon charity camper Max Woosey meets Prime Minister at
Number 10 Downing Street' (*ITV News*, 10 July 2021)

'Charity camper, 11, meets PM after pitching up in No 10 garden'
(*LBC News*, 9 July 2021)

There are two truths here which are unavoidable: children need support
and charities need to fundraise, and thus this campaign has proved to be
very successful in raising much-needed funds and attracting the support
of younger supporters (Gorczyca and Hartman, 2017). Nonetheless, my
concern here is the normalisation of charity as a response to children in need
and poverty, with politicians, the media and, at times, charities themselves
legitimising this discourse through the focus on the exceptionalism of a
young fundraiser, who is positioned as a moral role model for other children
and young people to follow. The child's role in this campaign is to use this
platform of exceptionalism to engage other young fundraisers across the
country, with very little attention or discussion about the wider political
and social issues impacting vulnerable children. It perpetuates a narrative
of the personally responsible citizen and fails to consider the broader social
context or examine the deeper structural causes impacting on children's
lives. Thus, it risks encouraging a repetition of the status quo rather than
encouraging children to critically engage in informed critique and make
collective decisions. At our most critical, we may suggest this action risks
legitimising governments cuts to vital services for children and young people,
while suggesting that philanthropy is the answer to fill these gaps in funding.
Indeed, these fundraising efforts are demonstrably pleasing to authority and
those in power with the invitation to the 'Boy in the Tent' to camp in the
gardens of No 10 Downing Street. This further normalises the concept of
personal responsibility and benevolence as the ideal citizen, while doing
very little to encourage children to critically engage in their fundraising
decisions and question the politics of funding for early intervention and
support services for vulnerable children further, and indeed what other
responses are appropriate, beyond that of charity. In short, what we are not
doing is stopping and asking why we are in the position where children
are left fundraising for vulnerable children, in the absence of adequate state
funding. Instead, this is seen as legitimate and moral, and even heroic action
by the media, charities and politicians.

If Max Woosey was being asked to share his views and voice on child poverty and how to support children in need, or indeed to challenge the Prime Minister on the systems and structures surrounding vulnerable children, to hold the government to account or even to call for wider political change, and engaging other children in that debate, the media discourse would likely look very different.

The 'right' kind of philanthropic citizenship

What about if we compare our celebration of child fundraiser exceptionalism against children's engagement in climate change protests (this topic will be explored further in Chapter 9). We start to unveil an entirely different narrative. I was invited to lead a talk on this issue, discussing children's philanthropic citizenship and eco-citizenship. I opened with a straightforward argument: "generally speaking ... our government, and many sections of our society applaud the child who leads a litter pick but deplore the child who joins a school strike for climate change". What I mean by this is that the narratives surrounding children's involvement and engagement with charities already points us towards favouring a virtuous, heroic, nonquestioning approach to supporting others – in this case, the environment. When children venture outside of this, responses are more critical (Dugmore, 2019). For example, in the UK, when asked whether the Prime Minister supported the schools strike for climate change, a Downing Street spokesperson said: "It is important to emphasise that disruption increases teachers' workloads and wastes lesson time that teachers have carefully prepared for" (McGuinness, 2019). This is a very different response from Prime Minister Johnson's statements to Max Woosey. Immediately children are being problematised and reduced to time-wasting rather than recognised as political and social actors. Andrea Leadsom, a Conservative MP and then leader of the House of Commons, tweeted: 'It's called truancy, not a strike' (https://x.com/andrea leadsom/status/1096441011914637312?lang=en-GB). And Conservative MP James Cleverly followed by tweeting:

> Climate Campaigner: 'Who wants to bunk-off school on Friday and join in with a climate change protest?'

> School kid: 'You had me at bunk-off school.' (https://twitter.com/ JamesCleverly/status/1096534591790346240)

None of this demonstrates that children voices or environmental concerns are high on the agenda. This is not just a UK phenomenon. Across the globe, the narratives formed around children's activism have been largely set to belittle and depoliticise children's voices, as will be explored further in Chapter 9.

In summary, all too often when children conform to virtuous modes of philanthropy, which are characterised by unquestioned notions of the good citizen and civic duty – media and societal discourses celebrate them as current and future heroes. When children move outside these bounded notions of citizenship in their philanthropic actions and when they challenge the status quo, the narratives become much more complex and much less celebratory, validating ideas of adult supremacy and shoving children back to the outskirts of political debates, under the discourse of 'it's for their own good' (Alexander et al, 2022; Jones et al, 2023).

Conclusion

In this chapter and the previous one, I have considered the relationship between fundraising and children. Beyond the immediate financial gains, child-led fundraising cultivates a host of positive outcomes. It empowers children, imparting a sense of agency, responsibility and critical engagement with social issues. This hands-on experience hones valuable life skills such as communication, teamwork and leadership, while fostering empathy and compassion. Moreover, it strengthens community bonds, promotes collaboration and nurtures a culture of giving. I discuss my own and colleagues research with 150 children, which reinforces the transformative potential of child-led philanthropy. When given the chance to critically assess charities and causes, children shift towards more thoughtful, cause-oriented giving, rooted in social justice principles. This not only showcases their heightened awareness of inequality but also sparks vital discussions about homelessness, poverty, climate change and educational disparities. Moving forward, it is crucial to empower young fundraisers as change makers by providing them with the tools, support and guidance to make informed giving decisions, such as that demonstrated by the case studies of SuperKind and First Give in Chapter 4. This approach recognises child-led fundraising as an integral part of children's philanthropic citizenship, contributing to a more compassionate and engaged society.

I have then argued that the media representation of young fundraisers reveals a dual narrative: one of exceptionalism and heroism attributed to a select few, and another of marginalisation and passivity often associated with the broader population of child fundraisers. This dichotomy perpetuates an inflexible set of moral values regarding children's roles in philanthropy and civic engagement, reinforcing notions of adult superiority while constraining children's agency in political discourse. Despite occasional acknowledgements of children's charitable endeavours, the prevailing media discourse predominantly centres on exceptional individuals, typically White, privileged and male, while neglecting the collective efforts of diverse children engaged in fundraising activities. Furthermore, the co-optation of children's philanthropic actions for political agendas or charitable marketing purposes underscores the superficiality of such narratives and their failure to address systemic issues affecting vulnerable children. By prioritising individual acts of charity over systemic change and critical engagement, media representations perpetuate a cycle of complacency and depoliticisation, relegating children to the periphery of meaningful political discourse under the guise of benevolence. In contrast, children engaged in climate change protests face criticism and dismissal, highlighting a bias towards a compliant, unquestioning approach to charity. Thus, children are often praised as present and future heroes when they adhere to conventional, virtuous forms of philanthropy, aligning with established notions of good citizenship and civic duty. However, when children engage in civic endeavours that challenge these predefined boundaries of citizenship, the narratives surrounding them become more problematic, reinforcing notions of adult superiority and pushing children's agency to the margins of political discussions. Thus, a re-evaluation of media portrayals is imperative in order to foster a more inclusive and nuanced understanding of children's agency in philanthropy and civic engagement, moving beyond the confines of exceptionalism towards a more equitable and participatory model of citizenship.

6

Education, education, education: a transatlantic focus on schools

With Amy Neugebauer

Introduction

Do you remember the last time you were asked to donate to a school fundraising campaign, maybe as a parent, family member or member of the local community? Maybe it was through baking a cake for the school fair, a Parent Teacher Association (PTA) charity quiz fundraiser, a nonschool uniform day, a sponsored activity or simply in response to a direct request for help? Indeed, barely a week seems to go by without a sponsor form for families to complete, requests for old toys or books, or some larger-scale fundraising campaign. These activities highlight how voluntary, community and philanthropic action is an important and multilayered part of everyday school life, with a combination of parents, grandparents, community members, teachers (and their friends and families!) and children coming together to raise funds and partake in charitable action to support a range of good causes.

Such activity enables schools to draw on a wide range of additional skills and resources, can strengthen a school community and can engage children in philanthropic activity from an early age. Unsurprisingly, voluntary action in education tends to be viewed as a positive and good thing, and is increasingly encouraged within policy and practice. Indeed, fundraising, volunteering and social action in primary schools are becoming progressively central to school activities, with many primary schools keenly seeking to strategically engage and grow this area of activity. Schools increasingly purposefully foster children's philanthropic citizenship in a bid to help cultivate prosocial habits now and in the future, as well as increasingly fundraising for their own needs (Body and Hogg, 2021).

Under this topic, I remember the first time I met the wonderful Amy Neugebauer, Executive Director and Founder of The Giving Square. We both featured on a podcast for the Urban Institute, funded by the Gates Foundation, entitled 'Teaching Kids How to Give' (Urban Institute, 2021). We followed up with a chat afterwards and I felt so inspired by the work they were doing – approaching philanthropic conversations with children from a social justice mentality – that we have stayed in touch ever since. Therefore, it only seemed sensible to come and invite Amy to share her experience and co-author this chapter to offer a transatlantic look at philanthropic citizenship education in middle childhood. Based on research in the UK (see Body et al, 2019, 2020), the work of The Giving Square in the US and drawing on a range of case study examples, we critically examine the relationship between civil society organisations and schools in developing and co-constructing children's philanthropic citizenship. Thus, in this chapter we start with an overview of the role of schools in educating our children as philanthropic citizens, followed by a look at what is happening in primary schools across England, and a deep dive into the work of The Giving Square in the US. We conclude with a discussion about what we can learn from these two examples, transcending geopolitical borders and focusing on a global community.

The importance of school

Schools stand out as crucial hubs for fostering philanthropic citizenship among children and adolescents, given children's widespread attendance in these institutions (CAF, 2013; Hogg and de Vries, 2018; Barrett and Pachi, 2019; Peterson et al, 2021). The role of civic learning programmes in schools, especially in the primary and early years, is of paramount importance, as these institutions often mark children's first experiences of collaboration with others beyond their immediate circles (Body et al, 2020; Payne et al, 2020). The Civic Action and Young Children Study (Payne et al, 2020) delves into the civic actions of three to five year olds from marginalised communities, asserting that recognising such civic behaviours can help schools nurture inclusive participation and visions of the common good. Emphasising the need for schools to provide ample opportunities for children to engage in civic activities, the research underscores that granting children agency expands their civic capabilities, allowing them to act in solidarity with their communities. Rather than instructing children abstractly about democracy and citizenship, the focus should shift towards creating embodied, lived experiences through experiential learning.

Swalwell and Payne (2019) stress the role of educators in helping young children comprehend current injustices and their root causes, articulate their vision of an ideal society and develop strategies to advance their ideas. School-based studies consistently underscore the importance of experiential, active learning in civic education. While discussions about civic issues may heighten awareness, research indicates that participative civic learning activities – such as service learning, community service, exposure to civic role models, political simulations like student council elections, role play and storytelling – significantly contribute to children's longterm civic engagement

(Westheimer, 2015; Torres-Harding et al, 2018; Brownlee et al, 2019; White and Mistry, 2019; Body et al, 2020; Payne et al, 2020). Eidhof and de Ruyter (2022) advocate for schools to play a role in fostering children's self-efficacy in democratic citizenship education. They highlight the importance of citizenship education extending beyond the classroom, involving activities in local communities or engagement in national-level political activities, such as community service-learning projects. Acknowledging the challenges faced by educators in balancing diverse student views, often rooted in family traditions or cultures, Eidhof and de Ruyter argue for promoting neutral politics while encouraging students to critically explore their own beliefs. In a US-based focus group study with 32 children aged 5 to 14, Torres-Harding et al (2018) found that even the youngest children developed sociopolitical awareness and critical consciousness through active participation in grassroots campaigns. The study revealed that children could acknowledge and understand how power differentials and inequalities impact their lives and communities. By facilitating children's decision-making capacities, action and reflection on social change efforts, Torres-Harding et al (2018, p 16) suggest positive outcomes for youth engaged in social action projects, benefiting both individuals and their communities, advocating for children's engagement as social change agents within a school-based, social justice-oriented curriculum.

The RSA's *Citizens of Now* (Tejani and Breeze, 2021) report details the evaluation of a three-year-long project, funded by Pears Foundation working with nine primary schools in the West Midlands, England, between 2018 and 2021, engaging a total of 519 Year 4 pupils to deliver youth social action programmes within a primary school context. They concluded that children (aged eight to nine) derive direct benefits from participating in social action, developing leadership, teamwork, problem solving and communication skills, as well as a sense of social responsibility and civic self-efficacy. Conducting a survey of almost 2,000 teachers as part of this project, Tejani and Breeze (2021) revealed that most teachers and headteachers believe in the importance of youth social action during the primary phase of education; nonetheless, schools located in the most deprived areas have fewer opportunities to take part in social action projects. Equally, this project highlighted significant barriers to engagement. The survey revealed a significant socioeconomic gap in how schools engage with youth social action. Only 27 per cent of primary school teachers in schools where more students come from families facing financial hardship (measured by the percentage of students receiving free school meals) said they incorporate youth social action into their teaching methods. In contrast, 57 per cent of primary teachers in schools where fewer students face such economic challenges said they integrate youth social action into their teaching.

Colleagues and I have also explored civic learning in primary schools in England through the notion of philanthropic citizenship, which we define, as outlined in Chapter 1, as a dimension of citizenship behaviour, associated with intentions and actions that intend to produce social and/or environmental benefits – for example, volunteering, social action, charitable giving, advocacy and activism (Body, 2021). We, and others, find that encouraging philanthropic acts, such as giving to charity, volunteering and social action, has become increasingly mainstream in education and more broadly in society (Power and Taylor, 2018; Body et al, 2020, 2024). This prompts a call for greater emphasis not just on teaching children to be civically engaged, but also on how schools and communities engage children in conversations concerning civic engagement as active citizens (Westheimer, 2015; Simpson, 2017; Body et al, 2021). Thus, as argued throughout this book, philanthropic opportunities should be used to help children challenge and come to their own views of charity, philanthropy, democratic action and associated virtues rather than simply training them to be 'good citizens'. This requires teachers and other facilitators to move away from encouraging transactional engagement and neutral consensus attitudes even at an early age, and instead nurture children's voices within the debates and complexities of charity and giving (Body et al, 2020).

An English perspective

Children's early experiences of active civic engagement and philanthropic citizenship have significant implications for their engagement as current and future citizens. Therefore, this is likely to have consequences for children's ongoing civic journeys and requires further attention within practice, policy and research. In 2021, I was lucky enough to be granted Economic and Social Research Council funding to extend our understanding of children's philanthropic citizenship education in primary schools. Working with my colleagues Dr Emily Lau and Dr Lindsey Cameron, the first stage of this project included a nationwide research project in England, representing over 2,000 primary school teacher's voices via two surveys. From this data we were able to map the 'what' that was happening in children philanthropic citizenship education across England. The findings indicate that there is significant disparity in the types of philanthropic citizenship engagement opportunities available for children within primary school settings, dependent on socioeconomic factors, ethnicity and teachers' own civic behaviours (see Body et al, 2023, 2024). We also see significant disparity in the types and frequency of active civic engagement activities available to children within these regions. In the following, I summarise the core trends from the study.

A focus on monetary donations

In virtually all primary schools, philanthropic citizenship education is an important aspect of the curriculum, aiming to involve children in acts of giving, volunteering, social action and advocacy. However, the crucial consideration lies not in whether children are encouraged to engage in philanthropy, but in the specific type of activity being promoted within the UK primary education system. Our research consistently highlights that primary school educators place significant emphasis on fostering active civic engagement as a vital part of the curriculum. Unfortunately, this emphasis tends to be predominantly centred on fundraising activities, revolving around the donation of money to national campaigns, school fundraising initiatives and local charities, with 67 per cent of teachers reporting children engaging in fundraising for school funds, 66 per cent saying children engage in national fundraising campaigns (for example, Comic Relief) and 53 per cent reporting children raising funds for local charities. This is framed within a discourse of contributory and personal responsibility, with less than a third of children being given the opportunity to discuss issues of justice in relation to fundraising. This often leaves many children with limited opportunities for participatory and critical engagement with the underlying causes of charitable needs.

Like the concerns I raised in Chapter 4, this constrained approach to philanthropic engagement in primary schools risks reducing it to a tokenistic and transactional act, particularly when it comes to helping or supporting others. This misses a pivotal opportunity to provide more profound and meaningful avenues for active civic engagement, connecting concepts of social good with essential social and environmental concerns. While around one half of the school's endeavour to cultivate participatory active civic engagement, it is important to note that these programmes do not inherently aim to enhance children's ability to analyse and critique the root causes of social issues. Indeed, only 15 per cent of primary school educators believe that children have a genuine chance to critically examine the underlying social problems behind the causes they support. For example, children are asked to donate towards the foodbank, but are rarely given the opportunity to consider or debate why food poverty may exist, and other potential responses beyond donating funds (Body et al, 2024).

Simultaneously, we observe a growing concern among teachers regarding the escalating cost-of-living crisis, heightened levels of poverty and families grappling with financial hardship. Consequently, educators are increasingly apprehensive about requesting financial contributions from families. Therefore, this narrow concentration on charitable giving via financial means as the primary avenue for philanthropic engagement poses an escalating challenge, particularly as teachers and schools are placing greater emphasis on poverty-proofing their educational environments. This highlights the need for a more comprehensive approach to active philanthropic citizenship education that encompasses critical analysis and addresses the root causes of social issues, moving beyond monetary donations and focusing more on collective action which is more inclusive.

An issue for equality, equity and democracy

Our research shows substantive differences in children's access to civic engagement opportunities, particularly in relation to socioeconomic status. This is perhaps most exaggerated when we look at private schools versus state schools; nonetheless, we also see stark differences based on the most affluent versus the least affluent school communities. Schools with the most disadvantaged communities are not only most likely to report experiencing multiple barriers to providing philanthropic engagement opportunities, such as engagement in fundraising, social action, campaigning and advocacy, and therefore unsurprisingly offer fewer opportunities as a result, but they are also least likely to offer children the chance to engage in participatory and justice-oriented approaches (Body et al, 2024). For example, children in the most deprived schools are 40 per cent less likely to have opportunities to engage in social action projects than children in the most affluent schools. Given the multiple issues facing these schools and their communities, this is hardly surprising and should not be taken in any way as criticism of these schools; instead, if we really value children's civic education, additional efforts need to be made to support all schools facilitating active civic engagement opportunities.

I argue that this is not just an issue for education, but also for societal equality and democracy, both now and in the future. Children from the most privileged backgrounds are most likely to have early access to active civic and philanthropic engagement opportunities, and therefore are most likely to be equipped with the skills and sense of empowerment for this type of citizenship engagement before secondary school. The potential implications of this are that certain socioeconomic groups are readied for participative philanthropic engagement more than others, increasing the likelihood of these voices being more dominant as they grow.

Engagement with external civil society organisations matters

Our data indicate that partnering with civil society organisations, particularly those focused on philanthropy from a justice-oriented perspective, can significantly enhance children's civic learning journeys. Schools collaborating with such organisations are twice as likely to adopt participatory and justice-oriented approaches compared to those receiving only resources. This isn't surprising, given that previous research suggests that schools often engage in fundraising campaigns with a focus solely on raising funds or goods, neglecting the underlying reasons for giving. In contrast, partnership programmes, like some of the case studies highlighted in this book and the two in this chapter, tend to be longer term and rooted in children's rights principles.

From a children's rights standpoint, fostering active civic engagement should go beyond mere financial contributions. Organisations working with schools should ethically engage children in action and debate to help them understand the moral justifications for intervention. Ideally, activities in schools should be co-created by the fundraising charity, the school/ teachers and the children themselves. This collaborative approach transforms civic engagement activities into a conscious effort to address societal issues comprehensively. Therefore, external organisations, even those focused on fundraising, should provide frameworks that facilitate schools in critically engaging children about the motives behind the need for help and alternative ways to address societal challenges beyond monetary donations.

Case study 6: The Linking Network

One small person can make the biggest difference.

Year 4 pupil following social action linking

The Linking Network brings children and young people together who would not otherwise meet, creating opportunities for them to build relationships with others who are in some ways different to them. Over an academic year, pairs of classes are connected and take part in a series of activities so that they can meaningfully explore the four key questions: who am I?; who are we?; where do we live?; and how do we all live well together? Having taken part in the introductory, 'getting-to-know you' activities in the first phase of the linking journey, the connection between the classes is then deepened as the children find out about each other's values through taking part in social action together.

Our work is rooted in Intergroup Contact Theory which has found that having shared goals, taking part in collaborative activities and meaningful positive interaction create the optimal conditions for the effective contact that can reduce prejudice and build confidence in connecting with others. The social action phase of The Linking Network's Schools Linking programme is designed to build shared understanding and values and draw out that we are all motivated by compassion, thus deepening the connection between the linking classes.

Social action in Schools Linking starts by asking the children: 'what do you care about?' They respond with their ideas which they record onto leaves. These then are displayed onto a 'kindness tree' in their classroom. A photo of this is sent across to their linking class. Teachers then draw out the commonalities between the children's responses, thus gently making the point that although their linking partners live in a different place, they not only care too, but also often care about the same issues. Based on their responses, the next stage is for the children to decide what they can do to make a difference. These ideas are gathered together and the children vote on which they think will have the most positive impact and are realistic and achievable. Again, these are then shared with their linking partner to reinforce the message that they have shared values.

Examples of social action project ideas generated by the children are varied and reflect the interests of the children and their local communities and have included a clean-up of the local community by organising a litter pick, helping younger children and their families increase their physical activity by designing and sharing Keep Fit routines. One Year 4 teacher shared how her class responded to the Social Action aspect of linking. "They have really taken the social action part of our linking to heart and have organised activities to raise money to plant trees. They feel 'just caring' is not enough and that they must speak their minds about issues which concern them and 'do something about it' too. Their activities have caught the attention of a local farmer who is keen to be involved."

Y4 pupils at another school shared their thoughts on the impact of the project: "I'm very proud of myself – sharing with other people that I can be confident and that I can tell you something." They also shared that they felt empowered and inspired by the positive impact they could have: "It's time for the next generation of children – they can change the world really and make the world a better place."

The Linking Network successfully brings young people together, across lines of difference, to build young people's empathy and understanding, and confidence that they can make a difference in the world.

The Linking Network and Dr Lindsey Cameron

Children's rights and voices are all too often overlooked

The data underscore a crucial disparity, one in relation to which I raised concerns in Chapter 4: while children are frequently educated about acts of giving, voluntary action and social engagement, they are less often involved in researching and making decisions about their own responses to social and environmental concerns, with only around half of schools saying that children get to lead on giving decisions. Embracing a children's rights perspective in this participation paradigm necessitates recognising children and young people as adept, socially engaged individuals who possess expertise in their own lives and experiences. They are not just future citizens to be shaped into pre-existing systems and structures; they are current citizens with the capacity to help shape the world they presently inhabit.

Engaging children and young people in active civic decision making goes beyond merely adopting a rhetoric about how to groom them as future participants, volunteers and donors within existing systems. It should fundamentally challenge us to consider the following question: how can we best support and enable children and young people to critically evaluate these systems and structures? This includes considering alternative ways of existence that foster notions of fairness and social justice. Moreover, it calls for a re-evaluation of the interconnectedness of all aspects of the philanthropic ecosystem in driving social change. This encompasses the vital roles of volunteering, advocacy and lobbying governments. Such an approach broadens the perspective, pushing for a more inclusive, impactful and equitable civic engagement framework that truly empowers children and young people to be catalysts for transformative societal progress.

Teachers as civic leaders

Our research demonstrates the pivotal role that teachers play in shaping civic engagement within the classroom. First, we ascertain that teachers, as a group, exhibit a commendable level of civic engagement and display a dedication to fostering active civic participation among children. Second, we establish a direct correlation – the more actively engaged teachers are in civic matters in their personal lives, the more likely they are to implement a participatory and justice-oriented approach in their classrooms. Third, we unearth a positive link between a teacher's own engagement as a civic actor during their own schooling years and their subsequent involvement in participatory and justice-oriented citizenship activities as an adult.

However, it is crucial to acknowledge that teachers encounter various obstacles when attempting to integrate active civic engagement opportunities into their classroom activities. These hurdles range from constraints on time to incorporate such activities to challenges relating to parental involvement, and the financial circumstances of families. While this continues to be an area that warrants further research, it is clear that primary school teachers should not only be acknowledged as civic educators, but should also be viewed in the light of civic leaders and agents.

When teachers perceive civic engagement and political participation as integral components of their personal civic journey, they are twice as likely to impart such knowledge and values within their classrooms than those teachers who are not as civically active. This underscores the importance of promoting lifelong citizenship education and learning among teachers themselves, serving as a means to cultivate inclusive and democratic spaces within the classroom. By reconceptualising teachers as civic leaders, we invite a shift in how schools interact with local communities. In this progressive paradigm, teachers are viewed as co-producers of civic knowledge, collaborating in partnership with children to drive social change. This approach not only amplifies the impact of civic education but also fosters a more dynamic and inclusive educational environment that empowers students to be active participants in the democratic process.

There are multiple moral tensions

The impact of socioeconomic disadvantage on children's civic learning opportunities has long been a concern, but recent times in England have seen these issues exacerbated by the cost-of-living crisis. Our research highlights a growing tension as schools increasingly assume roles as welfare providers while also promoting giving to those less fortunate. Addressing civic learning in schools necessitates confronting issues of poverty, inequality, civic responsibility and social justice – topics that many children are directly experiencing. However, teachers express concerns about the moral responsibility of broaching these discussions in the classroom, often avoiding such conversations. This avoidance of certain discussions and the identification of significant barriers to active civic learning disproportionately affects schools in the most deprived areas. Moreover, framing active civic engagement primarily around monetary giving risks marginalising and diminishing the voices of disadvantaged communities, portraying them as objects of charity. Thus, in our research, we argue for a redefinition of active civic engagement in schools, shifting the focus from benevolent acts to processes aimed at building a better world collaboratively. A participatory and justice-oriented approach fosters collective solutions, empowering children within their communities and lives.

In summary, our mapping of the opportunities across England underscores the critical impact of early experiences in civic engagement and philanthropy on children's future as citizens. The findings reveal a significant disparity in the types of philanthropic citizenship education available in primary schools, with a predominant focus on monetary donations. This narrow emphasis, while fostering charitable giving, risks reducing engagement to a tokenistic and transactional act, missing the opportunity for deeper understanding of social issues. Furthermore, socioeconomic factors exacerbate inequalities, with privileged backgrounds providing early access to civic engagement opportunities, potentially shaping the future dominance of certain voices in civic discourse.

Our study advocates for a more comprehensive approach to philanthropic citizenship education that goes beyond monetary donations, emphasising critical analysis and addressing root causes. It highlights the role of teachers as civic leaders and the need for a broader perspective that includes engagement with external civil society organisations, such as Young Citizens, as we will outline later on. Importantly, the research calls for recognising children as current citizens with rights and voices, urging a shift from viewing them solely as future participants to empowering them as catalysts for transformative societal progress. Lastly, the study identifies moral tensions arising from schools simultaneously playing the roles of welfare providers and promoters of civic responsibility, particularly in the context of the UK cost-of-living crisis, urging a redefinition of active civic engagement in schools to be more inclusive and justice-oriented.

Case study 7: Young Citizens UK

The Make a Difference Challenge is a child-led framework of activity developed by Young Citizens to engage groups of primary aged children in tackling issues they identify in their communities. Over the last 15 years, the programme has supported projects focused on a wide variety of issues: from knife crime to period poverty; plastic pollution in the sea to road safety; food poverty to tackling isolation in the elderly.

The programme's framework ensures that children are at the heart of decision making at every step. They identify and explore a range of issues before using democratic methods to choose one on which to focus. Children are encouraged to develop their understanding of the causes and effects of the issue, developing empathy for the people and situations behind the problem before coming up with creative ways to tackle it. In this way children learn about social injustices rather than simply parachuting in to try and 'solve' what are often complicated issues.

A key part of the Make a Difference Challenge framework supports children to look at key decision makers in their communities – who could (and should) help them with their cause, and how best to approach them. This could be engaging with the local council to tackle the issue of dog waste left in the park, lobbying their MP to take a campaign to Parliament, or presenting to local business leaders in order to secure a donation to help further their project.

One such school is South Hetton Primary, where children were horrified to learn that many girls and women on low incomes were forced to choose between buying sanitary protection or buying food. They researched the impact locally, including linking into homelessness charities and foodbanks, and decided to create 'Pants Packs' for distribution to those who needed them most. They set up donation points for local people to donate wipes, tampons and pads – and wrote to supermarkets asking for their support too. The children were interviewed on Heart Radio to raise awareness of the problem, and their teachers posted about the project on social media.

'People shouldn't be uncomfortable talking about periods.' (Year 6 pupil)

The class also contacted their local MP, Grahame Morris, who submitted an Early Day Motion to the House of Commons and tabled a question for the Minister for Women and Equalities asking if she would take steps to ensure the provision of free period products to low-income families:

'The students of South Hetton Primary should be immensely proud of the positive impact they have had in their local community. The pupils demonstrated remarkable maturity and social awareness in developing their Period Problems and Poverty campaign. South Hetton Primary school's campaign has been taken up nationally and I hope it will inspire others to participate in the Make a Difference Challenge.'

Stella Baynes, Programmes Manager, Young Citizens

A US perspective: The Giving Square

By Amy Neugebauer

An emerging model of school-based engagement in the US, The Giving Square's mission is to transform the civic role of children through a new, inclusive expression of philanthropy. Recognising philanthropy as the 'giving of yourself for the good of humanity', The Giving Square was founded to more meaningfully and impactfully connect children to their philanthropic capacities and identities. Primarily focused on seven to 13 year olds, the nonprofit works with elementary and middle schools across Maryland, Virginia and most recently Missouri. In 2024 we are estimated to be reaching students from over 60 schools across a diverse range of socioeconomic realities (from low-income public schools to private schools). Our programmes mostly take place during the school day as part of civics, social studies, homeroom or 'specials' (such as blocks for school counsellors). Alternatively, they take place during recess or out-of-school time (club time, before and after care, and so on). Using a 'train the trainer' model, The Giving Square trains and equips teachers or staff to facilitate the programmes at their own schools.

Why philanthropy?

Even though philanthropy is often associated with money or old rich donors, the origins of the word are much more expansive. 'Giving of yourself for the good of humanity' assumes a deeper, more meaningful, purposeful and impactful way of giving. This is how we want kids to understand their philanthropic potential.

Some suggest we stick to easier words (giving, service or kindness) to make things easier for younger kids. We unapologetically stick to the use of 'philanthropy' for three reasons:

1. Because helping others well is not easy and therefore needs a harder word. Similar to a child's skill development in maths, reading or even soccer, philanthropy is something that one can (and should) get better at doing. We cannot be satisfied with the notion that any help is enough or even helpful. At a school drive for household goods, I saw this first hand. Neighbours dropped off helpful pieces of lightly used furniture, bikes and home goods. In equal measure, people dropped off unusable items: tables with missing legs, outdated (and often broken) electronics and even a toddler potty that hadn't been cleaned. While many things were in 'dignity condition' (as asked), 40 per cent of what was donated was recycled or put in the trash. The resulting three truckloads of 'goods' for the local nonprofit were a mix of what the organisation needed and what the organisation now had the burden of handling.
2. Kids are natural philanthropists. More than other age groups, upper elementary students are empathic, open-minded, fluid thinkers and are deeply aware of the fact that life is not fair.
3. Kids can handle hard things and grasp complex concepts. Simply put, if kids can say 'pterodactyl', they can say 'philanthropist'! Children can also handle hard things because they are exposed to the challenges of life too. Shared one nine-year-old: "Adults think it is so easy to be a kid. When I was three my parents got divorced, then my dog died, and now my dad has cancer. My life is not easy!" Adults may try to shelter and protect kids from harder conversations, difficult topics in the news and pain in general. Yet, many kids are already aware of the issues parents seek to protect them from. One of the reasons we engage kids in philanthropy is to give them a way to channel their angst and distress in a positive direction.

Challenges within the US context

Traditional US models tend to focus on engaging kids as fundraisers, collectors and doers. Examples include Jump for Heart (renamed

Kids Heart Challenge), where kids go to family and neighbours to sponsor their jump-roping efforts, with the proceeds going to the American Heart Association. Adults remember UNICEF donation boxes they used to trick or treat with at Halloween. Many Americans break diets around Girl Scout Cookie sale season as troops sell cookies door to door, in front of grocery stores or now increasingly online. Additionally, there are numerous examples of kids hosting lemonade stands, canned food drives or bake sales. Within families, when asked how they engage kids in giving, many will refer to giving jars where kids divide their dollars into the categories of save, spend and donate.

From an early age, kids are incentivised to participate in service activities through prizes, points or other extrinsic motivators. As a mom I was thrilled when my son came home from school one day excited about donating a good portion of his Christmas money to Jump for Heart. When asked why he was so compelled, he eagerly showed me a photo of the t-shirt he would earn. Look at most school-based engagements and there is likely a prize sheet tied to it. In Maryland (and several other states), once a student reaches middle school, a big driver of service efforts becomes the earning of Service Learning Hours, which becomes a graduation requirement in high school. And finally, as students hit high school, doing good for others becomes part of how kids market themselves to get into college. These extrinsic motivations may lead to quality giving experiences, but they can also create a dependency on external drivers to fuel philanthropic actions.

Making philanthropic action meaningful

Thanks to Alison Body's research, we know that while most kids have been involved with service, immediately after helping, only 20 per cent of kids could tell you what it is for (Body et al, 2020). If service doesn't lead children and young people to form deeper connections to their own purpose or social issues, we risk them becoming apathetic about service. Therefore, The Giving Square is only satisfied if engagement is meaningful to kids, connects them to their purpose as a human and leads to a positive impact on the community.

Our curriculum is guided by four core CARE principles:

Community. We are part of a shared humanity which relies on all of us looking out for each other.
Accessibility. Everyone should be able to see themselves as a philanthropist. Everyone can be a contributor in their own, unique way.

Responsibility. Life is not fair. It is everyone's responsibility to make life better for others.

Empathy. In order to help, we need to develop empathetic connections to social challenges.

In designing our curriculum, there were several parameters we wanted to design for. The two most important were as follows:

1. While a lot of philanthropic programmes for kids are modified (or 'rolled down') versions of curricula for high schoolers or adults, we designed our programmes for specifically for kids. This meant that we needed to be able to humanize social issues in a way that would feel emotionally and intellectually meaningful to children. It also meant that we needed to test and develop new pedagogical frameworks. One example of a successful framework is the 'Philanthropic Body Part', a way for kids to see the many ways in which people can contribute with their brain, ears, mouth, muscles, eyes and hands. This framework helps kids get away from the idea that they can only help with money, an asset most kids don't have.

2. We also designed our curricula to be universally accessible. From the beginning, we were committed to ensuring that our programmes could work across socioeconomic realities and with kids with their own stories. This affected our language, our tools and the stories we chose to feature in the curriculum. It also took into consideration that kids might be experiencing some of the challenges we discuss. We needed to be sensitive to participants struggling to have their basic needs met, experiencing loss (such as divorce or a death in the family), or having health issues (or sick family members). Therefore, we make sure facilitators are sensitive to this issue ahead of running the programme. In a few cases kids or families have been pulled aside to see if they felt comfortable in a particular session. More broadly, we account for this by normalising the idea that we can all help, but that we all need help sometimes too. The curriculum allows for kids to share their own experience with their peers. During the programme, peers have learned things such as that their classmate experiences chronic headaches, is dealing with a sick relative, has parents going through a divorce, lost their dog and so on. One boy shared that "the reason I wear these glasses is that if I don't, all I can see are rainbows", at which point the room shared a collected "wow, we had no idea" reaction. In another classroom Jayden shared his early experience with cancer at which point

some kids exclaimed: "WE REMEMBER!" This led to a rich conversation about the scary stuff he remembers (especially the shots [injections]) and his classmates remembered. Jayden shared that he remembers the blanket his classmates made for him as it really brought him comfort, especially during follow-up visits. "We made that!", shouted out a few of the kids.

The Giving Square programme

All of our programmes are designed as eight 40-minute blocks. While each programme is unique, they all generally follow an arc that starts with personal reflection and discovery, leads to empathy-building sessions around different social issues, and then culminates in an experience or production of content.

Kids for Kids Intro

First piloted in 2021, the Kids for Kids Intro is a literacy-based programme for 2nd and 3rd graders. The programme consists of sessions organised around the themes of 'everyone has a story', 'there are many ways to help', 'we all give and receive' and 'kids can do a lot to help others'. Each session is based on a different children's book (carefully selected in partnership with the Children and Youth team at Politics and Prose, a revered book store in Washington DC, and then reviewed by kids). After each book, we introduce a game, exercise or project that makes the topic more personal for each kid.

The Kids for Kids Fund

The Kids for Kids Fund programme offers a dynamic civic experience for 3rd to 5th graders to develop their philanthropic identity and capacity. During this experiential journey, we focus on building an empathetic connection to the needs of others, exploring compassionate solutions to issues facing our communities and putting our philanthropic capacities into practice. The sessions include exploring the rights of all children, perspective taking about different social issues impacting kids (including health, basic needs and disabilities), and learning about great local solutions to these issues in their local community. The programme culminates in each school group determining how to allocate $1,000 to a local, kid-serving nonprofit. It should be noted that kids are not the fundraisers; rather, they have been given the responsibility to make an important decision about how to give away the money.

The Service-Learning Workshop

The Service-Learning Workshop is designed to give 5th to 8th graders a path to successful and meaningful service learning, and an opportunity to explore their own philanthropic identity. Our programme starts with exploring participant's unique story and purpose, building empathetic connections to different social challenges, and then exploring service pathways of meaning to them. A central component of this programme is a tabletop role-playing game that puts theory into practice in a format that is natural to young people.

The 'Kids are philanthropists, too' podcast

While there are many podcasts for and about children; 'Kids are philanthropists, too' is produced *with* children. It is designed to help people of all ages get closer to issues and solutions in our communities. Over the first two seasons we have interviewed people of all ages about health, immigration, disabilities, basic needs and grief. Season three has focused on solutions relating to loneliness, disaster relief and more.

Conclusion

Both the English and US perspectives underscore the pivotal role of schools in fostering active civic engagement and philanthropy among young people during middle childhood. The emphasis is on moving beyond monetary giving to instil a deeper, more meaningful form of philanthropy that involves active participation in addressing social issues. Both perspectives recognise the inherent empathetic qualities of children, particularly those in upper elementary grades, and stress the importance of tapping into these qualities to promote genuine civic engagement.

The discourse emphasises that the significance of schools in cultivating philanthropic citizenship extends beyond tokenistic acts, urging a shift towards a more profound and meaningful engagement that addresses root causes and nurtures critical thinking. While acknowledging the role of monetary donations, the call is for a comprehensive approach that actively involves children in conversations about civic engagement, social justice and the interconnectedness of the philanthropic ecosystem. The disparities in access to civic engagement opportunities highlight concerns about equality, equity and democracy. The discourse underscores the urgency for a more inclusive civic education landscape, emphasising the potential long-term impact of certain socioeconomic groups being readied for participative philanthropic engagement more than others.

Moreover, the engagement of external civil society organisations and the recognition of teachers as civic leaders emerge as critical factors. Teachers play a central role in shaping the civic engagement landscape within classrooms, and by reconceptualising them as civic leaders, a shift is proposed in terms of how schools interact with local communities. The Giving Square is a groundbreaking model reshaping children's civic roles through a distinctive approach to philanthropy in US schools. Rooted in the belief that philanthropy means 'giving of yourself for the good of humanity,' the organisation fosters meaningful connections between children and philanthropy. Unlike simplistic charity notions, The Giving Square views philanthropy as a skill, encouraging children to develop and excel in their giving endeavours.

Recognising children's innate philanthropic nature, particularly in the upper elementary years, The Giving Square taps into their empathy and awareness of social issues. Rejecting external incentives, the organisation focuses on intrinsic motivation, fostering a genuine commitment to positive community impact. Addressing challenges in prevailing models, The Giving Square's curriculum aligns with core CARE principles – Community, Accessibility, Responsibility and Empathy – ensuring meaningful philanthropic action that connects children to a broader purpose. The Giving Square's carefully crafted curriculum, featuring the 'Philanthropic Body Part' framework, goes beyond monetary contributions, emphasising diverse ways in which individuals can contribute. Universal accessibility ensures effectiveness across socioeconomic realities, creating an inclusive space for diverse backgrounds. Programmes like Kids for Kids Intro, the Kids for Kids Fund, the Service-Learning Workshop and the 'Kids are philanthropists, too' podcast provide structured avenues for children to reflect, empathise and take meaningful actions, fostering responsibility and connection to community issues.

In conclusion, the English and US perspectives converge in recognising schools as vital catalysts for instilling a profound sense of philanthropy and civic engagement in middle childhood. This shared emphasis extends beyond financial contributions, focusing on active involvement and addressing root causes. The discourse underscores the urgent need for a more inclusive civic education landscape, stressing the potential impact of disparate access to participative philanthropic engagement. Additionally, the roles of external civil society organisations and teachers as civic leaders emerge as critical factors, proposing a transformative shift in schools' interaction with local communities.

7

"I promise that I will do my best to do my duty": The Scouts

Introduction

So far in this book, I have explored several spaces and places within society where children and young people are encouraged to be and become good citizens. In this chapter, I turn our attention to the uniform groups, focusing initially on the Scouts and then the splinter group of the Woodcraft Folk.

The roots of scouting trace back to the leadership of Sir Robert Baden-Powell, who was born in 1857 in London. Inheriting a passion for outdoor activities from his father, Baden-Powell organised a camp on Brownsea Island in 1907, marking the experimental beginnings of scouting. In 1908 he released his seminal manual, *Scouting for Boys*, setting the standard for scouting activities, emphasising self-reliance, good citizenship and moral development. This ignited a global surge in scouting, culminating in the formal establishment of the Boy Scouts Association in 1910. The Scout Law, the Scout Promise and the motto 'Be Prepared' became guiding principles. Scouts diversified across urban and rural settings, later including girls through the establishment of the Girl Guides. The global movement now impacts youth worldwide and is currently active in 216 countries and territories, with a global membership of over 31 million, male and female, with two thirds of the international membership in developing countries.

In the UK, scouting played a crucial role in both world wars, offering vital support and exemplifying commitment to community and military service. After the Second World War, adapting to changing societal needs, scouting introduced various sections for different age groups. Today, UK Scouts state that they strive for inclusivity, welcoming participants from diverse backgrounds, although with varying degrees of success. They continue to receive strong support from the British royal family, symbolising British values of character, resilience and grit. Indeed, Bannister (2022) argues that scouting and guiding organisations play a crucial role in the ritual socialisation of young people in Britain, instilling values, norms and identity among their members, contributing to their socialisation into society, and shaping the moral and social development of youth within these organisations and their broader communities. Despite facing challenges, including a drop in youth membership during the COVID-19 pandemic, efforts by the UK Scouts to broaden their appeal have resulted in the establishment of new scout packs, troops and colonies in economically disadvantaged regions. Furthermore, as Mills (2021) identifies, the Scouts increasingly emphasise character education, tying language to life-course successes and focusing on values, with collaborations with government agencies, especially the Department for Education (DfE) and the Department for Digital, Culture, Media and Sport (DCMS), highlighting scouting's growing role in character development. Nonetheless, concerns persist about funding adequacy, especially in the wake of significant cuts to the youth sector. Thus, Mills (2021) argues that the closeness between the UK Scouts and the UK government reflects a broader focus on the character agenda and youth engagement, raising questions about the potential impact on youth responsibilisation.

Therefore, in this chapter I explore how the UK Scouts, rooted in tradition, navigate these contemporary challenges. As I explore the evolving role of uniform groups, including the alternative perspective of the Woodcraft Folk movement, I seek to unpick both the strengths and limitations of these organisations in shaping current and future ideas about active citizenship for children and young people today.

Research exploring uniform groups

While research clearly shows that uniform groups and positive youth development programmes benefit children and young people, the extent of these benefits is more debated. For example, engagement in the Scouts has been found to predict not just moral and performance character (Lynch et al, 2016), but also prolonged participation in Scouts is linked to active civic engagement during young adulthood. There's even evidence suggesting that this engagement can reduce substance use and violence among young individuals, and increase long-term health (Berrie et al, 2023). A study in the UK delved into the connection between attendance at scouting and girl guides and later mental health, taking into account childhood risk factors and social class (Bonell et al, 2015). It found that attendees of scouts and girl guides had 18 per cent lower odds of experiencing a mood or anxiety disorder at the age of 50 (Dibben et al, 2017). Furthermore, a study examining attendees of the Boy Scouts of America uncovered evidence of a long-term impact on subjective wellbeing during adulthood (Jang et al, 2014). This adds to the growing understanding of the potentially far-reaching positive effects of youth development programmes like the Scouts.

Indeed, several studies in the US have emphasised the significance of community-led programmes in fostering civic participation among presecondary school children. However, the outcomes regarding children's civic mindedness display a mix of results. For instance, engagement in scouting during the presecondary school years in the US is positively correlated with multiple indicators of civic engagement in adulthood, including community involvement, community volunteering (Kim et al, 2016; Kim and Morgul, 2017), community activism and environmental activism (Kim et al, 2016). Likewise, the Girl Scout Research Institute (2012) found that American Girl Scout alumnae were more active in their communities (through volunteering, community service and so on) and more likely to consider themselves leaders than nonparticipants. Despite this, research involving a cross-sectional sample of boys aged 6–11 who participated in US Cub Scouts failed to establish associations between the intensity or breadth of their involvement and children's helpfulness, kindness and trustworthiness (Champine et al, 2016). Similarly, in a sample of 1,398 Boy Scouts (with an average age of nine), Wang et al (2015) found that scouts' self-ratings significantly increased for helpfulness compared with non-scouts over a two-and-a-half-year period, but not for kindness or trustworthiness.

Lynch et al's (2016) study on presecondary school-aged scouts, which indicated that high levels of autonomy, emotional engagement and cognitive engagement in activities led to the most substantial increases in prosocial, moral and civic behaviours. Likewise, in the context of the UK, Tyler-Rubenstein et al (2016) highlighted the importance of uniformed groups in engaging children in social action, while Birdwell et al (2013) suggested that such activities offer crucial spaces for nurturing younger children's civic engagement. Moreover, several studies underscore the positive impact of involving children as agents of change within their communities as a vital component of civic life. Percy-Smith and Burns (2012), through participatory research with children, suggested that a pivotal aspect of promoting the growing role of children as agents of change in communities lies in providing spaces that are not solely controlled by adults or bound by adult agendas, but also offer opportunities for children to take action in response to issues they feel passionate about. Likewise, Nicotera's (2008) participatory action research study, where children were actively engaged in community planning processes, demonstrated statistically significant changes in children's civic engagement, awareness and civic skills, such as the assessment of the strengths and weaknesses of community projects and actions. Together, this research underscores both the importance of civic engagement opportunities and the ways in which these opportunities are enacted as important.

Furthermore, scouting organisations worldwide play a pivotal role in cultivating eco-citizenship, serving as a conduit for the development of environmentally conscientious and proactive individuals. While the organisation has modernised its badges, the core scouting ideals of adventurous, outdoor activities remain central to fostering grit and resilience. These activities are celebrated as examples of nurturing good and moral citizens (Mills, 2021). Through a structured combination of outdoor experiences, ecological education and community involvement, the intention is that scouts undergo a process that extends beyond passive environmental awareness, fostering a sense of duty towards environmental stewardship. Central to this is experiential immersion in natural environments, embarking on expeditions that traverse diverse landscapes, camping under the stars, and exploring the ecosystems of woodlands and water bodies. These immersive encounters serve as a foundation for cultivating an understanding and respect for the natural world, establishing a resolute commitment to its preservation.

Research conducted by Wells and Lekies (2006) reveals a noteworthy correlation between childhood engagement in activities with 'wild nature', such as exploring natural areas through walking, playing, hiking and camping, and the development of positive environmental attitudes and behaviours in adulthood. Notably, individuals who participated in these activities before the age of 11 demonstrated a greater likelihood of expressing pro-environmental attitudes and engaging in environmentally friendly behaviours later in life, highlighting uniform groups as a particularly important space within which children gain these experiences (Kim et al, 2016). The diverse pathways by which children encounter nature exhibit significant connections with their engagement in environmental citizenship actions and their dedication to nature-centred activities during adulthood. Among these pathways, childhood exposure to nature facilitated by structured programmes displayed the strongest association with environmental advocacy, activism and participation in environmental volunteer work (Asah et al, 2018). Nonetheless, while we witness multiple benefits of scouting the pedagogical framing of such activities, which favours a character, virtues-oriented approach, requires further scrutiny.

Scouting in contemporary times

For several years (2016–2019) I was a Beaver Scout Leader, supporting a very popular colony of six to eight year olds. My experience from this period has without doubt shaped some of my views on scouting today. I loved leading the Beaver group. We had wonderful adventures, got involved in so many engaging activities and had access to brilliant outdoor experiences, including adventurous sports such as rafting, canoeing, climbing and hiking, as well as camping and similar excursions. My oldest son benefited from these activities, gaining confidence, skills and friendships.

Nonetheless, regardless of my enjoyment of this time, it also provided me with the opportunity to witness some of the challenging realities of scouting. For example, the colony I managed was for the first two years of my time there entirely made up of White, middle-class children, and had a huge waiting list of, again, White, middle-class children, most of whom had been on that waiting list since birth. The first-come-first-served waiting list approach immediately favoured children from more privileged backgrounds, whose parents had enlisted them early and were well established in the relatively affluent community. Children from more transient backgrounds, who happened to move around more, or move into this community, were less likely to secure a place. Indeed, I remember raising and questioning this when two looked-after children moved into the area and were seeking a place. I was firmly told they would 'have to wait their turn'. Equally, as we tried to expand the group, or even run a second colony, a lack of volunteers meant this option was an impossibility. While it is important to acknowledge that Scout groups all over the country are run very differently and often dependent on the volunteers that run them, two issues arise; first, the persistent perception that scouting is a space for White, privileged children; and, second, that there are not enough volunteers to meet demand.

I wasn't alone in the recognition of these challenges and the UK Scouts have gone to lengths to seek to address this. In response to these pressing issues, UK Scouts have sought to confront the situation head-on, acknowledging that the organisation's diversity often doesn't mirror that of the local communities and may not reach all the children and young people who stand to gain the most from being members (Booth, 2019). This recognition sparked a determined effort to create new scout packs. From 2014 to 2019, this initiative bore remarkable fruits. The Scouts established an impressive 1,280 new packs, troops and colonies in some of the most economically disadvantaged regions of Britain, leading to a noteworthy surge in membership by over 20,000. Notably, more than a quarter (26 per cent) of these new units emerged in areas ranking among the bottom 20 per cent on the government's multiple deprivation index. This strategic shift was part of a broader campaign by the Scouts to broaden their appeal, seeking to dispel the stereotype that scouting is solely for White, middle-class individuals. Furthermore, the Scouts aimed to rebuild their once-strong ties to urban areas, where scouting was once a pathway for learning valuable skills to combat unemployment. Backing this endeavour into inner cities has come through substantial funding, with contributions exceeding £7 million from notable donors. These combined efforts, both in terms of outreach and financial support, aimed to signify the Scouts' commitment to a more inclusive and impactful future (Booth, 2019).

However, the COVID-19 pandemic, which hit the UK in 2020, witnessed a 23 per cent drop in youth membership. Nonetheless, in 2021/2022 the charity reported a resurgence of 16 per cent membership, largely down to the launch of Squirrel Dreys for four to six year olds in September 2021. This was the culmination of two years' piloting of early years scouting, building on pioneering work in Northern Ireland. Importantly, the charity prioritised opening these Dreys in areas of deprivation, with the aim of supporting children and families hardest hit by the pandemic. The Scouts report that in 2021/2022, 28 per cent of Squirrel Dreys opened in lower-income areas, with 34 per cent in Scout groups that already have 10 per cent or more young people from Black, Asian and minority ethnic communities, demonstrating a welcomed commitment to widening inclusivity (Scouts, 2023).

A military ethos with a colonial past

While the Scouts are a nonpolitical organisation, the blurring of state and organisational boundaries is arguably evident as they are increasingly co-opted into the normalisation and socialisation of children into a responsibilisation agenda, which is framed by a quiet military ethos, embodied by character virtues (see Chapter 2), and representation of civic duty (Mills, 2021), embedded within a colonial legacy. Indeed, scouting organisations both here and in the US have received criticism for their links with political parties. Notably, in the UK, the appearance of Bear Grylls on stage at the Conservative Party conference in 2017 caused a backlash for UK Scouts, as critics suggested it showed the scouting movement endorsing the party. Nevertheless, the very appointment of Bear Grylls as Chief Scout in 2009, and then later as World Ambassador in 2018, symbolises the scouting ideal. As the son of a former Tory MP and a devout Christian, his scouting ethos can be found in his military ties, personal values and survival expertise. He is perhaps the very embodiment of Baden-Powell in contemporary times (though with some notably more inclusive views). Bear Grylls himself draws upon the traditional values of scouting, as he told *GQ* magazine in 2017:

> 'The main reason I believe that scouting is such a positive force for young people is that it instils in us certain values that, if we carry them forward into our adult lives, can act as an anchor and a rock. They are as relevant now as they were when Lord Baden-Powell wove them into the scouting movement 108 years ago.' (Grylls, 2017)

Attached to this military ethos, scouting, like many uniform groups, has an uncomfortable amount of colonial baggage to manage as it seeks to redefine itself. The movement itself, founded by Baden-Powell, who served in the military and gained fame defending the town of Mafeking during the Boer War, has its roots in imperial values and loyalty to the British Empire. It rapidly expanded to various colonies, where it served as a tool for instilling discipline, loyalty and colonial values among the youth. The movement's emphasis on outdoor skills and preparedness also resonated with these colonial ideals. This association with colonial values has resulted in the scouting movement facing several controversies relating to colonial and imperialistic attitudes. Indeed, Baden-Powell himself has been accused of war crimes against local Africans, including unlawful executions and contributing towards starvation (Foster, 2008), and has faced criticism for historic views considered in contemporary times as racist, anti-LGBTQ+ and sympathetic to Hitler and the Nazis. Documents revealed Baden-Powell's favourable comments on *Mein Kampf*. In June 2020, controversy erupted over a statue of Baden-Powell in Poole amid anti-racism protests sparked by George Floyd's death bringing debates about modern scouting back under public scrutiny.

The colonial roots of scouting are further exemplified by the relationship between scouting and the British royal family. Members of the royal family, including the reigning monarch, have frequently served as patrons of scouting organisations. Their patronage has played a pivotal role in drawing attention to and garnering support for the movement, contributing significantly to its growth and visibility. The royal family's involvement provides a symbolic link to traditional values of duty and service, aligning closely with the ethos of scouting that emphasises civic responsibility and personal development. Moreover, the presence of royalty at scouting events and ceremonies brings a perceived level of prestige, often attracting media coverage and enhancing the public image of the organisation. Indeed, the 2023 Christmas speech by King Charles III included footage of Prince George, Princess Charlotte and Prince Louis volunteering at a scout hut with their parents in May, as he praised people for their service to one another.

However, the association between scouting and the royal family is not without its criticisms. One notable concern is the continued perception and perpetuation of elitism and privilege associated with this connection. Critics argue that the close ties to the royal family create an impression of scouting as an institution aligned with traditional hierarchies, potentially undermining the movement's commitment to inclusivity. Additionally, the historical links between scouting and colonialism raise questions about how the royal family's association may reinforce colonial narratives within the scouting movement. This is particularly relevant given scouting's origins in the British Empire and its historical role in promoting imperial values. Another critical aspect centres on the challenges of modernisation and inclusivity. In an era where institutions are actively working towards greater diversity and inclusivity, the close association with a hereditary monarchy can be viewed as incongruent with the progressive values that scouting seeks to embody. Moreover, the question of neutrality arises, as scouting organisations often emphasise values such as independence and political impartiality. The connection to the royal family can be seen as compromising the movement's ability to maintain a neutral stance, especially in constitutional monarchies where the monarch's role is intertwined with the state. Thus, as societal values evolve, the relevance of the association with the royal family comes under scrutiny, questioning the compatibility of scouting's values with an institution based on birthright rather than merit.

While over time, scouting organisations have adapted to changing social values, acknowledging the need to move away from imperialistic ideals, they remain caught between a space of progression and tradition. For instance,

UK Scouts admitted women in the 1970s, adjustments have been made to the Scout Promise to be more inclusive, and decisions to review the appropriateness of awards (Smart, 2023) or statues (Morris, 2020) named after scouting figures indicate a reassessment of their historical legacy. The reconsideration of these awards and statues reflects a broader societal dilemma faced by organisations, caught between honouring colonial figures as heroes by some while facing criticism for their roles in history (Smart, 2023). Despite Baden-Powell's enduring status as a hero and the global success of the scouting movement, scrutiny of his alleged antisemitic and racist attitudes, coupled with historical accusations of war crimes during the Boer War, has prompted a review of the appropriateness of how this historical figure is represented and celebrated within the scouting movement. The broader context involves various organisations confronting their colonial legacies, whether through the renaming of places or statues, exemplifying an ongoing process of public reckoning with historical figures and their complicated legacies (Smart, 2023).

This is not only an issue for scouting but also impacts philanthropic foundations more widely. Framing discussions around engaging children in understanding contemporary philanthropy poses crucial challenges. In today's philanthropic landscape, there is a tendency to idolise wealthy benefactors for their charitable deeds, often overlooking the ethical complexities of their financial success. This dilemma mirrors the debates surrounding statues of historical philanthropists like Edward Colston, whose wealth stemmed from the slave trade (Nasar, 2020). While some argue for the preservation of such statues to foster dialogue about contested pasts, others see their removal as an opportunity for critical reflection on philanthropic actions (Nasar, 2020). Incorporating these discussions into educational and community settings involves acknowledging philanthropy's evolving nature, akin to the historical evolution of scouting, and its deep-rooted connections to exploitation and inequality. By examining historical narratives, children and young people can actively participate in shaping a more transformative philanthropic future. However, blindly celebrating philanthropic gestures without scrutinising their origins perpetuates unjust power structures and reinforces existing imbalances (Daly, 2012). A nuanced approach is needed not only to appreciate charitable acts but also to critically evaluate the systemic issues surrounding wealth accumulation and the influence of philanthropists on societal priorities. By engaging in these conversations, children can develop a deeper understanding of the complexities inherent in philanthropy and philanthropic institutions.

UK Scouts: the embodiment of civic duty

Building on the traditionalism of scouting, scouts worldwide have become to be viewed as the embodiment of the good citizen and civic duty – the role models of good character – and, as such, concepts of character education and scouting have become increasingly intertwined. Mills (2021) highlights four contemporary trends within scouting symbolising its wider role in the character agenda. First, the Scouts increasingly adopt themes of character education within their campaigns, for example 'Be Resilient' and 'Skills for Life'. Second, this language is increasingly tied to experiencing success across the life-course – attributing major successes to the fact someone belonged to the scouting community – for example, a six-year-old boy called Henry heard a woman crying for help and, along with his father, raised an alarm and called an ambulance. Bear Grylls later in a statement immediately attributed these actions to the child's role as a Beaver Scout, stating: "Henry is a real hero, I'm so proud of his actions … Scouting has given him these skills and Sylvia is living proof of how important they are" (*BBC News*, 2016).

Third, Scouts UK have increasingly focused on values within their messaging, as Mills explains:

> For example, the centrality of 'values' in the additional alternative Scout Promise for atheists or agnostics introduced in 2014. Here, the line 'Duty to God' has been replaced with a pledge 'To uphold our Scout values'. This change, following an extensive consultation, reflects not only broader changes in British society in relation to religion but demonstrates the continued belief that they are somehow distinct and recognisable 'Scout' values, ones that would presumably 'set apart' members of the organisation from other young people. (Mills, 2022, p 72)

And finally, the growing partnership between Scouts UK, the Department for Education (DfE) and the Department for Digital, Culture, Media and Sport (DCMS). Indeed, over the last decade, collaborations between the Scouts and the DfE have grown significantly, particularly within the character agenda. Notably, the 'Character by Doing' initiative received DfE funding in 2014, introducing scouting in six schools and claiming to result in improved leadership abilities and behaviour among students (Scott et al, 2016). Scouts UK have also been actively involved in projects like the 'Scouts Early Years' pilot scheme, receiving partial funding from the DfE (UK Scouts, 2023). The National Youth Guarantee (NYG) and its £580 million investment, announced by the government in February 2022, stems from a Youth Review conducted by the DCMS. The aim is to ensure that every young person in England has access to out-of-school activities, adventures and volunteer opportunities by 2025. The funding is distributed through various streams, including £180 million for the National Citizen Service and £22 million for the Duke of Edinburgh Award and the #iwill fund (UK Scouts, 2023).

However, there are ongoing concerns about the adequacy of funding, especially in light of significant cuts to the youth sector in recent years (Cultural Learning Alliance, 2023). The funding emphasis on capital investment has raised worries about sustainability and the need for youth work revenue funding. While the government's investments are welcomed, they fall short of addressing the deep-seated issues faced by the youth sector, where austerity cuts have resulted in a 75 per cent decline in real terms funding for youth services since 2010/2011, reaching £1.1 billion by 2022 (YMCA, 2022), resulting in increasing challenges in terms of responding to the needs of children and youth, particularly those who are most disadvantaged (Body, 2020; Fretwell and Barker, 2023). Nonetheless, while issues around funding for youth support across youth services persists, UK Scouts secured a £6.35 million grant in 2023, demonstrating continued support for uniformed youth groups (UK Scouts, 2023). This suggests that mainstream uniformed groups, framed within the character discourse, are viewed as a solution to the challenges in youth provision and services. Critics would argue this adopts an approach which 'seeks to fix the kids' (Jerome and Kisby, 2019) rather than directly address inequalities in access to opportunities, which youth work seeks to tackle.

Mills (2021) offers excellent analysis of the growing closeness between UK Scouts, uniform groups more widely and the UK government. As she points out, the 'Character by Doing' programme was the first time ever that the UK government had funded this voluntary uniformed youth movement. The push on being resilient, developing 'skills for life', civic duty, determination and grit communicated powerful ideas about what it means to be a good citizen and character virtues in British society. The embodied promises within scouting of a 'duty to self, duty to others, and duty to God' is endemic of what the UK Conservative government (2010–2024) viewed as the good, law-abiding citizens. Thus, according to Mills (2021), scouting can be interpreted as part of the wider and renewed focus on the character agenda, framed under the auspices of youth engagement. Furthermore, the status of scouting in British society is powerful and symbolic, and therefore the blurring of boundaries between the state and uniform groups gives further credibility to the governments responsibilisation agenda (Mills, 2021). And as Jon Dean points out, the responsibilisation of youth is beneficial to the state and power:

> With a responsibilised youth, the power of the state is increased, as the possibility of a threat to authority from young people within is reduced, and the work of the state is taken up by conscientious empowered scouts or volunteers. Governmentality is a use of power which attempts to 'unleash the productive skills and capacities which enable young people to adapt to a modern society'. Successive governments in Britain have realised that youth volunteering is a relatively cheap and effective way

of delivering results that benefit not only the young person, but society and the power, financial or otherwise, of the state. A young population constructed to take responsibility for their communities will provide this long-term through social control regulated at the individual level. (Dean, 2011, pp 9–10)

Indeed, in Baden-Powell's (1908) own words: 'Explanation of Scouting – The Boy Scouts, developing character and sense of service' (1908, p 6) and:

The function of Scout training is to develop character in all aspects – physical, mental, moral and spiritual … Therefore, the aim of the Scout training is to replace Self with Service, to make the lads individually efficient, morally and physically, with the object of using that efficiency for the service of the community. (1908, p 3)

He also commented: 'We want to save our lads from drifting into this class of loafer who swells the ranks of the unemployed' (1908, p 319).

While there has been much modernising of scouting, through a focus on inclusivity, updating of badges and reward systems, an expansion of the programme to offer membership for boys and girls aged four to 24, the central symbolic and pedagogic relevance of character, grit and gumption remains (Mills, 2021). Examining scouting as part of children's philanthropic citizenship, the current principles propagated by scouting concerning ambition and aspiration, as well as the emphasis on tenacious resilience and the ability to recover from setbacks, fall short of addressing or even alluding to the structural inequalities that mould the experiences of children, youth and families (Jerome and Kisby, 2019). For example, while the association with the royal family has undoubtedly brought support and tradition to scouting, it remains subject to ongoing critical analysis, with considerations ranging from issues of elitism and colonial legacy to the challenges of aligning with contemporary values of inclusivity and neutrality. Such aspects are not critically explored within this framework. Indeed, when evaluating the impact of children's organisations like scouting in terms of philanthropic citizenship, it's essential to recognise that while they do promote positive values such as tolerance, kindness, ambition, resilience and perseverance, they do less to address the underlying structural inequalities that affect the lives of children, young people and families. A commitment to individual service works from a basic assumption that in order to solve problems in society, citizens must have good character and be honest, law-abiding, responsible members of the community. To be fair, most of these are considered good qualities; however, such an approach, embodied within a character education and responsibilisation agenda, seeks to preserve social traditions rather than question them, and fails to teach children and young people to critically assess social, political and environmental structures, or explore strategies for change that address root causes and address injustice (Westheimer, 2015).

Woodcraft Folk: an alternative perspective

The Woodcraft Folk, founded in 1925 by Leslie Paul, presents itself as a distinctive departure from traditional scouting organisations and uniformed groups. Advocating pacifist principles and rooted in a connection to the natural world, the movement actively sought unconventional alternatives to what it perceived as the shortcomings of 'civilisation'. Its activities encompassed camping, ceremonial events, hiking and handicrafts, garnering substantial membership during the interwar years and endorsements from notable figures from politics, the arts and science (Harper, 2016). Suffragette Emmeline Pethick-Lawrence, novelist H.G. Wells and biologist Julian Huxley were among the movement's esteemed supporters (Pollen, 2016). Positioned as a progressive educational movement, the Woodcraft Folk emphasises cooperative and inclusive learning with a focus on nature, social justice, equality, cooperation, environmental sustainability and community building (Prynn, 1983). While its ethos initially appears aligned with critical pedagogy and social activism, a closer analysis reveals nuanced strengths alongside limitations, especially in terms of access to funding. Notably, academic literature on this unique group remains lacking, with existing articles primarily exploring labour roots rather than its contemporary role in children's active citizenship, which is the main focus of our attention within this book.

Nonetheless, in the realm of uniformed groups, the Woodcraft Folk offers an intriguing alternative that aligns more with this book's exploration of children's philanthropic citizenship. MP Lloyd Russell-Moyle articulates a parallel sentiment, distinguishing capitalist education, scouting and liberal education, emphasising the transformative potential of a more socialist-informed approach:

> 'Capitalist education, like scouting, is about fitting people into society', he said. 'Liberal education is about creating an alternative world. The point of socialist education is ... you take people out so that [they] can go back into real world to not just reject the world we have, but change it.' (Russell-Moyle, cited in Landin, 2017)

The movement, which is organised into age bands, fosters outdoor activities, nature-based learning, arts and crafts, cooperative games and discussions about social issues. Its distinctive approach to cooperative learning stands out, emphasising collective decision making, shared responsibilities and inclusive learning, promoting diversity and inclusivity. The focus is not on character improvement within a predefined framework, but on empowering children to construct notions of good citizenship themselves. Woodcraft Folk aims to develop skills, build friendships, and instil a sense of social and environmental responsibility. With a commitment to addressing social and environmental issues, the movement engages in activities and discussions on topics like climate change, inequality, peace and social justice. Indeed, research by Devine-Wright et al (2004) indicates higher levels of self-efficacy among Woodcraft Folk-affiliated individuals regarding climate change.

However, the movement's emphasis on critical curiosity and social justice has led to conflicts. In 2005, after 40 years of Labour Party support, funding was withdrawn, ostensibly due to budget constraints, but many viewed it as punishment for the movement's anti-war stance in 2003 (Batty, 2005). While it received modest funding as part of the Uniformed Youth Social Action Fund grants under the Conservative and Liberal Democrat Coalition government, likely due to pedagogical reasons, it remains outside of the membership of Youth United Foundation. This network includes some of the UK's uniformed youth organisations, allowing access to specific governmental pots of funding. As of 2024, membership included Air Cadets, Army Cadets, Boys' Brigade, Fire Cadets, Girlguiding, Girls' Brigade, Jewish Lads' and Girls' Brigade, Scouts, Sea Cadets, St John Ambulance Cadets and Volunteer Police Cadets.

Indeed, this movement is interesting as it has historically and seeks to continue to carve out a distinctive identity to the other uniform groups through a fusion of principles, activities and organisational philosophies that set it apart in various noteworthy ways. At the core of this distinction lies a commitment to pacifist principles, steering clear of the militaristic, competitive and hierarchical notions often associated with other uniformed organisations. For the Woodcraft Folk, peace is not merely a facet of their activities, but a foundational element that underpins their entire ethos, alongside its democratic model and cooperative learning approach. Another defining feature is the movement's unique connection to the natural world. Unlike counterparts that may incorporate nature-based activities to varying extents, the Woodcraft Folk places an unmistakable and central emphasis on the natural realm. Nature isn't just a part of their activities; it's intricately woven into their identity and learning experiences. Furthermore, the Woodcraft Folk stands out for its values, prominently centred around social justice, equality, cooperation and environmental sustainability. In contrast to groups that may not explicitly integrate these principles into their mission, the Woodcraft Folk actively engages in discussions and activities addressing contemporary social and environmental issues. The movement's distinctive organisational structure empowers its members, including children, to actively participate in self-governance. Pledging allegiance to each other, rather than to traditional symbols, reflects a unique approach to governance.

While both Scouting and Woodcraft Folk incorporate nature in their teachings, Woodcraft Folk's pronounced emphasis on collective action and self-efficacy sets it apart. A notable aspect of the movement's distinctiveness is its early recognition and proactive stance on global issues. Ahead of mainstream awareness of the climate crisis, the movement was already integrating it into its core learning in the early 2000s. Research suggests that Woodcraft Folk children exhibited greater conviction about climate change compared to their peers. Initiatives like the C-Change project, led by young volunteers, further demonstrate the movement's commitment to engaging children in addressing the climate crisis (Harper, 2016). The Woodcraft Folk's innovative approach, highlighted by its early recognition of environmental issues, positions it as a unique and forward-thinking educational movement. These elements collectively position the movement as a unique and progressive alternative within the landscape of uniformed groups, nonetheless, equally exclude them from the spaces which are in receipt of significant government support and funding, which seek to focus on more traditional notions of service and civic duty, reinforcing the status quo.

Case study 8: Woodcraft Folk

Woodcraft Folk is a youth movement dedicated to social and environmental justice, developing practical skills, involving children in democratic decision making and campaigning for a better world. It was officially founded in 1925 by young people who had seen their families suffer WWI and demanded an end to war – combining activities for peace with class politics and an internationalist ethos. However, it also has its roots in older organisations such as the more utopian Kindred of the Kibbo Kift, who combined peace activities with folk imagery and traditions, learning crafts, and ecological work. At different periods it has adapted to the progressive politics of the day, becoming associated with the Labour Party and Communist Party in the first half of the twentieth century; the countercultural movements of the 1960s–80s, feminism, LGBTQI+ rights, anti-colonial and anti-apartheid struggles, class and anti-racist politics; and most recently spearheading action in the context of climate crisis, twenty-first century wars and human rights.

The Folk (as the name implies) has always approached children's place in the world as part of collective efforts and issues. Individual achievements and development are celebrated, but the emphasis is on friendship, working together, community and belonging. In its near century-long existence, it has never segregated by gender or race. It is part of a wider organisation – the International Falcon Movement-Socialist Educational International (IFM-SEI), with like-minded organisations from across Europe, Asia, Africa and Latin America – and runs international exchanges. It creates initiatives to give young people access to the outdoors, to hiking, camping and bushcraft education. Members earn badges but these tend to be worked towards as a group and built into the regular programme so that everyone can take part.

Most Folk activity revolves around our group nights. There are currently 213 groups active in the UK who meet in halls or outdoors every week – run entirely by volunteers and covering a wide age range. While there are group leaders (who plan and run, or in the case of the older groups facilitate, the activities) and helpers (often parents who commit regular time and energy), there is no set hierarchy. While there is a bank of activities and packs developed by members over the years, there is no fixed curriculum. Young people are directly involved in making decisions about what the group does, and are encouraged to take collective responsibility for their group and place in their communities.

In the last few years, our groups in East Kent have been camping, hiking, learned woodcarving skills, marched for Pride, campaigned against sewage being pumped into the sea, worked with organisations helping refugees fleeing war and poverty, helped out at community gardens planting and harvesting, researched endangered animals, learned how to forage safely and responsibly, taken part in beach cleans, danced with Morris groups, learned the basics of first aid, and generally done lots of arts, crafts and outdoors activities. Woodcraft is all about understanding the relationships between local action and bigger issues; making friends and being compassionate citizens of the world.

David Nettleingham, East Kent District Co-ordinator, Woodcraft Folk

Conclusion

In this chapter I have sought to examine youth movements such as the Scouts and the Woodcraft Folk, unveiling a significant interconnection between uniformed organisations and their role in moulding the citizenship and character of children in society. These movements operate as pivotal arenas for moral initiatives, intricately entwined with the cultivation of youth citizenship (Mills, 2021). With a consistent focus, these organisations aspire to train children and young individuals, instilling in them the principles of responsible citizenship for the nation and the broader global community.

The exploration of the UK Scouts as a reflection of civic duty reveals a multifaceted institution that intersects with contemporary societal shifts, historical legacies and evolving notions of citizenship. Mills (2021) provides a comprehensive analysis, highlighting how scouting has strategically positioned itself within the character agenda, echoing a broader governmental interest in fostering resilience, character virtues and civic responsibility among children. However, this alignment with state objectives raises pertinent questions about the degree to which scouting serves as a conduit for societal control, particularly when juxtaposed with the military ethos and colonial underpinnings that permeate its historical fabric. The symbiotic relationship between the UK Scouts and governmental departments underscores a concerted effort to embed scouting's values within broader national narratives of citizenship and duty. Yet, as funding challenges persist and structural inequalities remain unaddressed, the discourse around scouting's impact on youth development warrants critical scrutiny. The juxtaposition of investing in uniformed youth groups like the Scouts while slashing resources for broader youth services underscores an approach that prioritises superficial fixes over addressing systemic issues (I will expand on this further in Chapter 10).

The colonial roots and military associations of scouting further complicate its contemporary positioning. As symbols of power and tradition, the ties to the British royal family and figures like Baden-Powell reflect an institution grappling with its imperial legacy. While efforts to modernise and promote inclusivity are evident, scouting remains ensnared in a delicate balancing act between tradition and progressivism. Alternative movements like the Woodcraft Folk offers a compelling juxtaposition, highlighting divergent visions of youth engagement and civic education. The Woodcraft Folk's emphasis on cooperative learning, social justice and environmental sustainability presents an alternative paradigm that challenges the hierarchical, militaristic undertones associated with traditional scouting. By fostering critical thinking, collective action and a nuanced understanding of global challenges, the Woodcraft Folk exemplifies a potentially more holistic approach to youth development – one that transcends the confines of character education to cultivate informed, engaged citizens capable of challenging and transforming societal structures.

In conclusion, the examination of the UK Scouts as a microcosm of civic duty and cultivation of philanthropic citizenship highlights the complexities inherent in youth development, citizenship and societal values. While scouting's contributions to character education and community engagement are celebrated, its alignment with state agendas, historical legacies and institutional hierarchies necessitates critical reflection. As society grapples with evolving challenges and aspirations, the imperative to foster inclusive, empowering spaces for children to navigate, question and shape their world remains paramount. Whether through scouting, the Woodcraft Folk, or other innovative platforms, the pursuit of fostering informed, resilient and socially responsible citizens demands ongoing scrutiny, adaptation and commitment to equity and justice.

8

Children should be seen and ~~not~~ heard: community organising, politics, protests and children

Introduction

So far in this book I have sought to explore the many places in which children's engagement in philanthropic and voluntary action can be cultivated and encouraged. I have sought to argue that in many spaces, opportunities and learning continue to be bounded by concepts of civic duty, character and personalised responsibility. In this chapter, I seek to look at how children are encouraged and enabled to step outside of these bounded ideas of philanthropic action and actively participate in spaces of community organising, advocacy and activism. Drawing on the example of the Industrial Areas Foundation, which has inspired community-organising activities globally, I seek to consider how children's voices are increasingly being included in these spaces. I then turn my focus to the organisations concentrating on engaging children in political spaces, advocacy and protests, considering how can we increase children's engagement in an ethical way, which recognises their state as both being and becoming citizens (see Chapter 2).

Let's start though with the story of Francisco Vera, a young Colombian human rights defender and environmentalist, who founded 'Guardianes por la Vida' (Guardians for Life) at the age of nine to address the climate crisis. Highlighted as a young change maker by the Office of the High Commissioner for Human Rights (OHCHR), I summarise his story here (see OHCHR [2023] for the full story). Motivated by devastating fires in the Amazon and inspired by activists like Greta Thunberg, the organisation began with six children in 2019 and now boasts hundreds of members advocating for a healthy environment in Colombia. Their mission involves influencing public policies to combat pollution and climate change, and promote the right to a healthy environment. Francisco highlights the role children can play in enacting change and fostering intergenerational dialogue, articulating this beautifully in an interview for the OHCHR (2023):

'It doesn't matter if we are children or not, really. We can all be part of the change … [a]dults already have experience, so what we propose is to use that experience and take advantage of our energy, our desire, our enthusiasm to continue building a society as children, as teenagers, as young people ... I think the first step is to recognise ourselves as political actors, that we are citizens, that we have a voice, a voice that must be included.'

Here he emphasises that recognising children as political actors and citizens with voice is essential, but moreover that it is about including these voices alongside adults, as one, to tackle issues facing communities. Francisco's advocacy led him to meet with the UN High Commissioner for Human Rights in Geneva, where he presented a manifesto signed by over 3,000 children in defence of a healthy environment. And as a result, he believes he sees progress in this fight, attributing part of it to the Universal Declaration of Human Rights. Although his human rights work occupies much of his time, Francisco still also enjoys hobbies like football and spending time with friends. He believes that children should be seen simultaneously as both victims of injustice and agents of change, stressing the global nature of environmental issues and the importance of action for a better future, and I could not agree with him more. In short, his argument is simple: children need to be both seen and heard.

The political child

Too often, people assume because children do not vote, they are not ready to engage in politics, political issues or political spaces, and instead require shielding from the adult world. Their views and opinions are seen as naïve and uninformed. As was discussed in Chapter 2, even though the UNCRC acknowledged that children have entitlements as citizens with their own set of human rights, the idea of children being politically involved is a contentious topic in many Western democracies. There is a prevailing narrative concerning children as 'citizens in the making' who require protection rather than full rights and traditional ways of participating in politics. Conversely, however, children and young people can then be accused of not caring about politics or political issues, while others are criticised for having too strong an opinion. Despite not knowing much about how children participate in politics, this subject has not been a focus in research until recently. In the past decade, there have been efforts to move away from thinking about citizenship based on age and instead view it from the perspective of the child. In terms of our focus here on philanthropic citizenship, this has resulted in greater opportunities for volunteering, experiential learning and collaborative participation within communities, alongside efforts to mobilise children's advocacy and agency.

Our democracy hinges on active citizen participation and tolerance for diverse viewpoints (Sullivan and Transue, 1999). This vital democratic function connects aspects of citizenship such as political literacy, moral responsibility and community engagement (Crick, 1998). Research underscores the impact of civic, social and political knowledge on democratic principles, attitudes and participation, with schools playing an important role among young people (Pontes et al, 2019) and with many education systems across the world emphasising teaching rights, democratic values and human rights to prepare youth for responsible citizenship (Dias and Menezes, 2014). Furthermore, many scholars argue that engaging children in voluntary activities fosters a sense of community involvement, which is essential for active citizenship (for example, Body and Hogg, 2019). Multiple studies highlight that while discussing civic issues such as equality, environmentalism and poverty may raise awareness, it has little impact on children's long-term active civic engagement (Westheimer, 2015). In contrast, participative civic learning activities both inside and outside the classroom, where children actively engage in researching, leading and participating in social and community actions, working with civic role models, political stimulation activities (such as student council elections), role playing and storytelling, all positively contribute to children's political engagement and understanding (Dias and Menezes, 2014; Westheimer, 2015; Torres-Harding et al, 2018; Body and Hogg, 2019; Brownlee et al, 2019; White and Mistry, 2019; Body et al, 2020; Payne et al, 2020).

Further studies highlight how active participation improves educational outcomes (Ruddock and Flutter, 2004), enhances understanding of citizenship and democracy (Kerr and Cleaver, 2004), and supports the development of essential skills such as relationship building, confidence and trust (Nolas, 2014). Indeed, significant progress has been made by many civil society organisations in an effort to understand and support children and young people's participation rights outlined in the UNCRC (for example, Johnson, 2017; Tisdall and Cuevas-Parra, 2022). Indeed, the strength of children and youth participation's positive impact on both child and adult citizenship depends on its authenticity. Successful participatory engagement necessitates the role of youth workers or practitioners in creating conducive spaces, contexts and environments for meaningful and genuine participation (Nolas, 2014; Ritchie and Ord, 2017; Body and Hogg, 2019). Notably, factors like familial ties, out-of-school activities and broader community connections play a crucial role in fostering meaningful community engagement among young people (Rivera and Santos, 2016; Saunders et al, 2016).

Nonetheless, it must be recognised that participation in community decision making requires cognitive and social skills, as citizens navigate various contexts (Haste, 2004; Pontes et al, 2019). It is a learnt skill, necessitating opportunities for children to develop it and practice. Indeed, several studies highlight younger children as politically knowledgeable (van

Deth et al, 2011; Gotzmann, 2015; Abendschon and Tausendpfund, 2017). Van Deth et al's (2011) panel study of 700 children in Germany in their first year of school (aged six to seven) suggest several important findings, which are likely to resonate across similar educational contexts and challenge the conventional wisdom that adolescence is where children and young people gain political and civic orientations and competencies. Their findings suggest that these political and social orientations are formed much earlier, and that young children can express political opinions and attitudes, displaying key basic political knowledge and orientations, which are considered to be prerequisites of political involvement and participation, highlighting the middle childhood period between the ages of four to 11 as a critical age for civic learning (Dias and Menezes, 2014).

However, research also shows us that civic and political literacy is not evenly dispersed. While van Deth et al's study highlights the strength of children's civic and political literacy preadolescence, they also find that even at this earliest stage 'the basic requirements for political involvement such as political knowledge, competences, and normative orientations are far from equally distributed' (van Deth et al, 2011, p 166). Children from ethnic minorities and lower socioeconomic areas show relatively less developed political orientations, and they do not improve as much over the school year as other children. This suggests that current forms of political and civic education within this context *does not appear to level the playing field*' (van Deth et al, 2011, p 166). Such findings are supported by others, including Abendschon and Tausendpfund (2017), who also highlight gender-based differences in civic and political knowledge, with girls generally displaying significantly lower levels of political knowledge than boys. Together, this research highlights that children's capacity for political engagement evolves even from the youngest of ages, and active meaningful participation is central to increasing capacity.

Nonetheless, these advantages stand in contrast to tensions arising from the frequent inadequate incorporation of children and young people as authentic partners in decision-making processes, as has been explored throughout the previous chapters. Instances of tokenistic consultation or outright exclusion of young voices are frequently observed (Body et al, 2020; Body and Hogg, 2019; Cuevas-Parra, 2023; Spicer and Evans, 2006). Given this backdrop of research and literature supporting children's engagement within the political spaces and debates, I now move on to examine some of the organisations seeking to engage children as politically aware social actors.

Community organising, Citizens UK and activism

Community organising refers to a methodology of establishing and fostering social action and organisational development, originating in the US during the late 1930s (Beck and Purcell, 2013). This approach involves the creation of networks of entities, which typically encompass block clubs, associations, churches, labour unions, families and individuals, increasingly including children. The primary objective of these networks is to amass influence, with the aim of inducing changes in policies and practices within institutions, which significantly impact the community. This is achieved through a combination of political and nonpolitical strategies and manoeuvres, enabling engagement with decision makers within these institutions. In cases where mutually agreeable resolutions are not reached, more assertive methods come into play. These may encompass nonviolent disruption, public condemnation and economic measures – like strikes and boycotts, as well as widespread advocacy for reform initiatives and legislative actions. Additionally, the strength of mass participation is harnessed to cultivate collective support, along with the establishment of alternative institutions like cooperatives, credit unions and support groups (Beck and Purcell, 2013).

Considered one of the founding thinkers of community organising, Saul Alinsky founded the Industrial Areas Foundation (IAF) in the US with the aim of empowering citizens to address various social and economic issues. The philosophy works broadly on the idea of bringing people together to collectively address common concerns and advocate for change. Concentrating on a wide range of interconnected issues, the focus is developing local community leaders and creating networks and alliances between organisations and people. The IAF advocate direct action as a means of then demonstrating community power, as well as negotiating with public official and policy makers to bring about change. It is rooted in the principles of social justice, equality and democratic participation, with the aim of making a long-term impact.

Drawing inspiration from the IAF, Citizens UK (originally known as the Citizens Organising Foundation) formed in 1989 and took root in East London under the guidance of Neil Jameson CBE. At the core of both its past and present endeavours is a dynamic approach to social transformation, referred to as community organising. The foundation's ideology was rooted in the profound belief that ordinary people possess intrinsic power and that by uniting individuals from diverse walks of life, a shared platform could be found and meaningful change could be enacted. Since its inception, the organisation has achieved many impressive successes: for example, securing an extra £2 billion in wages for those at the lower end of the pay scale, championing an amnesty for 'legacy cases' encompassing 160,000 asylum seekers, and achieving numerous triumphs on the local and regional fronts (Citizens UK, 2023).

As part of their plan for social change, Citizens UK focus on the concept of community organisation, which they state is 'about bringing people together to win change. This means building community-led solutions to big and small problems, that work for everyone' (Citizens UK, 2023). Working on the basis that ordinary individuals possess the capability to influence their surroundings, they aim to restore the authority to the people, empowering them to hold those in charge accountable by establishing constructive partnerships among communities, elected representatives and businesses to ensure that every voice is acknowledged and no one is marginalised. The plan is simple: it is to re-allocate distribution of authority, uniting people across their divergences, uncovering shared understanding and achieving transformative outcomes.

Citizens UK (2023) outline '5 Steps to Social Change' and I repeat them here verbatim:

1. *Organise.* Start by building a team! This involves bringing together everyday people from local organisations such as schools, faith groups, universities, charities, unions and others. It's not about leaving our differences at the door – we value contrasting perspectives and bring each person into the solution for change by finding common ground.
2. *Listen.* Communities we work with are too often shut out from decisions that affect their lives, and not involved in finding the best solution to local issues. So, we listen to each other and our communities to find out what is putting pressure on everyday people and families. We spot issues of social injustice that make people's lives difficult but which they feel powerless to do anything about. Listening not only helps you grow your team but unites people around the issues that matter, making your campaigns more robust.
3. *Plan.* We want you to write the script for your community's future – where things change for the better. This includes planning for how your team will tackle the root cause of injustice, by identifying solutions and deciding which actions to take. This might look like researching more about the problem and understanding which power-holders to build relationships with.
4. *Act.* We take action through fun, imaginative and legal public demonstrations to hold those responsible to account. We do this to prompt a reaction, such as receiving an invitation to a meeting or a commitment to work together. We'll support you through the steps to identify your team, equip your organisation with training, and connect you to the power holders who can implement change. The hard work will be yours, but we're here to support you and take action.
5. *Negotiate.* Finally, we negotiate with decision makers in government, businesses, or whoever holds power to find a solution together. Citizens UK provides communities and power holders support to help change the debate and find a constructive way forward, making sure change is effective and sustainable. Communities participating in decision-making

contributes to the common good and helps us all build a better, fairer society. (Citizens UK, 2023)

Children are actively involved in Citizens UK. For example, as part of the Living Wage Campaign, the St Antony's Primary School choir wrote a song for one of the area's biggest employers. 'Realise, wake up, pay up' was performed for London City Airport during a campaign to get local employers to pay the London Living wage. Supported by the East London Citizens Organisation and Citizens UK, the campaign started with bringing together local organisations to listen to the key concerns of local families. A survey of Year 6 pupils from the school and church population revealed that almost half of the parents earned less than the living wage. Planning a response to this, the children of St Anthony's wrote a protest song, campaigning for change – taking a strong stance on low wages and rising costs:

> The government don't make it easy for anyone.
> That's why we've got to come together, everyone
> We work so hard to get the funds
> But all we get are dribs and drabs and crumbs.

In testament to the children's powers of persuasion, City Airport decided to 'pay up', resulting in a £1,500 a year pay rise for contractors, including cleaners and security staff, many of whom lived locally. Since then, the children at the school have performed a song every year campaigning for the Living Wage. In 2022, the protest song 'Look to the Sky' is very clear in its messaging to businesses finishing with the lyrics:

> And to those still on the fence,
> You're either for it or against,
> Do your businesses a timely favour,
> And honour workers for their time and their labour.

As the headteacher Angela Moore is quoted as saying:

'Whenever I see the children perform it confirms to me that we are actually fully educating our children. They fully understand the messages they are conveying and the impact that being paid less than the living wage has on their families. They have fathers and mothers who work two to three jobs and are not able to spend quality time with them. They are very clear about what the message is and that this is their platform. They are conscious of the social justice message and are always willing to come out at weekends, after school – they are very committed. For the last five years it has been their mission and their message.' (St Antony's Catholic Primary School, n.d.)

When consideration is given to the core components of philanthropic citizenship, as outlined in Chapter 1, for me, this engagement fulfils the criteria. The children are donating their resources of time and talent, leading the response to the issues they, their families and their community face. It is inclusive and is not based on who can afford to participate or not. The action is collective; it is entwined with both the national Living Wage Campaign, but is also collectively directed at local employers within their communities. It is empowering and helps the children to develop the disposition to be committed and motivated to help change society (Veugelers, 2007), to develop civic courage and responsibility for decisions taken. The intention – and indeed impact – has positive social benefits and the action is critically informed and based on evidence, tackling the root cause of the problem rather than the consequence of the poverty created by the problem.

Another example would be the campaign by the Project for the Registration of Children as British Citizens (PRCBC), another community group mobilised by Citizens UK, which seeks to reduce or waive the £1,012 child citizenship fee. The motivation behind this project came from the narratives of families contending with the financial strain imposed by this fee, as outlined here:

> These stories often detail families sinking into debt to cover the costs, agonising over the painful decision of selecting which of their children could be registered as British and which could not, or, in some cases, facing total exclusion from the process. The absence of Citizenship bears ramifications, as most children would be subjected to international tuition fees at universities, rendered ineligible for student loans, disenfranchised from the voting process, and barred from full participation in public life – a stark denial of their rightful place as citizens in the country they call home. (Citizens UK, 2023)

The fee has barred many children from citizenship, and research conducted by the PRCBC highlights how disproportionately high the cost is when juxtaposed with the actual Home Office processing cost of £372 per application. Effectively, the Home Office has been charging children an excess of £640 above processing costs to attain British citizenship, resulting in a profit of £102,749,216 from child citizenship fees between 2017 and 2020 for the government (Citizens UK, 2023).

Once again within this process, children are not sidelined, but are centre stage to the community action. On National Poetry Day, 4 October 2018, over 140 children from schools that were part of London Citizens came together outside the Home Office to perform poems about their experiences of struggling to become British citizens and hand an anthology of their work to Immigration Minister Caroline Nokes MP.

Daniel (aged nine) began by reciting his poem entitled 'HOME':

Having a passport is important to people
Only if I had one to explore the world like other people
My mum has to go through a long process to get us one
Either way, my mum was not born here ... so I am not a British citizen!

This pressure applied as collective action through community organising resulted in the Home Office publishing new guidance to allow a fee waiver for the registration of 'some' children as British Citizens on 26 May 2022. While the campaign continues to widen the definition of 'some' to increase inclusivity, Citizens UK, working in partnership with children, continue to call for the profit element of the child citizenship fee to be removed for all children. The power of children's voices as part of this movement remains evident.

Within both these examples, Citizens UK enabled children to hold those with the power to change the issue to account very publicly in front of their electorate, generating media coverage and raising the profile of both the campaign and community organising (Holgate, 2015). While I am not promoting Citizens UK as the only model for unleashing children's philanthropic citizenship, I do seek to present community organising as at least one way in which we can think differently about engaging children in causes which matter to them.

Protests, advocacy and campaigning

Community organising presents us with a very different way in which children and young people can engage in, and respond to, local issues which affect them, and extends our understanding of the philanthropic toolbox discussed in Chapter 4. Rooted in ideas of justice, it presents us with different approaches to activism which venture beyond simply thinking of activism as typical street protests. As can be seen through the example of Citizens UK, children's activism, as part of collective action, encompasses a spectrum of intentional, organised efforts to bring about social, political, economic or environmental change. It manifests in various forms, ranging from more indirect activism to more direct and confrontational methods. Less direct activism involves utilising platforms like social media for campaigns and artistic expression, conveying social and political messages through mediums like the visual arts, music, literature or performance (Haupt et al, 2019; Yeom et al, 2020; Redwood et al, 2022; Howard, 2023). Ethical consumerism and consumer activism come into play at another level, where individuals boycott products or support businesses aligning with their values (Nonomura, 2017). This may involve avoiding certain brands due to concerns about environmental sustainability or labour conditions, or actively choosing to support fair trade or eco-friendly options.

Moving to the community level, activism takes the form of grassroots initiatives, such as local clean-ups, community gardens or awareness campaigns. Town hall-type meetings and community discussions further contribute to addressing specific local issues. Advocacy and campaigns involve petitioning, letter writing and lobbying efforts to influence policy decisions on matters like healthcare, education or environmental regulations. Protest activism, a more direct form, includes street protests, marches and acts of civil disobedience to express dissent or support for a cause. These actions often focus on issues such as racial injustice, gender inequality or government policies. On an international scale, activism expands to global advocacy campaigns and participation in international conferences addressing issues like human rights abuses, poverty or climate change. Activists may engage in online and offline activities, petitioning for change and participating in discussions on a global stage. In short, activism, in its diverse forms, allows individuals to choose methods that align with their preferences and the nature of the cause. The combination of different levels of activism creates a comprehensive approach to social change, each contributing to a broader tapestry of efforts aimed at making a positive impact on society. Thus, activism is more about the lens through which we view our actions. It is about the choices we make in our everyday actions in society, from the goods we buy, to our interactions with others, to direct actions of protest.

Focusing on protest as one form of activism, I think it is important we acknowledge that children's engagement in protests is a complex issue. As was briefly explored in Chapter 5, and as will be discussed later on in Chapter 9, it is commonly met with scepticism and criticism by both the media and politicians. Nonetheless, empowering children to engage in protests is viewed by many as a fundamental aspect of democratic participation, especially when they lack the ability to vote. As was explored in Chapter 2, the UNCRC recognises the importance of children's involvement in campaigns. It upholds their rights to freedom of expression, association and peaceful assembly, providing a crucial framework for their active participation. Indeed, children and youth are increasingly assuming pivotal roles as advocates for justice and societal transformation, exemplified by their participation in global movements such as climate strikes and Black Lives Matter. Nonetheless, despite their influential contributions, debates persist regarding the appropriateness of children's involvement in protests, citing concerns about their comprehension, susceptibility to manipulation, and physical and emotional vulnerability.

Proponents of children's rights contend that their voices should be recognised, emphasising their ability to grasp the significance of protest actions based on their lived experiences. However, balancing the acknowledgement of children's agency with the imperative to ensure their peaceful participation poses ongoing challenges, particularly in terms of their potential exposure to less peaceful aspects of protests (Daly, 2013; Danka, 2019; McMurry, 2019). This discourse prompts a re-examination of the UNCRC, which, beyond historical emphasis on socioeconomic and protective rights, underscores children's right to be heard, as articulated in Article 12. This paradigm shift challenges preconceptions about children's capacities to shape their destinies, acknowledging their fundamental rights to freedom of movement, association and peaceful assembly. However, these rights, which are applicable to both adults and children, are not absolute and may be subject to limitations based on democratic societal interests. As young protesters exercise their right to peaceful assembly, complexities emerge, necessitating an exploration of safety concerns and the government's responsibility to safeguard children's wellbeing during protests (Daly, 2013; Danka, 2019; McMurry, 2019).

While children lack the right to vote, I, along with many other scholars, argue that engaging in peaceful protests, and indeed other forms of nonviolent activism, becomes a vital avenue for them to express concerns and interests, particularly in matters like the climate crisis. The right to protest not only aligns with international human rights instruments but also empowers children to actively shape their futures and voice apprehensions about decisions impacting them in the long term. Governments, and, indeed, in the context of this book, philanthropic funders and actors, therefore need to recognise children as informed decision makers and create environments that enable their active participation in discussions that affect them socially and politically. Acknowledging and addressing the challenges faced by children in protests is important for upholding their rights and ensuring their meaningful contribution to shaping democratic societies, as evidenced by the impactful School Strikes for Climate in 2019 (Daly, 2013; Danka, 2019; McMurry, 2019).

Nevertheless, unfortunately, children's rights defenders often encounter obstacles in their advocacy efforts. These challenges range from limited access to information about their rights to facing scepticism from adults, and even experiencing physical or verbal abuse, both online and offline. Additionally, familial, educational and legal constraints may hinder their ability to take meaningful action. Nonetheless, the involvement of children in protests has a rich history encompassing a wide array of causes, from nuclear disarmament and anti-war movements to Indigenous land rights, racism and child poverty, which is too often overlooked. Children have often been disregarded in the narrative of political change, yet they have consistently played pivotal roles in historical processes of transformation, as exemplified by movements like #schoolstrikeforclimate, but there are many other examples from across history long before we had heard of contemporary change makers such as Greta Thunberg.

Children leading change throughout history

Children have a history of taking a stand. From the late 1790s to the early 1820s, many Georgian children voluntarily gave up sugar to protest against slavery and support abolitionists, while others signed anti-slavery petitions and produced anti-slavery needlework (Bridge, 2021). In 1888, protesting against poor and oppressive working conditions, toxic phosphorous vapours, 1,400 girls and women at Bryant and May's match factory began industrial action. This move led to the prohibition of white phosphorous in matches (The Matchgirls Memorial, n.d.). In 1889 in Llanelli, Wales, 30 pupils from Bigyn School walked out of their classroom in protest at the unjustified caning of a fellow boy, sparking a strike wave across the Britain in 62 different towns and cities about the treatment of children in schools (Prior, 2021). A decade later in 1899 in New York, thousands of 'newsies' as young as seven began a strike against two newspaper moguls in a battle over a fair wage. Within two weeks the newspapers were forced to the negotiating table by drastic falls in sales (Bowery Boys, 2010).

In 1901, Polish children in Wreśnia boycotted a particular class resisting the 'Germanisation' of Prussian schools, where most subjects were taught exclusively in German. When religious instruction switched to German, pupils at the Katolicka Szkoła Ludowa (Catholic People's School) staunchly refused to sing or speak in German in these lessons. Twenty-five adults and children were arrested as the strike became a national issue, lasting in some cases up until 1904 (Haworth-Booth, 2021). September 1911 saw a surge of children's school strikes across the UK, mirroring a broader period of labour unrest. Inspired by a spirit akin to union camaraderie, students collectively demanded worker-style rights: shorter hours, homework limits, pay for attendance or tasks performed by class monitors, and an end to corporal punishment. 'Flying pickets' gathering strikers from nearby schools formed processions of hundreds and held impromptu mass meetings. While the strikes were generally short-lived, their spirit ignited a profusion of alternative schoolday activities, from street theatre to beach picnics. In 1985, the Liverpool School Strike saw 10,000 schoolchildren skipping school to protest against the Thatcher government's controversial Youth Training Scheme, which paid students £30 per week, which was viewed as exploitative (Jeffries, 2016). In January 1991, over 30,000 children in the former West Germany went on school strikes against the Second Gulf War, blocking traffic by walking round junctions in circles.

In 1963 a powerful display of civil disobedience, thousands of African American students in Birmingham took to the streets, forsaking their classrooms to march against segregation. Their courageous stand was met with harsh reprisals; hundreds were apprehended, while others endured forceful water hose blasts, police baton strikes and attacks by police dogs. While the wider Civil Rights Movement encouraged children's involvement, there was debate among leaders about their role in acts of civil disobedience. Following initial reluctance, Martin Luther King Jr eventually supported the idea, having been convinced by Children's Crusade organiser James Bevel. Bevel argued that children had less to lose and would benefit from feeling empowered to stand up to a racist society (Eskew, 1997; Haworth-Booth, 2021). This pivotal event, known as the Children's March or the Crusade, marked a turning point in the Civil Rights Movement. It exerted significant pressure on President Kennedy to endorse federal civil rights legislation, ultimately leading to the historic passage of the Civil Rights Act of 1964 (Eskew, 1997; Haworth-Booth, 2021).

However, as demonstrated by the Crusade, children's involvement in protest movements, while courageous, has not been without its share of risks and controversies. Some of the largest school walkouts occurred during the anti-apartheid struggles in South Africa and the US Civil Rights Movement. The 1976 Soweto Uprising began in response to the government's decision to teach all schoolchildren in Afrikaans rather than their native languages. The uprising was marked by an initial act of singing the African hymn 'Nkosi Sikelel' iAfrika' at school. The subsequent march of up to 20,000 schoolchildren was met with brutal police violence. In the aftermath, hundreds of protesters, including children, lost their lives (Haworth-Booth, 2021). We may seek to confine these events to the history books, but in certain parts of the world brutality against children's voices continues, with over 58 children tragically killed in the Iranian anti-regime protests in November 2022 (Parent et al, 2022).

Examining the history of children's activism, it becomes evident that the seeds of dissent planted by children have often grown into significant movements, shaping societal norms and challenging oppressive systems. From Georgian children boycotting sugar to the poignant Children's March during the Civil Rights Movement, the courage of young protesters has left an indelible mark. As we now move forwards to look at more contemporary understandings, exploring children's rights to protest in the present day, it is crucial to recognise both the triumphs and challenges faced by young advocates throughout history. However, the thread of resilience persists, connecting the spirited protests of the past to the ongoing struggles for children's voices in the modern world.

Funders leading the way

The relationship between participatory community philanthropy and community organising is symbiotic, enriched by the recognition that both are essential components for fostering just outcomes within communities and shifting power dynamics. As some philanthropic funders increasingly prioritise community organising, it aligns with the principles of community philanthropy, which emphasise locally driven development and the activation of community energies and assets. The Global Summit on Community Philanthropy in 2016 set the stage for this paradigm shift, fostering a global movement that values generosity, trust and solidarity over conventional power dynamics. There are several funders within the UK and beyond that embrace these collective efforts. For example, the emergence of the Civic Power Fund in the UK, dedicated exclusively to supporting community-organising efforts, reinforces the importance of redirecting philanthropic resources towards grassroots initiatives. This fund recognises the under-resourced nature of community organising and aims to strengthen democratic engagement while empowering communities to drive meaningful change. The rationale behind this shift is grounded in the acknowledgement that communities often feel disconnected from decision-making processes. For example, as Laren McArthur articulates in the American-focused *Stanford Social Innovation Review*:

> To realise the democratic promise of community organising, however, donors must cease to view the practice merely as an instrument for advancing their political and policy goals and appreciate the fundamental role it plays in the health of the American polity. Community organising teaches people the skills of democracy: how to build and sustain organisations together with others, listen to people with different perspectives, forge consensus, and understand where power lies in our political and economic institutions and how to negotiate with it. At a time when people have lost trust in democratic institutions, good organising provides people a sense of agency and a belief in their capacity to influence and reform those institutions. (McArthur, 2023)

The synergy between participatory community philanthropy and community organising becomes particularly evident when considering the lessons learned from successful funding approaches. The Civic Power Fund underscores the significance of long-term funder collaboration, mirroring the emphasis on building trust and relationships within community philanthropy. Both movements recognise the importance of supporting unseen and unsupported groups through intermediaries and collaboratives, acknowledging that sustainable and strategic resources are essential in order for organisers to flourish.

Furthermore, the emphasis on 'beyond the grant' support in community organising aligns with the broader perspective of community philanthropy, which places value not just on financial contributions but also on the collective capacity and connections within communities. The call to action by the Civic Power Fund, inviting fellow funders to engage in lessons on collective action and explore collaborative opportunities, resonates with the ethos of community philanthropy. Both movements recognise the need for collaborative approaches to address multifaceted challenges faced by communities. In essence, the collaboration between community philanthropy and community organising amplifies the potential for transformative change, allowing for a more inclusive, locally rooted and people-led approach to development. As these movements gain momentum, they contribute to a broader effort to reshape the power dynamics within the global civil society and the philanthropic ecosystem, and promote a more equitable and democratic future.

Nevertheless, in 2021, the Civic Power Fund enlisted Jon Cracknell to conduct a mapping of social justice grants in the UK, which is summarised in the Growing the Grassroots report. The initial examination of 47 identified social justice funders, representing approximately 8 per cent of foundation giving in the UK, yielded revealing insights:

- Only 28 per cent of social justice grant making is directed towards initiatives addressing the root causes of injustice, constituting a mere 2.3 per cent of all UK foundation giving.
- A minimal proportion – around 0.3 per cent – of social justice grant making is allocated to community organising, equivalent to 0.04 per cent of all UK foundation giving.
- The study underscored a pronounced bias towards London, urban areas and centralisation, with three quarters of social justice grants concentrated on national-level efforts. London's dominance is evident, receiving £137 in grants per 100 people, whereas numerous English regions receive substantially lower volumes of social justice grants, both in absolute terms and on a per capita basis.

Thus, despite ongoing discussions among funders about power dynamics and geographical considerations, early indications suggest that these conversations have not yet substantially influenced funding decisions. However, the study serves as a noteworthy reminder of how funding preferences impact the advocacy and pursuits undertaken within the realm of social justice, offering some avenues for further exploration and improvement. Thus, the Growing the Grassroots report (2021) research concludes by highlighting the challenge of aligning time horizons in community-organising efforts with the typical three to five-year organisational strategies and funders' cycles. Additionally, the research underscored challenges related to funding, particularly in terms of ensuring small grants reach community-level initiatives. While there are sources of funding available, albeit limited, disseminating awareness about these opportunities remains a hurdle. Collaborative efforts among funders and support coalitions were deemed crucial for effective strategic regranting. Examples like the Climate Coalition's micro-grants for the Great Big Green Week demonstrated impactful initiatives, but restrictions from some funders on regranting to local levels posed a challenge. The study suggests a need for increased collaboration among funders to support grassroots community organising, drawing inspiration from the Civic Power Fund's mission to empower civic leaders and nurture the ecosystem necessary for effective organising.

Community participatory grant making serves as a powerful strategy within philanthropy, fostering increased community ownership, leadership and grassroots decision making. Rooted in diverse models and insights, this approach involves ceding grant decision-making power to the communities directly impacted by the funding decisions (Gibson, 2018). The core belief is that by empowering communities to design and own grant-making processes, philanthropy becomes more effective, democratic and just. The community participatory grant-making sector has witnessed significant growth in the past decade, emphasising the importance of shifting decision-making power to those with lived experiences of the challenges philanthropy seeks to address. This transformative approach is particularly tangible in response to critiques of philanthrocapitalism, highlighting negative consequences of market-based solutions and the historical harm inflicted on marginalised communities (McGoey, 2015). While some funders are making strides in this arena, such as the UK BBC Children in Need and others exemplified by Patuzzi and Pinto's (2022) report titled *Child and Youth Participation in Philanthropy: Stories of Transformation*, they remain too few and far between to be achieving the radical change required, especially when it comes to engaging children's voices in grant-making decisions.

Conclusion

In this chapter I have argued that the traditional and conventional narratives (which have been summarised throughout Chapters 1–7) too often posit children as nonpolitical actors' confining children's opportunities within civic duty, service and character development, and hindering their potential in community organising, advocacy and activism. Thus, this chapter delves into the political engagement of children in democratic society, emphasising their rights as citizens and advocating for a shift from traditional views of 'citizens in the making', to 'citizens of now'. Research indicates the uneven distribution of civic and political literacy in children, with political orientations forming as early as the age of four, and the middle childhood years being crucial in children's development of political and civic literacies.

Nonetheless, disparities persist, particularly among ethnic minorities and children from lower socioeconomic groups.

However, there are organisations actively working to actively bring greater equity to children's civic engagement. For example, the involvement of children in Citizens UK's initiatives aligns closely with our conceptualisation of philanthropic citizenship, as the 'active' element of citizenship education, showcasing empowering engagement that addresses societal problems. Despite challenges in incorporating children in decision making, genuine youth participation positively impacts both young and adult citizenship, shifting children from beneficiaries to contributors in societal change. Children's activism becomes an integral part of collective action, spanning a spectrum from indirect, creative expressions to direct, nonviolent, confrontational methods. This inclusive approach encompasses ethical consumerism, grassroots initiatives, advocacy and international engagement, forming a tapestry of diverse strategies for social change. By embracing this multifaceted activism, children can align their efforts with their evolving values, contributing collectively to a more just and equitable society.

Nonetheless, if philanthropic funders really believe in the power of children as change makers and community organising, increased funding in community organising is vital for fostering societal change and empowerment. Historical and contemporary examples highlight children's capacity for transformative shifts through protests and campaigns. Recognising their rights to freedom of expression underscores the need for an environment facilitating peaceful participation in sociopolitical discussions. Even so, defenders of children's rights face challenges, including limited access to information and scepticism from adults. Community organising becomes an important opportunity for channelling children's voices into meaningful action, with a symbiotic relationship between community philanthropy and organising. Thus, philanthropic efforts must extend beyond traditional grants, recognising the power of collective action. As an example, the Civic Power Fund's emphasis on long-term collaboration aligns with participatory community philanthropy, valuing not just financial contributions but also collective capacity. Nonetheless, despite positive strides, challenges persist, such as biases towards centralised efforts in social justice grant allocation. Advocating for increased funding in community organising and collective action is a strategic investment in the future, requiring collaborative efforts among governments, philanthropic funders and civil society to reshape power dynamics and amplify children's voices globally.

9

Children as future makers and the climate crisis: fighting for a habitable planet

Introduction

Climate change poses an urgent and violent threat to current and future generations. Children will bear the biggest brunt, with immediate and lifelong impacts (United Nations, 2023). Nonetheless, it also highlights the power of children and young people who collectively come together around the world, united around a common cause. The term 'climate crisis' encompasses the devastating impacts of global warming, creating environmental havoc and emphasising the need for robust mitigation efforts. The global response is crucial. Climate change is escalating faster than anticipated, affecting every corner of the world, with rising temperatures causing environmental degradation, natural disasters, food and water insecurity, economic upheaval and more. Scientific consensus attributes climate change to human activities, particularly the combustion of fossil fuels and deforestation, leading to a rapid increase in greenhouse gas concentrations.

Global emissions, mainly from coal, oil and gas production, continue unabated, pushing temperatures over 1°C above preindustrial levels. Without intervention, the Paris Agreement's target of limiting warming to well below 2°C is increasingly unachievable, risking irreversible ecological harm. Melting glaciers, rising sea levels, ecosystem collapse and severe weather events threaten major cities and vulnerable coastal populations. Climate change also exacerbates global challenges, widening economic disparities, increasing resource competition and intensifying weather-related disasters. The impacts of climate change disproportionately affect low-income, Indigenous and marginalised communities, exacerbating existing inequalities. Nonetheless, the United Nations (2023) remains hopeful, advocating for sweeping societal transformations in agriculture, land use, transportation and energy production. Technology, particularly renewable energy and electric vehicles, offers solutions, while nature-based approaches like sustainable agriculture and land restoration provide relief. The UN calls for global collaboration across governments, businesses, civil society, youth and academia to forge a green future that mitigates suffering, upholds justice and restores harmony between people and the planet. Together, the UN asserts, we can turn the tide against the climate crisis, with children and young people often leading the charge.

Drawing on research and case study examples, I seek to present a critical exploration of how children engage in environmental issues outside of the education curriculum, from civil society organisations programmes to the school strikes. Particularly focusing on global youth climate action, the Greta Thunberg effect and the rise of young environmental activists, this chapter focuses on children as 'future makers', who initiate and lead political action and seek to set the agenda for their own future in light of the failures of adults to address the crisis meaningfully. For example, children launching legal action against the government for failing to protect their futures (Australia) and campaigning activities from across the world (Uganda, Malaysia, India, Afghanistan, Brazil, the UK, Germany and so on). Children's engagement in the environmental movement, under the banner of Greta Thunberg, has received unprecedented media attention, both in terms of praise and condemnation. These narratives say much about how adults perceive children's role as active social actors and recognise them as having (or not) political voices and rights of their own (Hayward, 2020). Through the climate change movement children are asking to be taken seriously as future makers challenging adult authority and control and asking for decisive change. In this chapter we critically explore this, the role of civil society in facilitating this activity and what this means for children's future as philanthropic citizens.

Children fighting back

Historically overlooked in national, regional and global political arenas, and often disregarded by the grandiose declarations of multilateral environmental agreements struggling to implement intergenerational justice in practical governance, children and young people are asserting themselves as advocates for both current and future generations. This advocacy is most well known as taking the form of protests, but also extends to more structured channels, where they purposefully assert their rights for intergenerational justice through legal systems (Kotzé and Knappe, 2023), pioneering a human rights-based approach to climate change (Gasparri et al, 2021; Rodriguez-Garavito, 2022).

Fridays for futures and beyond

> I want you to act as if our house is on fire. Because it is.
> Thunberg (2019, p 24)

Greta Thunberg has become an international household name. She has been covered in the international press, featured on the most popular national and international talk shows, become the object of social media memes, been on the front cover of *Vogue*, been in a social media spat with the US President, presented in music videos … well the list goes on. She is an international eco-celebrity who has attracted almost as much criticism as she has acclaim (Murphy, 2021).

The global movement sparked by Thunberg, rallying over 10 million people worldwide to demand decisive action on climate change, has not only elevated her to fame but has also significantly increased public concern about climate change to record levels. Her story has been retold in many children's books, positioning her as an environmental hero (Moriaty, 2021; Body and Lacny, 2022). Indeed, research by Sabherwal et al (2021) indicates that those more familiar with Thunberg express greater confidence in their ability to contribute to collective climate mitigation efforts. Familiarity with her story correlates with a higher likelihood of taking direct actions, such as contacting elected officials or supporting campaigns, driven by the realisation that ordinary people can instigate change. Despite Thunberg's association with young people and alignment with liberal policies, the Thunberg effect appears consistent across age groups and political spectrums, challenging conventional expectations. Lacking elite status, she has achieved success by embodying her empowering message and maintaining optimism amid climate change pessimism, insisting that there is still time for transformative change (Sabherwal et al, 2021).

Moreover, Murphy (2021) argues that Thunberg is the ideal eco-celebrity, challenging some of the conventional notions of eco-celebrity raised by scholars, who question the effectiveness of celebrity influence in addressing environmental issues and argue that celebrity culture tends to perpetuate individualised power and wealth concentration (for example, Goodman and Littler, 2013; Coughlin and Hauck, 2023). Accordingly, Murphy argues that Thunberg stands out as a different kind of eco-celebrity. Contrary to the stereotype, she actively engages in policy discussions, supports emission targets, advocates for collaboration, challenges existing power structures and pursues radical, systemic change to combat the existential threat of the climate crisis. Thunberg's connection to the natural world is marked by a controlled fury over its global degradation, emphasising a politics of youth-centred, righteous rage driven by a sense of urgency. Positioned as an 'ideal performer' within the contemporary youth-centred climate movement, Murphy argues that Thunberg's eco-celebrity status is not hollow or hypocritical; instead, it resists commodification and media co-optation. Thus, her authentic and credible persona, rooted in science, urgency and action, speaks not only for the planet but also for the world's children and young people, embodying a powerful force for environmental change.

Based on this celebrity status, Fridays for Future, spearheaded by Thunberg, has burgeoned into a global youth movement where students skip school on Fridays to rally for urgent climate action. Starting in 2018 with Thunberg's lone protest in Sweden, it swiftly gained international traction, uniting students from diverse backgrounds in a collective call for change. Beyond street protests, it serves as a catalyst for experiential learning, empowering young activists to engage in civic processes, articulate opinions and comprehend climate complexities. The movement's success in garnering global attention has propelled these voices into influential spaces, compelling governments and corporations to address climate change. More than a protest, it acts as a gateway, inspiring participants to undertake broader environmental initiatives. The movement's evolution, marked by its fifth anniversary in November 2023, has shifted focus from climate action to climate justice, addressing inequalities exacerbated by climate change. Embracing a justice-centric lens, it now encompasses issues such as the Global North/Global South divide and Indigenous rights. Despite challenges, including racial dynamics, the movement diversified and strengthened during the COVID-19 pandemic, emphasising solidarity with intersecting crises. Youth-led climate justice networks now target systemic issues through legal and direct action, aiming for a just and sustainable future.

Furthermore, when discussing young climate activists, Greta Thunberg is often foremost in people's mind, but building on and helping to create this momentum, there are numerous remarkable children and young people championing global climate action. For example, here are just ten inspiring activists making a difference (identified by Lai, 2022):

- Xiye Bastida. Born to environmentalists, this 19-year-old Mexican activist lobbies for aggressive global climate action and greater Indigenous visibility, leading initiatives like Fridays for Future.
- Licypriya Kangujam. Starting at the age of six, Licypriya, from India, advocates for climate action, addressing world leaders, giving TEDx talks and founding 'The Child Movement' before the age of ten.
- Daniel Koto Dagnon. Focused on protecting Benin from climate change, this dynamic activist empowers women through the 'Green Amazones' programme, recognising their crucial role in climate action.
- Xiuhtezcatl Martinez. A vocal advocate for Indigenous and marginalised communities, this 21 year old was one of the plaintiffs in *Juliana v. United States*, which challenged the government's use of fossil fuels.
- Ella and Amy Meek. These UK sisters founded 'Kids Against Plastic' at the ages of 10 and 12, picking up over 100,000 pieces of single-use plastic and launching initiatives against plastic pollution.
- Nyombi Morris. This Ugandan activist, who faced threats for climate justice campaigning, passionately defends the environment and fights for freedom of speech.

- Lesein Mutunkei. The Kenyan teen combines his love for football with reforestation, planting trees for every goal scored, while also advocating for sustainability in schools and football clubs.
- Luisa Neubauer. An organiser of Germany's Fridays for Future, often called the 'German Greta Thunberg', Luisa advocates for climate policies surpassing the Paris Agreement goals.
- Autumn Peltier. This 17-year-old Indigenous activist fights for clean drinking water, having addressed the UN General Assembly and emphasising the universal right to clean water.
- Qiyun Woo. This Singaporean artist uses stylised illustrations to raise awareness of climate issues, engaging diverse audiences on sustainability and collaborating with various sectors for climate education.

Utilising legal systems

As I write the last chapters of this book, I have been watching the case of the six young climate activists from Portugal who are taking 32 nations to court, arguing in the European Court of Human Rights that governments across Europe are not doing enough to protect people from the harms of climate change and are therefore violating their fundamental human rights. So far, it is the largest instance of activists taking governments to court to force climate action, but most certainly not the last.

In August 2023, young climate activists in the US won a legal battle against the State of Montana's government for violating their right to a clean and healthful environment. The judge concluded that the activists "have proven that as children and youth, they are disproportionately harmed by fossil fuel and climate impacts" (*BBC Newsround*, 2023). In 2015, young people in the Netherlands sued their government for inaction on climate change, forcing the court to rule that the government had explicit duties to protect citizens' human rights in the face of climate change and to order the government to significantly increase the amount of carbon cuts it was making. In Colombia in 2018, 25 young people won a lawsuit against their government for failing to protect the Colombian rainforest. Despite the ruling, the deforestation in the Amazon increased and the young people returned to court in 2020 to continue pressure on their government to act. In 2016, seven-year-old Rabab Ali sued the Pakistani government for violating her rights, and the rights of her generation, to a healthy life by extracting coal in the local district and increasing carbon dioxide emissions.

In 2023 the highest court in Germany rendered a verdict in a case that mandated revisions to the nation's climate legislation. The court instructed the government to establish unambiguous targets for emissions reduction beyond the year 2030. This legal action was initiated by nine young climate advocates who contended that the existing law, in its present configuration, contravenes their fundamental entitlement to a viable future. They argued that the law's provisions are insufficient in terms of mitigating emissions and constraining the global temperature increase to 1.5°C. Legal scholars characterised this ruling as unforeseen and noted that it marked an unprecedented development within the German legal context. And in Australia in 2021, the federal court found that Sussan Ley, the Minister for the Environment, had a duty of care to protect young people from the climate crisis. Eight teenagers and an octogenarian nun had sought an injunction to prevent Ley approving a proposal by Whitehaven Coal to expand the Vickery coalmine in northern New South Wales, arguing that the Minister had a common law duty of care to protect younger people against future harm from climate change. This was the first time such a duty of care had been recognised (Morton, 2021).

Nonetheless, the road to legal challenges is not easy. Exploring 32 cases of youth-centred legal challenges against governments across 14 different countries, Parker et al (2022) argue that states have a legal duty, both domestically and internationally, to safeguard, respect and fulfil the rights of children in the face of escalating climate change. Their analysis demonstrates that these cases represent a distinct category of climate change litigation, focusing on equity between generations, as children and young people are disproportionately impacted by the climate crisis, facing specific vulnerabilities and discrimination linked to their age. This unequal burden is compounded by societal, legal, political and economic structures that marginalise their interests and voices globally. Assessing this surge in climate litigation, they identify a concerning pattern in which youth-focused cases are dismissed on procedural grounds, such as lack of justiciability or standing. The reluctance by courts to address the substance of these claims not only undermines the agency of young individuals but also constitutes a denial of their right to seek redress for human rights violations resulting from worsening climate change (Parker et al, 2022).

The participation of children and young people in the climate change movement, be it as an eco-hero in terms of some of the names I mentioned earlier, the everyday actions of children joining marches or participating in action or those utilising legal systems to hold those in power to account, is exemplified by the global mobilisation led by figures like Greta Thunberg and the legal challenges being launched by children. It directly challenges conventional perceptions of childhood as passive and future oriented. This youth-centred activism is a direct response to the perception of adults' failure in addressing the climate crisis. It has not only ignited a global public debate but has also elevated children as future makers (Spyrou, 2020). This provides a valuable opportunity within society to acknowledge that children, far from being passive, are knowledgeable social actors capable of influencing change. The challenge for us all then is to recognise children as active participants and co-authors in shaping alternative and just futures, exploring the political potential of children as future makers, which extends beyond the boundaries of the climate movement, aligning with an 'ethics of possibility' and a 'politics of hope' that expand the horizons of possible responses and contribute to informed, creative and critical citizenship (Spyrou, 2020).

Changing the dial

In the face of the ongoing climate emergency, children and young people, supported by vital civil society organisations, are rising as leaders in the fight against climate change. Despite being the least responsible for environmental degradation, they bear a disproportionate burden in terms of its consequences. The global movement for climate justice underscores the need for equitable tools for survival, acknowledging the unique vulnerabilities of marginalised communities, including children and young individuals. The devastating impacts of climate change highlight the urgent need for meaningful participation and inclusion of young voices in decision-making processes. While children and young people face challenges, they are not only victims on climate catastrophe but also agents of change, demanding action. As they advocate for climate justice, these passionate youth are reshaping the narrative and paving the way for a sustainable and inclusive future for all, shifting focus towards addressing the structural and systemic causes of climate change (Cloughton, 2021). Research further suggests that while ageist and paternalistic responses still exist in response to children's engagement, for children, positive impacts – including fostering hope and connection with global groups, movements and organisations – prevail (Cloughton, 2021).

Nonetheless, research continuously highlights that while individual activists have made significant advances, their impact is amplified by supporters such as prominent figures like David Attenborough, Jane Goodall, NGOs, politicians and climate campaigners. Movements are most successfully mobilised by a broader network of sympathisers who champion their normative arguments, disseminating them to wider audiences and reinforcing them for those already familiar. Indeed, an adviser to the United Nations Climate Change Conference (COP26) President Alok Sharma acknowledged in an interview that youth activists' arguments shape the President's understanding of the crisis. Recent studies also highlight the explicit impact of youth climate activism on voting behaviour, contributing to increased support for environmentally conscious political parties (Nisbett and Spaiser, 2023). As societal norms shift, efforts to denormalise fossil fuel usage face resistance from vested interests promoting climate denial and action delay arguments.

Nevertheless, the perseverance and commitment of children and young people, the civil society organisations supporting them, social movements and their supporters remain essential for sustained success in challenging the status quo (Spyrou, 2020; Trott, 2021).

Yet, regardless of successes achieved, narratives surrounding children's climate change activism remain challenging. Alexander et al's (2022) research on this topic, exploring narratives of childhood in Australian media representations of the School Strike for Climate, came to a similar view. Typically, children are excluded from formal political systems. When they do participate in acts such as school strikes, their engagement is in general met with one of two narratives. The first, known as anticipatory, revolves around the idea that children should conform and grow into responsible adults. This viewpoint argues that the strikers should be attending school, facing consequences for skipping school and are essentially just young individuals who should not have their voices heard. This falls into the idea discussed earlier of the personally responsible citizens, who obeys laws and norms – here the children are considered to not be acting within this virtuous framework, as was discussed in Chapter 5, so they are criticised. On the other hand, protectionist narratives aim to shield children from adult issues. These narratives suggest that the strikers were influenced and manipulated, raising concerns about their wellbeing. Nonetheless, both narratives fail to recognise children as capable citizens with the ability to participate politically, even though these children are actively shaping a future in which their political engagement is valued (Alexander et al, 2022). Extending this idea further, Jones et al (2023) identify seven ways in which children and young people are storied within climate change discourses; innocent, vulnerable, heroic, alarmist, inheriting, apathetic or narcissistic. Only one of these narratives – heroic – recognises children as social actors, whereas all the others seek to remove their agency. The authors argue that these storylines are chiefly shaped by and tailored for adults, propagated through prevailing political, policy making, media, educational and social research, contributing to the longstanding sidelining of children's voices in contemporary Western societies.

In sum, the global movement for climate justice emphasises the need for equitable tools for survival, particularly for marginalised communities. While facing challenges and ageist responses, young activists foster hope and connection globally. Notably, their impact is amplified by influential figures and supporters, shaping political understanding and influencing voting behaviour. However, despite successes, narratives around children's climate activism remain challenging, often framed through anticipatory or protectionist lenses that fail to recognise their political agency. Research highlights the need to shift prevailing storylines that sideline young individuals, fostering a sustainable and inclusive future for all.

Civil society organisations leading the charge

Civil society organisations play a vital role in empowering children as catalysts for change in the climate change agenda. Recognising the unique perspective and untapped potential of children, these organisations, ranging from local initiatives (like the next case study) to global entities like the Youth Climate Justice Fund, view young individuals as active contributors to environmental advocacy. By creating platforms for youth engagement, providing educational programmes, mentorship and resources, these organisations enable children to voice their concerns and ideas relating to climate change. Initiatives such as youth-led campaigns and partnerships with schools cultivate a sense of responsibility among children, encouraging them to be agents of positive environmental change. As the climate crisis disproportionately affects children despite their minimal responsibility for environmental harm, recognising their unique needs and involving them in solutions is crucial. Children possess valuable skills and perspectives essential for creating safer, more sustainable societies, making their active engagement a necessity rather than an option in addressing the consequences of climate inaction. Engaging, facilitating, supporting, empowering and amplifying the voices of these young change makers, civil society organisations contribute significantly to building a sustainable and inclusive future.

I could spend a week just talking about the different civil society organisations supporting children in this area, but instead will just name a few here as an example. To start with, the United Nations International Children's Emergency Fund (UNICEF) works globally to address various issues affecting children, including climate change. They support initiatives that promote climate education, resilience and sustainable development. While the Youth Climate Action Network (YCAN) is a global network of youth-led organisations working on climate change issues. They empower children and young people to take action, participate in international climate negotiations and contribute to global climate policy discussions. The Zero Hour youth-led organisation focuses on centring the voices of diverse young activists in the climate movement. Zero Hour works to address climate change through education, mobilisation and advocacy, empowering young people to lead initiatives in their communities. Plant-for-the-Planet was started by a young boy, Felix Finkbeiner, with the goal of planting one trillion trees globally. Plant-for-the-Planet UK focuses on empowering children and young people to contribute to the global movement. Earth Guardians is a global movement led by youth activists advocating for environmental and social justice. They empower young people to become leaders and effective advocates for climate action in their communities. While the Children's Environmental Literacy Foundation, similar to the Ministry of Eco-Education, focuses on integrating sustainability and environmental education into school curricula. By providing resources and training, they empower children to understand and address environmental challenges, including climate change. Another organisation, Kids Against Climate Change, aims to educate and mobilise children and youth to take action against climate change. It provides resources, organises events and encourages young people to participate in climate advocacy.

The Global Youth Biodiversity Network (GYBN) is an international network of youth organisations and individuals from every global region who have united with a common goal: preventing the loss of biodiversity and preserving Earth's natural resources. While other organisations focus regionally, such as the Arab Youth Council for Climate Change (AYCCC), a nonprofit initiative led by the Arab Youth Center (AYC). The council is dedicated to bolstering youth-led climate action, fostering the active participation of young Arabs, and encouraging the creation of innovative and sustainable solutions to address the challenges posed by climate change. While the Green Africa Youth Organisation's goal is to address urgent environmental challenges by conducting research and offering solutions through the empowerment of children and young individuals, skills development and public education initiatives. It engages directly with local communities to mitigate the vulnerability of groups susceptible to climate impacts, such as children, youth and women facing comparatively lower adaptive capacities due to social and structural inequalities. And these are but a few examples of organisations championing not just for action against climate change, but also working with children to lead that charge – the full list of such organisations would likely fill many volumes of this book.

And while we recognise and celebrate many of these global entities, there are also hundreds of thousands of small groups and community-based activities engaging children proactively at a local level in contributing to environmental sustainability, conservation and nature-led learning, alongside leading change. Led by the Wild, outlined in the following case study, is an organisation my husband and I founded in 2018. Inheriting some land, we recognised both the privilege we had as landowners and also the responsibilities we had as custodians of land. So, we set out on a simple mission: how could we maximise biodiversity and biodensity here, and how could we bring others on a learning journey with us. The following case study outlines some of our activities, but this personal experience also acts as a microcosm of issues that can be faced as an organisation operating within this area, particularly the lack of funders supporting environmental work. For example, at Led by the Wild, less than 5 per cent of our funding comes through environmental routes. Our funding is made up of various programmes for education, emotional wellbeing, support for refugees and asylum seekers and family support services, services we deliver through engagement with the environment. This for me highlights two issues: first, that while I discuss in the next section how little philanthropic funding goes into the environmental sector, I do think it is perhaps under-represented somewhat, with some funding ending up in this space as a secondary consequence of other programmes; and, second, that while by luck, some minimal additional funding may end up targeting the climate emergency, it is clearly not a priority among philanthropic funders – conversely, over 80 per cent of young people are moderately or significantly worried about climate change, with 75 per cent frightened about the future and 83 per cent feeling that people have failed to take care of the planet (Hickman et al, 2021). Thus, there is a clear misalignment between philanthropic funders' priorities and those of children and young people.

Case study 9: Led by the Wild CIC

Led by the Wild CIC was established in 2018 with the mission to be an outstanding example of community conservation. Set in Aldington in Kent, England, the 30-acre site sits up on a hill, enjoying views out across the Romney Marsh. Supported by a wonderful set of dedicated and skilled volunteers, we bring together a wide combined skill set from teaching to farming, research to funding and a shared ambition to show how engagement with nature can benefit individuals from all walks of life, and nature itself. The roots of our enterprise and at the heart of our community organisation is to support, empower and facilitate children, parents and communities as eco-citizens through nature-led learning, experiential learning, creativity and wellbeing activities.

Working on a democratic model of governance, our community of volunteer participants help direct and organise our activities which includes early years groups, nature-inspired storytelling and creativity days, an eco-citizenship programme for primary schools, wild women's group, twilight campfires, hands-on conservation days for families and regular conservation volunteering opportunities. In doing so we have grown an intergenerational, diverse community around the organisation of likeminded individuals and volunteers who come together to help us achieve our shared vision of a more holistic and regenerative relationship between people and nature.

We are committed to conservation. In the UK even our most iconic species are in decline including the bumblebee, hedgehogs, and many native birds. We depend on each of these species to maintain a healthy ecosystem, especially our pollinating insects. We have been committed to taking whatever steps we can across our 30-acre site and beyond to help promote as healthy a balance of wildlife as we can. Working with local expert wildlife organisations and the children, young people and families who work alongside us, we developed a rolling 5-year conservation plan. Careful year-round monitoring, again actively led by children as co-researchers, has allowed us to not only track the species living on and around the site but also gauge the size of populations.

Our eco-citizenship programme, working in partnership with primary schools, facilitates children to visit our site and through hands-on experiential learning such as bio-blitz, pond-dipping, bee monitoring, planting and eco-research helps children understand the ecosystem and their part within it. Through arts, creativity and story-telling we explore the threats to nature, the potential consequence and together action plan our responses. Children then lead on creating responses within their own area as they see fit. Projects have included creation of new wildlife and habitat areas in their schools, petitioning MPs, creation and sharing of campaign songs and poetry, and fundraising for the World Wildlife Fund, to name but a few.

Directors of Led by the Wild CIC

Funding eco-citizenship

Regardless of the growing awareness of the climate crisis, philanthropic funders from across the globe are falling short in their efforts to combat climate change, despite the growing impact of climate-related challenges on high-priority philanthropic issues such as education, health, human rights, equality and food security. The negative effects of climate change are expected to intensify, with increased frequency and intensity of climate hazards, unless there is a drastic reduction in global greenhouse gas emissions. However, historical philanthropic allocations to address climate change have been relatively small, for example, accounting for less than 1 per cent of total philanthropic giving in the US.

To effectively mitigate the most dangerous effects of climate change, scientists emphasise the need to restrict warming to 1.5°C, requiring trillions of additional dollars in capital spending. According to Climateworks (2023), in the fiscal year 2022, the data indicate a minimal increase in global philanthropic contributions, with foundations and individuals collectively disbursing approximately $811 billion, of which climate change mitigation received an allocation ranging from $7.8 billion to $12.8 billion. Indeed, the overall funds dedicated to climate change mitigation remain woefully low, with less than 2 per cent of the total global philanthropic giving going towards this cause area. Thus, philanthropy is not yet realising its potential for advancing transformative global climate solutions – working in partnership with communities, movements and organisations to move funds to where they are most needed (Climateworks, 2023). And while we must acknowledge that this issue cannot be tackled by philanthropy alone, with urgent greater contributions by companies, governments and investors needed, philanthropists can play a crucial role by leveraging funds quickly and nimbly: they are uniquely placed to foster policy environments and civil societies dedicated to fighting climate change, including those supporting and led by children and young people; they can invest in climate solutions; and they can protect people from climate risks while promoting environmental justice.

Nonetheless, as has been observed throughout this chapter, the impact of young activists and advocates is significant, and while I note that philanthropic funding to climate change movements is low, the scarcity of funding allocated to children and young people's initiatives, given the evidential impact these movements, exposes a major failure in philanthropy. An in-depth quantitative analysis conducted by the Youth Climate Justice Fund, an organisation which works to strengthen existing organising efforts and support emerging youth movements with a focus on bridging funders and organisers to enable flexible and impactful support, shows that a mere 0.76 per cent of grants from major climate foundations reaches youth-led climate justice initiatives – that is, 0.76 per cent of the 2 per cent given to climate change by all funding given by foundations and individuals. This corresponds to an approximate annual global value of $14.2 million.

Therefore, and unsurprisingly, the Youth Climate Justice Fund highlights three significant steps that philanthropic funders can take to address the issues relating to the lack of funding for child and youth movements. I repeat them verbatim here, as in keeping with the rest of this book, they call for more funding, increased youth-friendly practices and the incorporation of children and young people in decision-making and operational activities:

1. Increase funding for youth-led climate justice action:
Around the world, we can see the impact that youth-led action is having. Young people are influencing policy, setting legal precedents and attaching new urgency to how people think about climate change. Many youth-led organisations have relatively modest funding needs, and have proven capable of extracting maximum value from every grant dollar. However, only a tiny fraction of philanthropic giving makes its way to youth-led groups, especially those based in regions most vulnerable to climate impacts. The movement's strong tradition of volunteerism often serves to amplify its power, spontaneity and reach, but the scarcity of financial resources can prove untenable in the longer term, contributing to burn-out and limiting participation among young people who are unable to donate their time for free.
2. Enact youth-friendly grantmaking practices:
A lot of youth-led climate action takes place at grass-roots level, carried out by small, new or informal organisations that are often in a state of flux as leaders' transition or age out. This dynamism is consistent with the movements' organic growth but can make it challenging for youth-led groups to access funds – especially from grantmakers whose practices are set up to support larger civil society groups. As well as

making themselves more accessible, funders can invest in networks or other movement infrastructure that serves to nurture, sustain and connect individual groups. They can also think carefully about how their grant and governance processes foster trust, participation and other values of importance to youth-led organisations.

3. Integrate young people into decision-making and day-to-day operations: Young people from climate justice backgrounds are not well-represented on the staff or boards of most philanthropic organisations. For funders, this is a missed opportunity to learn from a generation of activists whose understanding of intersectionality and collaboration runs deep, because they have often worked in these ways themselves. At a time when the environmental movement urgently needs to expand its skills, mindset and demographic reach, it is essential that young people see the sector as a viable place to build a career. Given that younger generations will bear the heaviest impacts of environmental harm, it is also right that climate-focused philanthropies define their strategies and priorities with the active input of youth.

(Youth Climate Justice Study, 2023)

While positive shifts in climate philanthropy have been observed in recent years, the fiscal year 2022 reflected minimal progress. The glaring inadequacy of funds dedicated to climate change mitigation, constituting less than 2 per cent of global philanthropic giving, underscores a substantial shortfall in realising philanthropy's potential for transformative global climate solutions. The impact of young activists is significant, yet philanthropic funding to climate change movements remains even lower, with a glaring failure evident in the scarcity of funding allocated to children and young people's initiatives. The urgency of the climate crisis demands that philanthropic funders no longer remain passive or depend solely on corporations and governments for solutions. With a limited timeframe to stabilise the climate, immediate actions are crucial for humanity's future. We have already witnessed the power children and young people can have in this global movement, influencing social, political and cultural understandings. Therefore, it is now vital for funders to listen to children and young people, and actively channel funds to address the pressing challenges at hand.

Conclusion

In this chapter I have sought to underscore the critical role of children and young people as influential actors in the global climate change movement, situating them as indispensable change agents in the face of the urgent and severe climate crisis. The examination extends beyond formal education, portraying children as 'future makers' who not only initiate but also actively lead political action. This conclusion is rooted in three core arguments. First, this chapter has highlighted the transformative power of youth-led movements, emphasising the shift from mere climate action to climate justice. This transition accentuates the disparate impact of climate change on marginalised communities and advocates for solutions that rectify social and ethical injustices. Despite encountering challenges, youth-led climate justice networks forge robust connections, exhibit solidarity and adapt their strategies to address broader systemic issues through legal and direct actions, all in pursuit of a just and sustainable future.

Second, this chapter has explored the pivotal role of civil society organisations in empowering children as catalysts for change. These organisations, recognising the unique perspectives and untapped potential of children, establish platforms for youth engagement, furnish educational programmes, and provide mentorship and support with resources. The active involvement of children in addressing the consequences of climate inaction is posited not merely as an option but also as a necessity, given their valuable skills and perspectives in forging safer, more sustainable societies.

Finally, in this chapter I have sought to highlight the insufficiency of philanthropic funding dedicated to youth-led climate justice initiatives. Despite their significant impact, young activists grapple with problematic narratives framed through anticipatory and protectionist lenses, which fail to recognise their political agency. Moreover, a quantitative analysis reveals a glaring discrepancy, with a mere 0.76 per cent of grants from major climate foundations allocated to youth-led initiatives, amounting to an annual global value of approximately $14.2 million. This stark reality underscores a major shortcoming in philanthropy, necessitating immediate and transformative action.

In conclusion, the urgency of the climate crisis demands unwavering commitment and decisive actions. Children, positioned as powerful change agents, actively contribute to shaping a narrative that transcends borders, cultures and generations, emphasising the interconnectedness of humanity in the face of a shared planetary challenge. While civil society organisations play a crucial role in enabling children's empowerment, persistent challenges in media narratives and philanthropic funding underscore the imperative for transformative measures to ensure the active involvement of youth in building a sustainable and just future.

PART III

Where next and future possibilities

10

Creating a responsive philanthropic ecosystem: voices from the sector

Introduction

Commencing my career as a children's participation worker, I engaged in numerous local social action projects with children and young people, striving to develop their skills while seeking to enable them to catalyse meaningful change within local communities on issues they cared about. This practical experience fuelled my commitment to children's voice and participation, a theme central to my academic research since entering academia in 2013. A pivotal moment occurred in 2018 when my colleague Eddy Hogg and I revisited a project I'd been involved in a decade earlier, exploring its lasting impact on participants (see Body and Hogg, 2019). The findings revealed that engagement in local social action projects had a 'transformative' effect, shaping participants' present-day citizenship. Relationships with supportive adults, a key factor in facilitating their role as change makers, a sense of achievement and the ability to effect change were defining aspects of their experiences. Over 90 per cent of these participants, now adults, remain actively involved in voluntary action within their communities (Body and Hogg, 2019), a common feature in individuals' civic journeys when engaging from a young age (McFarland and Thomas, 2006; Musick and Wilson, 2007; Flanagan, 2009), and two thirds of the participants were actively working with the younger generation in order to enable them to have a voice and empower them within their community.

Throughout this book, I've critically examined how children are socialised into our philanthropic ecosystem, emphasising its impact on achieving a fairer, more just and equitable society, particularly for children and young people. This concluding part delves into key components for fostering a more transformational approach to philanthropy, aligning it with justice and activist orientations (Johnson and Morris, 2010). Drawing upon insights from 40 leaders actively engaged in the philanthropic ecosystem, including educators, practitioners, leaders of charities and funders dedicated to supporting children as change makers, this chapter synthesises extensive interviews conducted for this book. Six interviewees represented leading philanthropic foundations and funders, 18 were leaders of organisations focused on children's citizenship and empowerment, while 16 were practitioners within the philanthropic ecosystem.

Summarising diverse perspectives, findings are presented under five key subheadings: shared belief in the power of children; a broken system; the role of education; following the money; and exploring organisational opportunities and challenges. Each section offers insights from civil society leaders into empowering children as change makers within the philanthropic context. The chapter includes practical tips for philanthropic actors, aiming to actively shape a philanthropic landscape that nurtures the potential of children and young people as impactful contributors to our shared societal future. As we then transition to the conclusion of this book, these insights pave the way for a broader exploration of cultural shifts needed to propel philanthropy towards a more inclusive, transformative and child-centred approach.

Shared belief in the power of children

For those of us committed to empowering children and young people as change makers, there is much to celebrate. Civil society leaders from across the spectrum of philanthropic funders, practitioners and educators are united in their commitment and belief in the power and importance of working with children and young people as agents of change. Indeed, as we have witnessed in the many case studies and examples discussed throughout this book, while there is much work to be done, many stakeholders within this ecosystem are already dedicated to working towards helping children unleash their real philanthropic power. They are engaging children and young people in critically considered, justice-oriented actions to support their local and global communities, and causes they are passionate about. Collectively they are committed to empowering children and young people as philanthropic citizens and helping to cultivate their civic engagement, and this work starts with the power of helping to elevate children's voices. Nonetheless, while campaigns like #iwill and National Citizen Service have seen some focus in youth participation, there is a shared recognition that preadolescent children are often neglected in these conversations. A civil society leader notes that "too often it's simply easier to fund and access older young people, as they are often able to be engaged separate from their families and schools. Engaging young children is harder and requires more work". This neglect demands increased attention to ensure a more comprehensive approach to engaging children across different age groups, and particularly younger children that are the focus of this book.

Across the interviewees, the power of children's voice was recognised as a cultural norm. For example, as one funder of social action programmes commented:

'I always go to conferences and hear the terminology that we need to share power with children and young people – that's the terminology that is so commonly used. I think it is actually the other way round. I think children and young people hold the power, and we need them to share their power with us – because we need it. Think of all the biggest social movements in the past decade – they have been driven by children and young people. And they have created social and narrative change on a scale which we in the charitable sector have not been able to achieve. Children and young people hold the power, and we as civil society need to think of ways to help them release and unleash that power.'

And another commented:

'I really believe we are missing out on the role of children and young people in society. They really, really care about the world and we would benefit from their blue sky thinking, ideas and sometimes straightforward views of what needs to be done. We would all benefit enormously if we work in partnership with children and young people, as we all bring something to the table.'

These observations draw attention to the transformative impact that the inclusion of young voices can have on societal dynamics. From fundraising enterprises (see Chapter 5) to engaging in community organising (Chapter 8) and climate advocacy (Chapter 9), the positive impact children can have as social and political actors is recognised across leaders within this space. Importantly, we know these early experiences have a lifelong impact on our civic engagement as adults (see Chapter 1), so it is perhaps unsurprising that when all interviewees were asked why they felt so passionately about this issue, many, echoing previous research (Body and Hogg, 2019), recounted their own childhood experiences of taking action in issues which mattered to them as a pivotal turning point in their lives. For example, a leader of a national organisation promoting civic engagement discussed their personal experience, recounting the discovery of the ability to influence change during a local secondary school campaign regarding gender identity rights; another talked about the social action they were involved with through their local church; while another discussed their early engagement in anti-war protests in the 2000s. More often than not, the leaders of civil society of today were the change-making children of yesteryear. Thus, it is then not too far-fetched to suggest that investing in children as the change makers of today is an investment in the civil society leaders of tomorrow.

Furthermore, while there are many challenges to contend with, which I will expand on later in this chapter, there was a recognition that we are experiencing a resurgence in interest in children's voices from across civil society and the philanthropic sector, which was welcomed by all interviewees. Thus, we are witnessing the journey towards unleashing the power of children's voices as a collective endeavour, with civil society leaders recognising the transformative potential within the youngest members of our society. Children are unilaterally recognised here as being able to create ripples of change throughout our communities, and many funders, organisations and educators not only acknowledge their power but also strive to create an environment where their voices can resonate, creating ripples of positive change that echo through generations. Nonetheless, this does not mean that the work is easy, and therefore in the next few sections I will critically explore some of the challenges faced in achieving this aim.

A broken system

The examination of challenges and opportunities for cultivating children's philanthropic citizenship rests heavily on a thriving children and youth work sector. Closer exploration of this sector reveals a problematic and, at times, broken system. Civil society leaders collectively decry the current state of the ecosystem of services surrounding children and young people, recognising its inadequacies and the urgent need for systemic change. "Everyone accepts that the system is really at best problematic, at worst, utterly, utterly broken and not serving children and young people", stated a civil society leader, highlighting the critical evaluation that underpins the call for transformation.

The discussion about the role of organisations supporting children and youth civic and philanthropic engagement cannot occur in isolation; it necessitates a broader consideration of the youth sector in the UK. The intersection of youth engagement and youth service provision by voluntary sector organisations is integral to understanding children's philanthropic citizenship and their opportunities for active civic engagement. Encouraging and supporting children and young individuals to participate and volunteer not only offers immediate benefits but also serves as a gateway to a lifelong commitment to community involvement. Positive experiences in voluntary action, such as fundraising, volunteering, collective action and community organising, shape a constructive attitude towards civic engagement (Musick and Wilson, 2007; Brodie et al, 2011; Hogg, 2016). The enduring value of youth service provision extends beyond immediate support, potentially paving the way for sustained commitment and associated advantages (Body, 2020). However, the landscape of youth services in the UK has undergone substantial changes since the election of the Conservative and Liberal Democrat Coalition government in 2010, and the later Conservative government in 2015. Austerity measures and service re-alignment have resulted in a 75 per cent decline in real terms funding for youth services since 2010/2011, resulting in a decrease of £1.1 billion by 2022 (YMCA, 2022). The annual spend per head on 5–17 year olds in England plummeted from £158 in 2010/2011 to a mere £37 in 2020/2021. Over 750 youth centres have been closed and over 14,000 youth workers have lost their jobs.

This drastic reduction has reshaped youth services on a local level, which is driven more by unique circumstances than a nationally agreed vision, leading to divergent models of service provision across the country (Ritchie and Ord, 2017). The absence of a cohesive national youth policy has further compounded the issue, steering youth work towards a more reactionary model of interventions, often merging traditional approaches with social care intervention (Body, 2020).

The remaining experienced and qualified youth workers find themselves increasingly engaged in caseload-based interventions or targeted programmes, reflecting an evolving recognition of their traditional skills base. However, this shift represents a departure from the delivery of universal services with integrated specialist support (Body, 2020). The consequence is a significant impact on the trajectory of children's philanthropic citizenship, with their opportunities and avenues for active civic engagement being significantly curtailed. A poignant observation from an interviewee encapsulates the broader sentiment:

'The whole of the youth sector is on its knees. We're really passionate about youth agency and voice, but it takes resources, people, and support, and most of our energy is currently spent on emergency work around mental health, poverty, and rising youth crime.'

Alongside these cuts to the youth sector, the *#iwill* initiative was launched, introducing Step up to Serve in 2013, and as a response to former Prime Minister David Cameron's vision for a 'decade of social action' as part of the responsibilisation agenda. The initiative aimed to double youth participation in social activities by 2020, enjoying bipartisan support and endorsement from the (then) Prince of Wales. It orchestrated a seven-year endeavour that secured substantial funding, conducted extensive research and established advisory boards. However, despite these efforts and the endorsement across central government, there has been no discernible shift in overall youth participation in social action. The engagement levels remain unchanged since the early 2000s, with some key providers in the youth social action sector ceasing operations or failing to scale up (Reed, 2020).

The *#iwill* initiative, character education agenda (see Chapter 2), and uniformed groups (see Chapter 7) collectively sought to instil civic duty and service in young individuals. In response to the 2011 London riots, former Prime Minister David Cameron highlighted the need to confront a perceived slow-motion moral collapse. Controversially, assuming a deficit of moral fibre in young people, and thus focusing on youth social action to foster commitment to community engagement and service to the country, the programme prioritised practical involvement in community-based activities (Body, 2020). This approach centred on viewing children, young people and families as the problem rather than addressing broader structural issues, marking a shift from supporting them through children and youth services to a focus on short-term outcomes to tackle 'troubled families' (Gillies, 2014).

Critics noted issues in this approach like a lack of focus, short-termism and a government-controlled conceptualisation of social action that lacks meaningful connection with young people (Dean, 2013). The emphasis on a responsibilisation agenda reinforces a focus on fixing troubled youth rather than viewing children and young people as positive agents of change and collectively inviting them to actively engage in building a fairer society, prioritising civic duty over critical scrutiny of political structures or ideologies. It is an approach which is about retaining the status quo, reminding us of Dean's (2013, p 58) quote:

> Successive governments in Britain have determined that youth volunteering is a relatively cheap and effective way of delivering results that benefit not only the young person, but society and the power, financial or otherwise, of the state. A young population constructed to take responsibility for their communities will, it is hoped, provide this long-term through social control regulated at the individual level.

While the *#iwill* programme made significant investments in youth social action initiatives, largely driven by philanthropic funders, the reduction in funding for comprehensive youth services remains a substantial challenge. The struggle between addressing pressing, visible concerns such as the cost of living and mental health while investing in the foundational building blocks of citizenship education is evident. As one interviewee aptly put it, "funders are focused on the cost of living. They're focused on mental health and well-being. So, things like citizenship and civic learning can feel like a nice-to-have and not a have-to-have", while another said:

> 'The systems supporting children now are inadequate to say the least. Children's mental health is spiralling out of control, poverty rising and standards dropping. We want to empower children and young people as change makers, but first we must make sure they are fed, warm, sheltered and safe ... And that in itself is a big job. Statutory services are utterly failing and the responsibility for all of this now rests squarely on the shoulders of schools and charities. It shouldn't do, but it does.'

And another stated:

> 'Philanthropy cannot replace what has been lost through government funding. There is so much we want to do, so much we know needs doing, but we simply do not have the resources to do it.'

While another added:

'We face challenges in navigating the changing landscape where traditional services are no longer funded, and charities are expected to step in, often becoming quasi-welfare states.'

This sentiment underscores the fundamental conversation needed among professionals working with children and young people regarding the imperative for transformative shifts and reveals the nuanced struggle between immediate concerns and the need for comprehensive, foundational citizenship education and support.

Universal youth service provision serves as a holistic approach, offering diverse programmes and resources, including mentorship, counselling and skills-building opportunities. This comprehensive approach caters to the multifaceted needs of the children and youth population, going beyond the focus on targeted social action projects. While small investments in social action initiatives can yield positive outcomes, they inherently fall a long way short in terms of compensating for the extensive cuts to universal youth service provision. The reduction in funding undermines the foundational infrastructure needed to support a broad spectrum of young people, hindering their development of agency, voice and active citizenship. The paramount role of staff and volunteers in establishing positive relationships with young people for enduring impacts is highlighted in the literature. Participants consistently attribute their positive experiences not to specific services or organisations, but to individual practitioners, emphasising the central importance of relationships in service provision. These relationships serve as pivotal hubs, facilitating open discussions on diverse topics from personal challenges to broader aspirations. Crucially, they extend beyond project timelines, forming integral components of ongoing support networks for participants, and offering solace and care (Body and Hogg, 2019).

In conclusion, the challenges and opportunities for cultivating children's philanthropic citizenship are deeply intertwined with the state of the current ecosystem of support surrounding children and young people. The drastic reduction in funding for youth services has reshaped the landscape, resulting in a patchwork of support for children and young people. Consequently, schools and educational institutions, which are also financially constrained, have been left to shoulder an increasing share of this responsibility.

The role of education

The importance of education has been discussed elsewhere in this book (see Chapters 1 and 6). Nonetheless, here I seek to draw attention to the intersection between the role of community organisations and schools in developing children's philanthropic power. The education philosopher John Dewey (1900, 1902, 1909, 1916) reminds us that a healthy democracy requires citizens who care. Nonetheless, Dewey's perspective on democracy was anything but stagnant. He saw it as a dynamic, evolving force, a living embodiment of community life. In his view, schools were more than just places of education; they were miniature communities, incubators for the development of democratic citizens. These institutions played a crucial role in preparing children for an ever-changing, larger democratic society beyond their classroom walls. In his vision, schools were the engines of this transformative process. They were meant to be models of community life, offering students opportunities to learn in ways that reinforced their social interconnectedness. He believed that true learning wasn't just about acquiring knowledge, but was also about internalising it as moving ideas that guided one's actions. He urged schools to see each child as a member of society in the broadest sense, equipped to recognise and actively engage with their social relations.

In a democratic society, Dewey emphasised that the culture of schools should mirror democratic principles, especially in citizenship education. For him, students were citizens and citizens-in-training, and the formal aspects of citizenship should be seamlessly integrated into the fabric of school life. This, he believed, was the aim of education. Ultimately, he underscored that education wasn't just about imparting knowledge and skills; it was about nurturing the bonds that held a culture together, ensuring its continuity and vibrancy. In his view, a true democracy wasn't merely a system of governance, but a mode of collective living, a shared tapestry of experiences. By participating in this complex web of associations, citizens would not only grow individually, but would also contribute to the broader fabric of society.

The strategy of embedding opportunities within schools emerges as a key aspect of Deweyan education, empowering children as change makers. The integration of philanthropic citizenship into the curriculum creates a safe space for diverse groups of children to participate actively, as one leader commented:

> 'Social action should create space for conversations and share experiences, which you might not normally be able to have in the classroom, under the standard curriculum. For example, there was a great story of a student who spoke about their experience of being a young carer for the first time ever with their peers as a result of the action, inspiring her peers to develop a model of support for young carers.'

The emphasis on embedding such initiatives within the curriculum, rather than treating them as optional add-ons, aligns with Dewey's vision of schools as dynamic agents in fostering democratic ideals. Civil society leaders are keen to work in partnership with schools, building in experience, skills and capacity into the programme. Indeed, research shows a positive correlation between school and voluntary sector partnerships, helping children engage in active citizenship and understand social justice (Body et al, 2023). There is a shared recognition that teachers and school culture play pivotal roles in this transformative process. Nonetheless, leaders note that success in implementing philanthropic citizenship education is framed more by values and culture of the school than a specific curriculum, echoing Dewey's emphasis on the broader social interconnectedness that schools should instil in their students. For example, as one civil society member observed:

> 'When it works, it's usually because of teachers. It's because they understand and live the concept and the values. They bring together the school community, parents and the local community. They lead social change. They get the importance of this kind of work, it's not about filling out worksheets, it's about fostering a culture of inclusion and change. It's about who they are, not so much what they do. Their passion can be infectious, empowering children to believe they can make a difference.'

While another commented:

> 'You can totally tell the difference between the school that is doing something because they think it looks good, and the school that really, really believes children can be change makers. The whole approach is different. The school doesn't just "do" social action, it engages children democratically in the whole school'.

However, universally across the interviewees, there was a recognition that challenges persist, primarily due to time constraints imposed by the curriculum. Frustration is evident in the quotes, such as that from a civil society leader, who worked in partnership with schools to deliver a philanthropic programme of activity and explained:

> 'I think the biggest problem we face as an organisation is actually the curriculum time, the amount of time we have ... they're trying to divide it up into these little sections and it's so frustrating for children not to be able to get into those issues and discuss them properly – it just becomes a tokenistic tick box exercise and the children don't really learn anything!'

Thus, as was discussed in Chapter 2, the organisational challenge highlights the tension between educational goals and the constraints of formal curriculum requirements. For example, as one leader highlighted, 'something being embedded within the curriculum time rather than being an added extra is a really key thing for me'.

Addressing these challenges requires a nuanced approach. The importance of active, participative citizenship education starting at a young age is emphasised throughout this book and across the interviewees, with many organisations like the case studies shared in this book aiming to provide quality education for active civic engagement, but it has to be a secured and recognised part of the curriculum. The discussion with civil society leaders also underscores the significance of values, culture and leadership within schools for successful civic education. Citizenship education is positioned as a key component in preparing children for modern society, providing skills for life and work, and fostering problem-solving abilities. While philanthropic citizenship is a distinct part of citizenship education (see Chapter 1), it is most prominently associated with the 'active' part of citizenship – the 'doing', which emphasises the need for a cultural shift within educational institutions. The vision of the majority of the civil society leaders, and indeed associated funders, is that 'every young person should have the opportunity to go through a user-led social action project before they leave primary school to help show children their own power early on', highlighting the aspiration to create informed and engaged citizens from an early age.

The critical role of education in fostering active and philanthropic citizenship involves embedding opportunities, integrating active, philanthropic citizenship seamlessly into the curriculum, addressing time constraints, starting citizenship education early, and emphasising values and culture within schools. Despite challenges, the overarching vision of preparing children for a critically engaged and active role in society remains a crucial and inspiring educational and community endeavour.

Following the money

As was explored earlier, empowering children as change makers faces significant challenges in the realm of funding, exposing the complex dynamics between funders and the organisations they fund, alongside the communities they wish to serve. There appear to be two central issues. First, while it is very welcome that funders are increasingly interested in children's citizenship, civil society leaders still consider that there are too few funders within this space, and the pressure on those funders is large, given the government cuts in funding for youth services. For example, as one civil society leader commented, "there are several philanthropic funders stepping into this space and shifting their focus, but it is not at the scale required given government cuts". Another stated that "whilst powerful, the funders who are passionate about and prepared to support children and young people's agency are really very niche. They are a creative bunch but we're not seeing their actions create the rippled effect we'd like where other funders follow suit".

This comes coupled with a second concern that some (though not all) of the funders who do fund within this space come with their own agenda – co-opting organisations delivering children's empowerment projects to align with donor priorities. One example cited was project funding given to an organisation to engage children in issues they cared about. When children chose to focus on poverty and social housing in their area, this was considered by the funder as being 'too political'. The organisation delivering the project was told to refocus the children onto a different topic, such as litter picking and planting trees locally. Indeed, several interviewees raised concerns about funders adopting specific models or focusing on specific demographics, raising questions about the potential limitations imposed on the scope of funded initiatives: "we have to be careful about how very specific people drive the agenda and to what purpose". Another commented that "too many funders have a set view on what they think good social action is – and so instead of saying to kids, right what matters to you – it is more about, this is what matters to us, so this is what we are telling you, you must care about".

Indeed, these are not outlier examples, with civil society leaders raising concerns that most funders within this space are happy to support participative, social action projects, usually revolving around local community development or environmental projects; however, significantly fewer were viewed as being happy to support activism and campaigning by children and young people. As one interviewee commented, "activism hasn't really been a theme of youth social action discussion. In truth it is a term we largely avoid", while another pointedly said that "the problem with this agenda is we want children and young people to be charitable, to be good volunteers and donors in their community, but we don't want them questioning the systems and structures at play which necessitate that need for charity". This calls for a more inclusive and comprehensive perspective, underlining the need for flexibility and adaptability in the funding landscape to truly empower children as effective change makers in society.

Another central issue, highlighted by interviewees from across the board, revolves around the scarcity of truly unrestricted, core funding, with some progressive funders advocating for flexibility, but organisations consistently encountering a prevailing trend of having to align their work with the donor's priorities, short-term projects and "collecting data" rather than being led by the communities they sought to serve. The dilemma is succinctly expressed in the following observation: "many of them [funders] are still not well you know really behind the idea ... basically they say we wanna do something cute and like that serves our need really, which translates as, something that makes us look good on social media and in the press". Another interviewee shared that "we've a couple of funders who really respect us as the expert – they ask 'what do you need and how can we help you' but those funders are rarer than hens teeth".

These discussions underscore some of the difficulties experienced by organisations in securing funding that genuinely aligns with the authentic needs and goals of organisations dedicated to fostering philanthropic citizenship. Moreover, interviewees place significant emphasis on funders comprehending the necessity for long-term and continuous support to embed civic education in schools and community projects rather than short-term interventions, acknowledging a potential misalignment when some funders focus on scalable models that may not cater to the ongoing needs of educational institutions and communities. As one civil society leader suggested:

'I think where we see difficulties are when funders who are really interested in the topic, but just focused on things like scale and creating hands-off models. Encouraging children as change makers relies on a hands-on, intense model – it relies on relationships, it looks different everywhere. It's a societal cultural shift in thinking, not a product we can package, shelf, sell and copy.'

A final issue raised by civil society leaders was the need for philanthropic funders themselves to be both transparent about the origins of their funding and how they distribute grants. As one leader put it:

'We have funders who preach social justice to us and participatory practice, whilst sitting on funds which derive from colonial injustice, distributed by a board of extremely wealthy, older, White family members. Well it's a bit bad. It completely lacks authenticity.'

There was a strong feeling among the interviewees that funders should model the values they seek in delivery organisations and that this too is part of the shift needed within the philanthropic ecosystem to truly empower children's voices.

In conclusion, the journey towards empowering children as change makers encounters several challenges within the funding landscape, revealing complex relationships between funders, organisations and the communities they aim to serve. Two pivotal issues emerge: the scarcity of funders dedicated to children's citizenship and the potential imposition of donor agendas on empowering projects. The limited scale of philanthropic involvement, exacerbated by government funding cuts, underscores the urgent need for a broader commitment to supporting children's agency. The concern about funders co-opting projects to align with their priorities raises questions about the true independence and inclusivity of initiatives. Moreover, the reluctance among some funders to support activism and questioning of systemic structures hinders the development of critical thinking in children. The second central issue revolves around the lack of unrestricted core funding, with organisations facing pressure to align with donor priorities and short-term projects rather than being community-led. The call for genuine collaboration and long-term support to embed civic education underscores the necessity for funders to embrace a hands-on, adaptable model that respects the expertise and needs of organisations dedicated to fostering philanthropic citizenship. This discussion highlights the imperative for a flexible and comprehensive perspective in the funding landscape to authentically empower children as effective change makers in society, some of which is addressed by the 'top tips' given in the next section.

Top tips: funding for hope

While acknowledging the challenges, civil society leaders from across the ecosystem recognised the pivotal role that philanthropic funders can play in transforming the landscape of initiatives aimed at cultivating children as change makers. I asked each of them what a positive funding landscape for children's philanthropic and active citizenship looks like, and in the following list I summarise the excellent insights:

- *Emphasise active participation.* Funders should support organisations that prioritise active involvement of children in project design and delivery. Evaluations should consider the extent of children's participation, fostering a genuinely child-centric approach.
- *Prioritise children's narrative and lived experiences in evaluation.* Place greater emphasis on storytelling and sharing lived experiences by children in evaluative processes. Go beyond quantitative outputs, focus on qualitative impacts and empower children to share their journeys.
- *Acknowledge the time needed for cultural shifts.* Recognise and support organisations undergoing cultural shifts that prioritise diverse ways of engaging with children. Long-term funding is crucial, acknowledging that this shift is a journey requiring time.
- *Broaden engagement avenues.* Support organisations actively engaging with community and youth groups across diverse communities, ensuring a more inclusive and comprehensive impact beyond traditional school channels.
- *Unrestricted and sustainable funding models.* Provide unrestricted and longer-term sustainable funding to build a socially responsible future generation. This allows flexibility in programme adaptation, fostering social responsibility, empathy and active participation.

- *Supporting the sector.* Invest in the overall development of the youth sector, enabling comprehensive programmes that address education, health and personal development. This holistic approach strengthens the impact of philanthropy and contributes to sustainable social change.
- *Modelling.* Actively model collaboration and partnership with children in grant-making decisions, especially those from marginalised communities, creating a democratic and community-centric approach in funders' own grant making. Involving children in decision making empowers them and aligns grant making with community needs.
- *Championing children's voices.* Serve as advocates for children's perspectives and experiences, encouraging a more equitable and child-centred philanthropy. Actively promote prioritising children's input in funding decisions.
- *Support collective action and community organisation.* Actively support children's engagement in collective action to cultivate community responsibility, empowerment, and social awareness. Foster collaborative initiatives for leadership development and a deeper understanding of societal issues.
- *Transparency.* Prioritise openness and transparency about the origins of funds, addressing historical roots and associated social injustices. By openly discussing the origins of their resources, funders create opportunities for children to critically engage in conversations about philanthropy, wealth and social justice. This fosters a deeper understanding of the complexities surrounding financial privilege and encourages a more informed and conscientious generation that actively participates in shaping a fair and just society.

Exploring organisational opportunities and challenges in engaging children in philanthropic citizenship

Even amid the stark reduction in youth services across the UK, the aspiration to empower children as change makers persists among all the individuals interviewed, acknowledging that such aspirations face an array of challenges. The discourse, grounded in the perspectives of interviewees, unveils issues of socioeconomic disparities, lack of trust, representation, and the crucial distinction between authentic child-led leadership and mere engagement.

The interviewees consistently underscored the existence of disparities in opportunities and civic engagement, with socioeconomic status emerging as a persistent challenge. Some of these have been explored throughout this book, including unequal access to opportunities through school (see Chapter 6), a focus on character and service (see Chapters 2, 3 and 7) and a lack of recognition as children as active citizens within society (see Chapters 2, 8 and 9). Nonetheless, several further challenges persist. A quote captures this concern: "it always worries me that participation programmes privilege the already privileged children. Those who show up, are most commonly those who regularly have voice and power. It's the ones without voice and power which we need to be working with". Within this, socioeconomic barriers are recognised as having significant impact on children's opportunities, particularly within schools (Body et al, 2024). This raises a dual concern for civil society leaders: first and foremost, it's about who shows up. As one leader put it:

> 'So much of organising and involvement in society is just on who shows up. It's such a powerful thing, to have that confidence to feel your voice matters, to help shape what does and doesn't get spoken about. It comes with a sense of entitlement, from those who have access to spaces, places and tools to enact their voice, which is often found in the most affluent in society, the privileged families, the private schools, etc. So for those children and young people it is like "of course I'm gonna show up. Of course. People care what I have to say". But when you have families who are working three jobs and worrying about practical everyday things such as food, warmth and survival, you know like Maslow hierarchy of needs, the physiological issues, they don't necessarily spend time fostering that sense of entitlement, they've more important, more immediate things to worry about. Or worse, you have someone telling some children, you don't matter … Then the disparity in who shows up is already instilled from such a young age … Our job is to make sure all children know they are entitled to show up and be listened to.'

The call here is clear – targeted efforts are essential to ensure inclusivity, as socioeconomic disparities should not be a deterrent to civic engagement. Articulate individuals can override the diversity of voices, as another interviewee emphasised, referring to youth participation: "if you're articulate and engaging, etc, you will put yourself forward for these types of roles, say on the school council, in a campaign or in a social action project … but if you are not, your voice remains hidden and, well and unheard".

This highlights the danger of certain voices dominating the conversation, necessitating proactive measures to amplify diverse perspectives. Moreover, a pervasive lack of trust among children and young people in established institutions, as voiced by several interviewees, demands deliberate attention. Addressing this trust deficit requires efforts to provide alternative models and reshape narratives around institutional involvement, fostering a sense of reliability, legitimacy and authenticity. Thus, a crucial distinction is drawn between authentic youth leadership and mere engagement.

The second significant challenge pertains to striking a delicate balance in decision-making responsibilities for children engaged in philanthropic citizenship. Recognising this concern, civil society leaders advocate for the creation of an environment that allows children to explore their views without shouldering the full weight of responsibility for those issues. For example, they commented:

'But I mean, you know, time and time again, they'll [children] say, "I don't know. That's your job. Like, can I be young, please. Can you make sure this environment is conducive so that I can get on with being young. I definitely wanna share my view and I definitely wanna feel counted but it's not my job to make decisions on every level because otherwise what is your job and the adult or the organisation in this space".'

And:

'We're not and should never be trying to obfuscate our responsibility and put it on young people all in the name of youth empowerment.'

And:

'But you don't put the weight of the decision on them. You make it super clear. Like we're the ones that have to bear the brunt, we'll deal with it. They can be confident about sharing their views, knowing that the weight of the decision is not on their shoulders. And I think we cloud that when we're engaging with children and young people sometimes, all in the name of authentic, genuine engagement. When on top of that, by the way, they are also just being young. They are also navigating hormones trying to figure out friendship groups, etc.'

In response to these challenges, the organisations frequently adopt a twofold approach to empower children, applying a social justice lens to initiatives, ensuring alignment with principles of fairness and equity, while empowering children by allowing them to choose their projects and cause. As one interviewee explained, "this strategy aims to instil a sense of agency and ownership among the children, emphasising the importance of personal investment in projects that align with their passions and concerns". Alongside this, another challenge addressed by the interviewees is the need for sustained engagement to build relationships to really enable children to feel confident to begin to develop their philanthropic citizenship. To overcome this, leaders emphasise the implementation of longer projects that encompass a thorough process, skills building and real-world engagement. This approach acknowledges the multifaceted nature of philanthropic citizenship and seeks to equip children with the necessary tools and experiences for effective and impactful participation, but as one leader said, "it takes time".

Finally, in recognition of the cultural dynamics within the UK's multifaith and nonfaith context, civil society leaders acknowledge the impact of religiosity in different communities. This highlights a recognition reflecting an understanding of the nuanced influences on children's engagement, contributing to a more inclusive and culturally aware approach to philanthropic citizenship.

In conclusion, empowering children as change makers is a complex endeavour, fraught with challenges such as socioeconomic disparities, voice dominance, lack of trust and neglect of preadolescent engagement. Navigating these challenges demands a holistic and strategic approach, ensuring inclusivity, authenticity and a genuine sense of trust in the democratic process. Organisations can contribute to this endeavour by committing to meaningful involvement, balancing decision-making responsibilities, adopting a comprehensive strategy, and understanding the cultural and religious nuances within diverse communities. By doing so, these organisations pave the way for a generation of empowered children actively shaping positive change in their communities.

Top tips: cultivating children's philanthropic citizenship

As has been argued throughout this book, research shows us even the youngest of children have the capabilities of engaging critically in discussions regarding political, civic, environmental and social issues. However, it is important that opportunities created are age-appropriate and supportive of children's evolving capabilities and thinking. Initiatives that voluntary sector organisations, educators and philanthropic actors can consider may include the following:

- *Raising education and awareness.* Create educational programmes that promote philanthropic citizenship, embracing the core components of active participation, collective action, empowerment, critical thinking and justice orientation (Westheimer, 2015), and help children learn about social issues and how to imagine and create different ways of being. This also involves raising awareness among children about the power of their actions in making a difference.
- *Child-oriented activities.* Develop specific philanthropic initiatives and projects tailored with and for children and youth, offering age-appropriate opportunities for children to get involved in a range of philanthropic initiatives, connecting critical thinking with actions, such as charitable giving, social action, volunteering, fundraising, advocacy, campaigning and protesting activities (Body et al, 2020).
- *Evaluation and learning.* Philanthropic institutions and nonprofits should continuously reflect on their initiatives to help cultivate children's philanthropic citizenship, working with children, as co-producers of

knowledge, to help inform future activities. This should include open and honest critical reflection on philanthropic institutions themselves, for example, are activities orientated towards changing systems, or reproducing and retaining the status quo.

- *Inspiring role models.* Facilitate children to engage with positive role models and mentors who can collaborate with, and inspire, them on their philanthropic journey. Fostering interactions with community leaders, volunteers and successful philanthropists, who adopt collective and activist orientations, helps encourage children to lead on philanthropic decision making (Body et al, 2021).

- *Collaborating with educational institutions.* Establish partnerships with schools to incorporate philanthropic citizenship into the curriculum. Body et al (2023) highlight how partnerships between schools and justice-oriented nonprofits support schools in adopting more justice-oriented approaches to philanthropic citizenship.

- *Acknowledging children's contributions.* Recognise, commend and celebrate the philanthropic efforts and achievements of children in ways that are meaningful to the children themselves. As research highlights, this increases philanthropic engagement in the long term (Weller and Lagattuta, 2013; Ongley et al, 2014).

- *Nurturing global perspectives.* Stimulate children to look beyond their local communities and comprehend global issues as 'citizens of the world' (Nussbaum, 1998). Expose them to diverse cultures and viewpoints, fostering a sense of global citizenship.

- *Supporting skills development.* Provide resources and training opportunities to enhance children's philanthropic skills, leadership abilities and understanding of social issues. For example, Payne et al (2020) highlight through their research that even for the youngest of children aged three to five, as children are given more agency to practise everyday civicness, children's civic capabilities expand.

- *Advocating child participation.* Promote policies and practices that respect and encourage children's right to participate in decision-making processes concerning philanthropy and social issues (Body et al, 2021).

- *Empower children's leadership.* Encourage children's engagement in leadership and involve children in decision-making processes. Participatory activities can include the creation of youth advisory boards or committees where children can meaningfully influence philanthropic strategies and grant allocations (see Patuzzi and Pinto, 2022).

Conclusion

In recognising the potential of children as active contributors to philanthropy and civic engagement, the philanthropic ecosystem stands at a crossroads. It can continue as normal, sidelining children, or it can turn its attention to holistically engaging children in a meaningful way. By valuing children's voices and nurturing their philanthropic citizenship, philanthropy can significantly impact the trajectory of societal progress and cultivate a generation of compassionate and empowered change makers. However, in order for this vision to materialise, philanthropic funders must undergo some profound reflection themselves, re-evaluating funding models, modes of operation and priorities regarding the inclusion and empowerment of children. First and foremost, philanthropy must reassess its funding models to prioritise initiatives that directly engage children in philanthropic endeavours and active civic engagement. Traditional grant-making approaches often overlook children's agency and perspectives, favouring projects led by adults or established organisations. By allocating resources specifically for programmes that empower children to initiate and lead philanthropic initiatives, philanthropy can catalyse a transformative shift towards more inclusive and participatory practices.

Moreover, philanthropic funders must reconsider its modes of operation to amplify children's voices and agency within their own decision-making processes. Too often, children are sidelined in discussions concerning philanthropic investments and strategic planning, despite being key stakeholders in issues that affect their lives and communities. Philanthropic organisations should actively seek out opportunities to involve children in governance structures, advisory boards and grant-making committees, ensuring their perspectives are not only heard but are also given due consideration in shaping philanthropic priorities and interventions. Additionally, philanthropic funders must re-align their priorities to recognise the intrinsic value of children's contributions to social change and community development. Children possess unique insights, creativity and empathy that can enrich philanthropic efforts and drive innovative solutions to complex societal challenges. By reframing children not merely as beneficiaries, but as active agents of philanthropy, philanthropic organisations can foster a culture of mutual respect, collaboration and reciprocity, where children are valued as equal partners in the pursuit of collective wellbeing.

Furthermore, philanthropic funders have a responsibility to invest in capacity-building initiatives that equip children with the skills, knowledge and resources necessary to effectively engage in philanthropic citizenship, and organisations with the knowledge, skills, systems and structures to enable that to happen. This entails providing opportunities for leadership development, civic education and experiential learning that empower children to advocate for social justice, promote equity and enact positive change within their communities. Philanthropic support for youth-led organisations, mentoring programmes and peer-to-peer networks can nurture a generation of resilient and visionary leaders who are equipped to address the complex challenges of the 21st century.

Ultimately, by embracing a child-centred approach to philanthropy, the philanthropic ecosystem can harness the full potential of children as catalysts for social transformation. As philanthropic organisations grapple with pressing global issues such as inequality, poverty, climate change and injustice, they must recognise that children are not merely passive recipients of charity, but active agents of change with the capacity to shape the future of our world. By valuing children's voices, investing in their empowerment, adopting more democratic modes of operation and fostering a culture of inclusion and respect, philanthropy can fulfil its promise of creating a more just, equitable and compassionate society for generations to come.

11

Children as change makers: unleashing children's *real* philanthropic power

Introduction

I am not the first person, or indeed the last, to seek to question the systems and structures under which our children are raised. Nor am I the first (or last) to seek to critique the role and understanding of philanthropy in our society. Nonetheless, I do hope this book brings a renewed focus on the role of children as change makers through the lens of philanthropy and philanthropic citizenship.

In this book I have sought to question how we raise our children as philanthropic citizens. Philanthropy, often associated with power and privilege, is a subject of intense debate and criticism. While acknowledging these concerns, I argue for a shift in focus towards the central question of what it means to be philanthropic and why it matters. While Chapters 1 and 2 seek to outline some of the concepts and challenges behind these ideas, Chapters 3–7 focus on the spaces and places in which children can begin their philanthropic and citizenship journey, but, as argued, too often framed in a very particular discourse. Chapters 8 and 9 focus more on engaging children in collective action, community empowerment and change making, while Chapter 10 draws on the voices of civil society leaders to consider: where next? Across these chapters I have sought to challenge traditional views of philanthropic engagement, especially in terms of how children are socialised into philanthropic behaviours, and I have advocated for a model of children's philanthropic citizenship that encourages different ways of engagement rooted in critical thinking, collective action and social justice.

Ultimately this book argues that fostering an active and thriving civil society is crucial for a fair and just world. Therefore, in this last chapter I will outline what I think (some of) the most pressing tasks are that lie ahead of us all within the philanthropic ecosystem:

1. We must hold, and indeed defend, the space for children and young people (and us all) to consider, debate, deliberate, voice and act on issues they care about.
2. We need to ensure we challenge and continue to challenge institutionalised notions of what is seen as good and selfless, and support children and young people's critical engagement in the causes that matter to them.

3. We should foster collective action and seek a greater redistribution of power.

1. Holding the space

'Holding the space' is a phrase often used in the context of providing emotional support and creating a safe, nonjudgemental environment for individuals to express themselves. This is important. I argue that it also means a physical, literal defence of the spaces and places where children can critically explore, express and act upon their own opinions. In both senses, we need to hold the space for children's voices, both with and on behalf of children. If you are reading this book, then it is likely you are already an actor within the philanthropic ecosystem; maybe you run a charity or nonprofit; maybe you support, educate and engage children and young people as a teacher, parent, carer or practitioner; maybe you fund work with children and young people; or maybe you are simply an interested member of a community. Nonetheless, your responsibility towards helping children to unleash their real philanthropic power remains.

Defending the right to voice

As I outlined in Chapter 2 of this book, I, along with many others, argue that there is a concerning narrative forming around protest and many forms of activism, which is closing the spaces and places in which all people, including children, can meaningfully explore and voice what type of world they wish to live in and the type of citizen they need to be in order to make that vision a reality. My argument in this book is not to say what that world should look like, but to argue that we should root this thinking in ideas of justice, inclusivity, fairness, compassion and equality, for the good of all in society.

Nevertheless, the focus of media, education policy, literature, uniformed groups and (some) political voices mean that spaces for children, and indeed for us all, to critically engage in these debates and voice their opinions are narrowing. It is therefore down to us to hold the space, to come together to defend children, and all our rights to protest, rights to voice and rights to peacefully advocate for others without fear of persecution. This means civil society organisations, foundations, philanthropists and voluntary action groups campaigning for proactive policies which protect that right, and holding governments and politicians to account when those spaces are under threat. While this activity does take place to some extent, those actors raising their heads above the parapets remains niche – while too many voices still remain silent as other institutions come under attack for 'wokism', when trying to address issues of social justice, in a socially constructed 'culture war'. Indeed, research from King's College, London (Duffy et al, 2022) suggests that the growing perception of a 'culture war' dividing the UK populace is strikingly evident, with a majority of 54 per cent now subscribing to this belief – an increase from 46 per cent in 2020. This shift has decisively wielded and is indicative of the rising prominence of terms like 'being woke' and 'cancel culture', alongside a notable transition in how the term 'woke' is perceived. A total of 36 per cent of the population view it as an insult, while only 26 per cent consider it a compliment. These shifts parallel a remarkable surge in media utilisation of phrases such as 'culture wars', 'cancel culture' and 'white privilege'. To illustrate, 'cancel culture' made its debut in UK newspapers in 2018, featuring in only six articles. By 2021, this number had skyrocketed to 3,670 articles referencing the term (Duffy et al, 2022).

In a world marked by escalating inequality, persistent discrimination, armed conflict, authoritarianism and governance crisis, along with mounting global threats to livelihoods and the environment, protests have become increasingly prevalent. Sadly, instead of addressing urgent concerns and fostering dialogue to rectify injustice, abuses and discrimination, states across the globe often resort to stigmatising and suppressing peaceful protesters through endorsing this culture wars narrative. Protecting the right to protests and engage in nonviolent activism is essential in order to foster a society that values dynamic and public expressions of human rights. As was discussed in Chapter 8, throughout history, protests have served as a powerful platform for children and young people to voice dissent, share opinions, expose injustice and demand accountability from those in power. This collective mobilisation, which is marked by creativity and peaceful defiance, acts as a necessary check on entrenched and unaccountable power structures, and seeks to propel the advancement of human rights. Many significant strides in global human rights have been made thanks to the bravery of individuals who dared to advocate for a more inclusive and equal society, despite the risks and challenges they encountered. Everyone, including children, should be afforded the opportunity to engage in protests safely and without discrimination.

Defending the space

Protest is one form of activism and it is important that we defend legal encroachment which seeks to diminish that space for voice, for all our sakes. However, holding space for children's voices extends beyond legal and political realms. It involves creating environments in homes, schools, communities and various platforms where children can freely express themselves, advocate for their beliefs, and act philanthropically and participate in civil society. It is the bedrock of supporting children's voices, spaces where they can practise their everyday civicness and develop their citizenship. It requires us to both maintain and create spaces which encourage active listening, respect and encouragement without imposing judgements, empowering children by valuing their perspectives, fostering trust, and providing safe and inclusive environments. Nonetheless, these spaces are shrinking, particularly in the UK context as austerity bites, crucial services are lost and culture wars reduce discussions to binary, divisive narratives which lose space for nuanced and critical discussion. In addressing this, I suggest we need to focus on three key areas of activity, younger voices, youth services and education.

A focus on younger children

As has been argued throughout this book, there is an urgent need for us to focus on younger children when seeking to cultivate lifelong philanthropic citizenship. This is crucial for several reasons. The challenges faced by civil society in the UK and beyond, such as persistent poverty and the decline in natural spaces, have far-reaching implications for children's futures (Thunburg, 2024; HM Government, 2018). Philanthropic action is acknowledged as one mechanism to address these challenges (Payton and Moody, 2008), especially for the younger generation who are excluded from formal democratic processes such as voting. While there has been an increased focus on adolescents as future political and social actors, there is a notable gap in attention towards younger children. Nonetheless, research suggests that involving children in philanthropic actions before the age of ten significantly increases the likelihood that they will sustain such behaviours throughout their lifetime (Arthur et al, 2017). Promoting children's rights and providing positive experiences in their early years helps them develop a personal ownership and identity in their beliefs, actions and responsibilities (George et al, 2017). While intrinsic motivation and natural development play a significant role in prosocial behaviour, socialisation remains crucial in furthering the development of empathy, compassion and altruistic acts (Feigin et al, 2014; Berliner and Masterson, 2015). Nonetheless, civic participation demands cognitive and social skills, which are crucial for navigating diverse contexts (Haste, 2004; Pontes et al, 2019). Studies emphasise that political knowledge in children is developed early on (van Deth et al, 2011; Gotzmann, 2015; Abendschon and Tausendpfund, 2017), underscoring the importance of civic learning during middle childhood (the ages of four to 11) for future social, civic and political engagement (Dias and Menezes, 2014). Therefore, by focusing on middle childhood, we have an opportunity to help cultivate their philanthropic behaviours positively, encouraging them to help others and to engage in philanthropic activities from a young age (Warneken and Tomasello, 2008; Wildeboer et al, 2017). Taking this then a step further, encouraging active participation and critical curiosity, framed in a discourse of justice, lays the foundations for a lifelong commitment to justice-oriented, civic engagement, framed by allyship and solidarity, potentially contributing to the overall wellbeing of civil society and democracy.

Advocating for and supporting youth services

In response to the urgent need for systemic change in the support systems for children and young people, this book is a call to action for all stakeholders to stand in solidarity in order to advocate for the governmental prioritisation for children and young people's support services. As was argued in Chapter 10, the current state of the support system surrounding children and youth is widely acknowledged as problematic, with civil society leaders recognising its inadequacies and calling for transformation. Indeed, the damaging impact of austerity over a decade (2008–2018) is tracked in a previous book I wrote (Body, 2020), and the situation has only worsened since then. Thus, the discussion about organisations supporting children and youth civic and philanthropic engagement cannot occur in isolation; it requires a broader consideration of the children and youth sector in the UK. Youth services have long provided an important and valuable space for children and young people to engage in social action, develop their agency, and receive support for proactive participation in community and democratic decision-making. These services encompass a wide range of activities, from expressing themselves through art, sports, and literature to participating in campaigns, volunteering programmes, youth participation projects and formal democratic processes such as youth councils. The role of the youth worker is particularly important for engaging children and youth from the most disadvantaged backgrounds (Body and Hogg, 2019). The significant decline in funding for youth services in the UK since 2010, coupled with the absence of a cohesive national youth policy, has resulted in a fragmented and reactive approach to youth work. This has led to the closure of over 750 youth centres and the loss of over 14,000 youth workers, fundamentally reshaping the landscape of children and youth services.

Simultaneously, initiatives like *#iwill* aimed to instil civic duty and service in young individuals, but faced challenges in terms of achieving meaningful shifts in youth participation in civil society. While the programme made significant investments, these were tiny compared to the reduction in funding for comprehensive youth services. Thus, the struggle between addressing immediate concerns, such as mental health and the cost of living, versus supporting children's philanthropic citizenship weighs heavily on civil society organisations. Philanthropy, while crucial, cannot replace the losses incurred through government funding cuts, creating challenges for charities to navigate the changing landscape and fulfil quasi-welfare roles. The reduction in funding for universal youth service provision compromises the holistic approach needed to support diverse children's needs, hindering their development of agency, voice and active citizenship. Thus, addressing the challenges and opportunities for cultivating children's philanthropic citizenship requires collective advocacy for the restoration of funding and a holistic approach to children and youth services.

Focus on citizenship education in primary schools

The paramount importance of citizenship education in schools, as opposed to a narrow focus on character and the individual, is underscored throughout the book (see Chapters 2, 4 and 6), and supported both by the literature and across the voices of civil society leaders. In this book I advocate for schools as dynamic agents in fostering democratic ideals, where the culture of school's mirrors democratic principles, especially in citizenship education. Research shows us the importance of fostering civic and political literacies early on and the impact of meaningful, experiential active citizenship opportunities in middle childhood. Thus, primary schools become a core focus for this engagement. This views schools not merely as places of education but also as miniature communities, incubators for the development of democratic citizens who actively engage with their social relations.

However, as was seen in Chapter 6, while many schools are committed to offering civic learning opportunities for children, this is far from universal, and both the quantity and quality of opportunities are unevenly dispersed, as schools face increasing pressure to act as quasi-welfare state providers, deliver an ever-increasingly transactional, test-facing curriculum and balance their own books (Body et al, 2024). Children from the most privileged backgrounds are most likely to have early access to active civic and philanthropic engagement opportunities, and thus are most likely to be equipped with the skills for this type of citizenship engagement as they enter secondary school. The potential implications of this are that certain socioeconomic groups are more readied for participative active citizenship engagement than others, increasing the likelihood of these voices being more dominant as they grow, rather than an approach which fully embraces *all* children's voices. Thus, I place emphasis on embedding philanthropic and active citizenship into the curriculum, alongside supporting teachers to develop the skills and confidence to deliver such opportunities and recognising the positive potential of partnerships with civil society organisations to achieve the transformative potential of schools.

Civil society leaders also recognise schools as crucial partners and the need for active citizenship to be built into a values-driven curriculum. The role of teachers, their understanding and embodiment of the concept echo this vision of broader social interconnectedness within schools. Citizenship education is positioned as a key component in preparing children for modern society, providing skills for life and work, and fostering problem-solving abilities, yet remains ambiguous at best within primary education. Philanthropic citizenship, as a distinct part of citizenship education, emphasises the 'active' part of citizenship – the doing – and calls for a cultural shift within educational institutions.

Despite challenges, the overarching vision shared by civil society leaders, educators and associated funders is clear: every child and young person should have the opportunity to engage in user-led collective, community action projects early on, helping to cultivate informed and engaged citizens. As was identified in Chapter 6, we know that the power of civil society organisations working with this space, helping to support programmes of activities, particularly in areas of deprivation, which adopt justice-oriented, experiential approaches, will reap big rewards in terms of engagement of children as active, philanthropic citizens. This should become an important focus of funding for foundations and funders interested in this space. While in the longer term, our focus together should be on securing and recognising active citizenship education as a key part of the formal curriculum, while giving schools the freedom and support to design this with their children and engage in partnerships to help children unleash their true philanthropic power.

2. Challenge institutionalised notions of the good citizen

Previous narratives relating to how children learn to give often propose a deficit model of care, starting from a standpoint which suggests that as values break down in society, institutions must find ways to nurture children's philanthropic spirit. Over 25 years ago, in his book *Learning to Care*, Wuthnow argued that if young people were not taught to do good deeds through 'instruction and reflection', they would become 'cynical and self-serving' (1995, p 10). Wuthnow also stated that 'kindness is seldom easy to instil in children, as parents know, as it is usually overshadowed by petty jealousies, egoism, and self-interest' (1995, p 22). Bentley (2002) raises concerns about who will teach children to be philanthropic, while implying societal breakdown:

> Where do children learn to care for others? Traditionally, we think of home and school as important socialising partners. But home is not what it used to be. Today's child is likely to grow up under the loose guidance of an overworked, financially strapped single parent. Many schools, struggling just to provide a safe educational environment, are in no position to fill the gaps in a child's philanthropic education. (Bentley, 2002, pp 21–22)

I reject this deficit of care model. Having worked with children for a significant period of my career, from all backgrounds and all walks of life, I, like the civil society leaders in Chapter 10 and exemplified by the countless examples contained in this book, find a collective of young individuals who are passionate about various causes, justice and equity. It is when we shut down their voices and views on these topics that we disempower them. I come from a standpoint which assumes that most children care significantly, but too many people do not always care enough about those children to listen.

I once got into a debate with a fellow academic about my work, who accused me of wanting all children to become protesting activists. I felt he missed the point of my argument. I don't want every child to take to the streets in protest or engage in peaceful activism. What I want is every child to know they can do so if they wish to, and in doing so, they will be safe in the knowledge that their voice and rights are being respected. I argue for them to understand the full range of tools at their disposal in their philanthropic toolbox (see Chapter 4) and to be supported to wield these effectively, as they see fit. It is a subtle difference. It is not my job or that of any other adult to tell our children and young people what to think and how to respond to every issue, or to tell them what social and/or environmental causes they should care about or prioritise most. But it is all our jobs to equip children and young people with the tools, knowledge, curiosity, wisdom and skills to be able to critically consider and question the world around them, to investigate, to be intrigued and to be passionate about what they care about. And it is our job to ensure that when children seek to express their voice, they are safe, they are listened to and they are respected.

Dean points out that charity and philanthropy 'exist in a larger social, political, and cultural swirl that defines the rules of what is seen as good or selfless' (Dean, 2020, p 157). It is from this viewpoint that I argue that currently what we view as the good citizen is being carefully curated in certain spaces, including political discourses, educational spaces and some civil society organisations themselves, to limit and suppress children and young people's notions of citizenship. Too often, children's philanthropic and active citizenship is bounded in notions of duty, service and virtue. I am not against the ideas of civic duty, service and virtues per se; what I am against is this being used to close down the additional spaces children have to explore these ideas further. Challenging institutionalised notions of what is seen as 'good' and 'selfless' while supporting children and young people's critical engagement in charitable, social and environmental causes requires a multifaceted approach. Children should be encouraged to foster a sense of critical thinking, questioning and the skills to critically analyse societal norms and beliefs. This involves actively teaching and encouraging children to research and explore different perspectives of history and social movements, including instances where conventional beliefs are challenged.

Chapter 3 underscores that while kindness is a crucial starting point, it should not serve as the sole endpoint for fostering a more equitable and just society, and helping to transition children from kindness to solidarity and allyship aligns with the broader goal of cultivating active, justice-oriented citizens. Nonetheless, Chapters 4 and 5 highlighted how traditional engagement in activities such as fundraising often confines children to virtuous modes of philanthropy, celebrated as heroes in media and societal discourses, reinforcing notions of the good citizen in a discourse of individualistic civic duty and service. However, when children challenge these bounded notions in their philanthropic actions through actions such as campaigning and protest, as seen in Chapter 9, narratives become complex, less celebratory and risk reinforcing adult supremacy, pushing children to the outskirts of political and social debates, under the guise of adult protectionism. These narratives risk being reinforced through education (see Chapter 6) and uniformed groups (see Chapter 7), increasingly emphasising character and individual virtues.

I argue that reconsidering notions of the good citizen involves moving beyond mere kindness towards allyship and solidarity, which are crucial for genuine social justice and equality. While kindness operates universally, allyship goes beyond individual acts, where in being a good citizen we recognise our moral responsibility to actively support and advocate for marginalised groups. If we return to our parable of the river in Chapter 4, it is about teaching children that good citizenship encourages us to pull the babies out of the river, while simultaneously questioning and seeking to rectify why the babies are ending up in the river in the first place! Solidarity, when individuals unite in support, is grounded in a commitment to dismantling oppressive systems and promoting equity, while allyship involves individuals outside marginalized groups using privilege for positive change. The distinction lies in involvement: solidarity entails direct experience, and allies act based on a commitment to justice. Embracing allyship and solidarity as part of our citizenship broadens civic responsibility, encouraging citizens to dismantle oppressive structures and promote a more just society. Nonetheless, both allyship and solidarity share a fundamental connection – the need for collective action.

3. Foster collective action and collective power

The imperative to foster collective action and redistribute power intertwines intricately with defending the space for children's voices and challenging institutionalised notions of the good citizen, forming a final import thread for the engagement of children in societal transformation. Fostering collective action, which actively engages children, as exemplified by impactful initiatives such as Citizens UK and the dynamic youth-led climate movements highlighted in Chapter 9, emerges as an important catalyst with significant transformative potential. This approach, which is rooted in coordinated efforts and collaboration, involves children in diverse forms of social action, community organising, advocacy campaigns and participation in social movements. Through community organising efforts, such as those depicted in the case studies of St Lawrence Primary School, First Give, the Linking Network and Led by the Wild CIC, children actively contribute to addressing local issues ranging from improved school facilities to environmental concerns. Simultaneously, the advocacy campaigns portrayed in the case studies of Young Citizens and the Woodcraft Folk showcase young activists participating in broader movements for climate action, social justice and human rights. Aligning with international frameworks, notably the UNCRC, the inclusion of children in collective action becomes a manifestation of their rights to freedom of expression, association, and peaceful assembly. It becomes a strategic effort to nurture a sense of civic responsibility, agency and empowerment among children, which can be supported by all philanthropic actors within the philanthropic ecosystem. This inclusivity not only recognises their unique perspectives but also positions children as valuable contributors, both now and in the future, to decision-making processes that shape a more inclusive, equitable and just society.

As Edgar Villanueva (2018) points out in his excellent book *Decolonizing Wealth*, philanthropic organisations across the globe continue to perpetuate the social architecture inherited from colonialism. All too often, decision makers are made up of individuals who do not represent the communities they serve, and funding priorities are donor and founder-centric rather than based on community-led identified needs. These trends feature across all levels of the sector, particularly within many of our traditional, longstanding organisations and foundations. Seeking to share power with children and young people within these spaces becomes one way in which we can begin to dismantle these systems. Engaging children in these conversations is a powerful way in which we help them recognise that deep-seated inequalities have roots in past injustices, compelling us to confront the advantages certain groups have enjoyed due to years of economic, social, gender and racial bias. These advantages have made generational success seem more attainable for some, while others are left struggling. Collective, justice-oriented approaches to this provide a powerful space in which we can perhaps begin to right historical wrongs, we can rebalance the scales and move away from narratives of the fortunate and less fortunate, and we can shift away from ideas of 'us' and 'them', and discourses which 'otherise' certain groups of individuals, instead embracing more collective responses of 'we'. A social justice approach to philanthropic citizenship focuses on addressing the root causes of systemic injustices, such as racial discrimination, economic inequality, gender bias and other forms of oppression. It recognises that true change requires collective efforts to tackle the underlying structural issues that perpetuate inequality.

To achieve this, we need to start by being transparent about philanthropy and the roots of wealth. In part, it is now down to philanthropic foundations and other funders to help children view philanthropic endeavours through a different lens. Indeed, significant progress has been made in this direction with several large foundations actively seeking to address and redress their sources of wealth, which are rooted in colonialism. Nonetheless, in the majority of cases, power continues to reside in nonrepresentative decision makers and funding priorities designed by donor and founders rather than based on collective, community-identified needs.

To achieve this, as the final thread to achieving cultural shifts, we need to change our funding and grant-giving practices; transitioning philanthropy from individualised donor-centric approaches to collective decision making necessitates a multifaceted and intentional strategy, emphasising the empowerment of children, young people and communities. Adopting participatory decision-making processes, like establishing empowered youth decision-making boards, is a foundational step in shaping philanthropic agendas. Community-centric, child-led methodologies prioritise unique community needs through deep listening and co-designing initiatives with children and young people. Investing in capacity-building programmes for children equips young individuals with skills and knowledge, enhancing their agency and contributing to community-driven initiatives. A paradigm shift in resource allocation is crucial, emphasising equitable distribution based on authentic community needs. And as was highlighted in Chapter 10, cultural competence and inclusivity, long-term partnerships, holistic impact measurement and education efforts amplify the transformative potential of inclusive and participatory approaches. Evolving practices, marked by buzzwords like equity and social justice, prompt crucial questions about funding distribution and the identity of funders and decision makers. The true power shift involves acknowledging historical contexts, addressing systemic barriers and supporting the most marginalised communities through fair funding distribution, as well as actively engaging children, especially those with direct lived experience, in these discussions and processes, emphasising justice over charity. Fundamental to the power shift is humility, recognising that children have the right to be included in decision making which impacts their lives.

Limitations

There are of course weaknesses and limitations within the arguments contained in this book to acknowledge. First, there is a lack of child-led, child-oriented literature within this space, especially within the field of philanthropic studies. While I argue that for too long children's voices have been excluded from the philanthropic decision-making processes and responses more generally in society, so too have we as academics, scholars and researchers overlooked their voices within this field. We know very little about the lived experiences of younger fundraisers and change makers (especially those who are of primary school age), the long-term impacts of different forms of engagement or indeed how children interpret, digest and respond to ideas of charity and philanthropy within schools, in the media and online. We know too little about how engagement in active citizenship impacts emotional wellbeing, long-term engagement or community participation, and thus as with most research, it requires further investigation and exploration.

Second, this book largely focuses on the role of civil society organisations and educational spaces for active citizenship. In doing so, wider discussions around the impacts of family, religiosity, diversity, gender and so on are touched upon but not given full consideration. Indeed, each topic could itself command a whole book or more in discussing the implications of these factors on children's philanthropic citizenship, and again warrants further research and investigation.

Third, this book adopts a child's rights-oriented approach rooted in a progressive understanding of philanthropy and justice. While advocating for child-led approaches, some may argue that a challenge lies in the potential for paternalism, where adults may inadvertently impose their perspectives on children, limiting their autonomy. Additionally, others may argue that there is a risk of instrumentalising children as symbols of virtue, overshadowing the genuine motivations behind their philanthropic actions. Striking a balance between fostering a sense of justice and ensuring age-appropriate engagement becomes imperative to avoid these pitfalls and to cultivate a genuine, informed commitment to philanthropy among children.

Finally, such a framing is open to criticism, most notably from proponents of more traditional forms of donor-centric philanthropy or critics of an analysis which is rooted in a socially just-orientated, progressive ideology.

Nonetheless, I offer this book up as a conversation starter, a space and a stimulant to provide discussion and debate, and most importantly as an energiser to rethink, reignite and reinvigorate the conversation around children as change makers, placing children centrally within and leading on the discussion, and working with them to release their philanthropic power, as both current and future social actors.

Conclusion

Martin Luther King (2019) himself said: 'Philanthropy is commendable, but it must not cause the philanthropist to overlook the circumstances of economic injustice, which make philanthropy necessary.' To this statement I would personally add 'and possible'!

Indeed, King's words highlight a central contradiction within philanthropy and philanthropic giving – that 'big' philanthropy, for all it hopes to achieve, arises from vast inequalities in wealth and our market systems from which individuals reap grossly unequal rewards, yet it is often at the forefront of addressing these exploitations and inequalities. Traditional views of philanthropy situate it as a spectrum with charity at one end and social justice at the other. Charity is commonly perceived as the acts of the many, whereas philanthropy is reserved for the privileged few who we situate as philanthropists. This model means these wealthy individuals wield significant power in determining what justice is, while most people – those most commonly with the lived experience of injustice – are left in the realms of both, donors to and beneficiaries of charity, often oscillating between the two. At least, this is the world of philanthropy into which we socialise our children. In this book I hope to have challenged these assumptions and to have asked what would happen if we switched that scenario around. What if power sat within the collective voices of the many and not the privileged few? And what if philanthropy and philanthropic actors helped make that happen?

While there has been widespread discussion on the idea of philanthropy for justice, what I hope to have shown over the course of the discussions in this book is that often the way in which we socialise children as the philanthropic citizens of today and tomorrow is still embedded in a framework that grounds and bounds children's philanthropic actions in charity, not justice. A framework rooted in charity alone encourages our children to give and respond to social ills while ignoring the realities, both past and present, that force communities and individuals into oppressive situations. Furthermore, it reinforces the giver with rewards for their benevolence, further depoliticising the conversation of injustice and inequality. It does little to question the perpetuation and reproduction of inequality, inequity and oppression. Children are often introduced and socialised into bounded notions of citizenship, which are imbued with notions of civic duty and service.

What I propose is a fundamental shift towards a framework of justice that engages children and young people not only in the act of philanthropy, but one which questions the role of philanthropy itself. Throughout this book I do not argue that benevolence is not admirable; indeed, the virtues underpinning the character traits that encourage giving are important. What I am saying is it is not enough to teach philanthropy as benevolence; it limits children's voices and removes them from the mainstream discussion about their own lived experiences. By teaching and engaging children in philanthropy in a framework of justice, such as the examples in the latter chapters of this book and in many of the case studies explored here, we retain space to question prevailing attitudes, to question beliefs, and to question societal and governmental responses to social and environmental concerns. Unleashing our power as philanthropic citizens should not confine any of us to the realm of benevolence; it should be a space in which we can interrogate and break down social divides and institutional policies which promote and maintain inequality.

In conclusion, this book calls for a re-evaluation of our approach to philanthropy and the socialisation of our children as philanthropic citizens. It challenges the inherent paradox in philanthropy, resulting from vast wealth disparities, and calls for a transformative shift from charity-rooted perspectives to justice-oriented frameworks. The narrative of privileged individuals dictating what justice is must give way to a collective power dynamic in which every voice, including those of children, holds influence. The ideas put forward in this book suggests a profound shift towards this framework of justice – one that actively involves children and young people not only in the practice of philanthropic actions as one way in which to address societal issues, but also in critically questioning the very nature of philanthropy itself. Confining our children's voices to the realm of benevolence alone, stifles their voices and excludes them from the broader discourse about their own lived experiences. Instead, it should be a space where alongside expressing generosity and kindness, we can also support them to actively and critically question and challenge social divisions, structural inequalities and institutional policies that propagate and sustain inequality. By supporting and engaging children in philanthropy within a framework of justice, we create room to challenge prevailing attitudes, beliefs and policies – and we help them and us to create a fairer society for all.

References

Abendschön, S. and Tausendpfund, M. (2017) Political knowledge of children and the role of sociostructural factors. *American Behavioral Scientist*, 61(2): 204–221.

Adriani, F. and Sonderegger, S. (2009) Why do parents socialize their children to behave pro-socially? An information-based theory. *Journal of Public Economics*, 93(11–12): 1119–1124.

Agard, K.A. (2002) Learning to give: teaching philanthropy K–12. *New Directions for Philanthropic Fundraising*, 2002(36): 37–54.

Aksoy, P. and Baran, G. (2020) The effect of story telling-based and play-based social skills training on social skills of kindergarten children: an experimental study. *Egitim ve Bilim*, 45(204): 157–183.

Alexander, N., Petray, T. and McDowall, A. (2022) More learning, less activism: narratives of childhood in Australian media representations of the School Strike for Climate. *Australian Journal of Environmental Education*, 38(1): 96–111.

Allen, K. and Bull, A. (2018) Following policy: a network ethnography of the UK character education policy community. *Sociological Research Online*, 23(2): 438–458.

Allred, A. and Amos, C. (2018) Disgust images and nonprofit children's causes. *Journal of Social Marketing*, 1(8): 120–140.

Allsop, B., Briggs, J. and Kisby, B. (2018) Market values and youth political engagement in the UK: towards an agenda for exploring the psychological impacts of neo-liberalism. *Societies*, 8(4): 95. doi: 10.3390/soc8040095

Arnstein, S.R. (1969). A ladder of citizen participation. *Journal of the American Institute of Planners*, 35(4): 216–224.

Arthur, J., Harrison, T., Taylor-Collins, E. and Moller, F. (2017) *A Habit of Service: The Factors That Sustain Service*. Jubilee Centre for Character and Virtues, University of Birmingham Report. Available at: https://www.jubileecentre.ac.uk/1581/projects/youth-social-action/a-habit-of-service (Accessed: 24 August 2023).

Asah, S.T., Bengston, D.N., Westphal, L.M. and Gowan, C.H. (2018) Mechanisms of children's exposure to nature: predicting adulthood environmental citizenship and commitment to nature-based activities. *Environment and Behavior*, 50(7): 807–836.

Baden-Powell, R. (2004 [1908]) *Scouting for Boys: A Handbook for Instruction in Good Citizenship*. Oxford: Oxford University Press.

Bannister, C. (2022) *Scouting and Guiding in Britain: The Ritual Socialisation of Young People*. London: Springer Nature.

Barnardo's (2022a) 'I am concerned about young people's mental health and that they have less hope for their future': practitioners' emerging concerns for young people between June 2019 to November 2021. Available at: https://www.barnardos.org.uk/research/practitioners-concerns-iss ues-facing-young-people (Accessed: 1 September 2023).

Barnardo's (2022b) More children at risk as councils forced to halve spending on early support. 22 July. Available at: https://www.barnardos.org.uk/ news/more-children-risk-councils-forced-halve-spending-early-support (Accessed: 1 September 2023).

Barrett, M. and Pachi, D. (2019) *Youth Civic and Political Engagement*. Abingdon: Routledge.

Bates, A. (2019) Character education and the 'priority of recognition'. *Cambridge Journal of Education*, 49(6): 695–710.

Batty, D. (2005) Youth movement lost funding 'because of anti-war protests'. *The Guardian*, 16 March. Available at: https://www.theguardian.com/ society/2005/mar/16/childrensservices.politicsandiraq (Accessed: 11 August 2023).

BBC Children in Need (2023) *Annual Report and Accounts*. BBC Children in Need.

BBC News (2016) Bear Grylls hails six-year-old hero scout who helped save a life. 11 August. Available at: https://www.bbc.co.uk/news/educat ion-37047048 (Accessed: 31 August 2023).

BBC News (2021a) 'Lemonade stand' boys get Gold Blue Peter badges for Yemen fundraising'. 25 February. Available at: https://www.bbc.co.uk/ news/uk-england-london-56202255 (Accessed: 24 August 2023).

BBC News (2021b) Max Woosey: Devon camping challenge boy pitches tent at No 10. 9 July. Available at: https://www.bbc.co.uk/news/uk-engl and-devon-57782725 (Accessed: 31 August 2023).

BBC News (2023a) Boy in the Tent': Max Woosey sets Guinness World Record for charity camp-out. 29 March. Available at: https://www.bbc. co.uk/news/uk-england-devon-65110616 (Accessed: 31 August 2023).

BBC News (2023b) Sunderland boy, 5, is 'youngest' to finish Coast-to-Coast. 3 September. Available at: https://www.bbc.co.uk/news/uk-engl and-tyne-66700736 (Accessed: 4 September 2023).

BBC Newsbeat (2023) MrBeast: why has YouTuber faced criticism for blind surgery video?' 1 February. Available at: https://www.bbc.co.uk/news/ newsbeat-64490431 (Accessed: 22 October 2023).

BBC Newsround (2023) Montana children win fossil fuel court case against state. 16 August. Available at: https://www.bbc.co.uk/newsround/59829 183 (Accessed: 12 October 2024).

Beaty, A. (2019) *Sofia Valdez, Future Prez*. New York: Abrams Books.

Beck, D. and Purcell, R. (2013) *International Community Organising: Taking Power, Making Change*. Bristol: Policy Press.

Ben-Ner, A., List, J.A., Putterman, L. and Samek, A. (2017) Learned generosity? An artefactual field experiment with parents and their children. *Journal of Economic Behavior & Organization*, 143: 28–44.

Bentley, R.J. (2002) Speaking to a higher authority: teaching philanthropy in religious settings. *New Directions for Philanthropic Fundraising*, 36: 21–36.

Berliner, R. and Masterson, T. (2015) Review of research: promoting empathy development in the early childhood and elementary classroom. *Childhood Education*, 91(1): 57–64.

Bernholz, L. (2021) *How We Give Now: A Philanthropic Guide for the Rest of Us*. Cambridge, MA: MIT Press.

Berrie, L., Adair, L., Williamson, L. and Dibben, C. (2023) Youth organizations, social mobility and health in middle age: evidence from a Scottish 1950s prospective cohort study. *European Journal of Public Health*, 33(1): 6–12.

Bhati, A. (2021) Is the representation of beneficiaries by international nongovernmental organizations (INGOs) still pornographic? *Journal of Philanthropy and Marketing*: e1722.

Bhati, A. and Eikenberry, A. (2016) Faces of the needy: the portrayal of destitute children in the fundraising campaigns of NGOs in India. *International Journal of Nonprofit & Voluntary Sector Marketing*, 21(1): 31–42.

Birdwell, J., Birnie, R. and Mehan, R. (2013) *The State of the Service Nation: Youth Social Action in the UK*. London: Demos.

Body, A. (2020) *Children's Charities in Crisis: Early Intervention and the State*. Bristol: Policy Press.

Body, A. (2021) Teaching philanthropic citizenship. *Compact Guides*. Available at: https://my.chartered.college/wp-content/uploads/2021/10/Body_philanthropy.pdf (Accessed: 22 May 2024).

Body, A. (2024) Raising philanthropic children: moving beyond virtuous philanthropy, towards transformative giving and empowered citizenship. *Journal of Philanthropy and Marketing*, 29(1): e1833.

Body, A. and Breeze, B. (2016) What are 'unpopular causes' and how can they achieve fundraising success? *International Journal of Nonprofit and Voluntary Sector Marketing*, 21(1): 57–70.

Body, A. and Hogg, E. (2019) What mattered ten years on? Young people's reflections on their involvement with a charitable youth participation project. *Journal of Youth Studies*, 22(2): 171–186.

Body, A. and Hogg, E. (2021) Collective co-production in English public services: the case of voluntary action in primary education. *Voluntary Sector Review*, 13(2): 243–259. doi: 10.1332/204080521X16231629157096

Body, A. and Lacny, J. (2022) Philanthropic tales: a critical analysis of how philanthropic citizenship is represented in children's picture-books – problems and possibilities. *Education, Citizenship and Social Justice*, 18(2). doi: 10.1177/17461979211061798

Body, A., Lau, E. and Josephidou, J. (2019) *Our Charitable Children – Engaging Children in Charities and Charitable Giving*. University of Kent. Available at: https://research.kent.ac.uk/philanthropy/wp-content/uplo ads/sites/2278/2020/04/OUR_CHARITABLE_CHILDREN_ENGAG ING_CHILDRE-FINAL-2019.pdf (Accessed: 2 December 2023).

Body, A., Lau, E. and Josephidou, J. (2020) Engaging children in meaningful charity: opening-up the spaces within which children learn to give. *Children & Society*, 34(3): 189–203.

Body, A., Lau, E., Cameron, L. and Ali, S. (2021) Developing a children's rights approach to fundraising with children in primary schools and the ethics of cultivating philanthropic citizenship. *Journal of Philanthropy and Marketing*, e1730.

Body, A., Lau, E., Cameron, L. and Cunliffe, J. (2023) *Educating for Public Good: Part 1. Mapping Children's Active Civic Learning*. University of Kent. https://research.kent.ac.uk/children-as-philanthropic-citizens

Body, A., Lau, E., Cameron, L. and Cunliffe, J. (2024) Mapping active civic learning in primary schools across England – a call to action. *British Educational Research Journal*. doi: 10.1002/berj.3975

Bonell, C., Hinds, K., Dickson, K., Thomas, J., Fletcher, A., Murphy, S., Melendez-Torres, G.J., Bonell, C. and Campbell, R. (2015) What is positive youth development and how might it reduce substance use and violence? A systematic review and synthesis of theoretical literature. *BMC Public Health*, 16: 1–13.

Booth, R. (2019) Scouts march back into Britain's inner cities as membership soars. *The Guardian*, 15 May. Available at: https://www.theguardian.com/ society/2019/may/15/scouts-march-back-into-britains-inner-cities-as-membership-soars (Accessed: 8 January 2024).

Bowery Boys (2010) Newsies vs the world! The newsboys strike of 1899. 11 June. Available at: https://www.boweryboyshistory.com/2010/06/news ies-vs-world-newsboys-strike-of.html (Accessed: 24 September 2023).

Brasta, Y., Mollidor, C. and Stevens, J. (2019) *National Youth Social Action Survey*. UK: #Iwill.

Breeze, B. (2021) *In Defence of Philanthropy*. Newcastle upon Tyne: Agenda Publishing.

Bridge, M. (2021) Georgian children refused to eat slave sugar. *The Times*, 31 March. Available at: https://www.thetimes.co.uk/article/georgian-child ren-refused-to-eat-slave-sugar-0frk8mcqn (Accessed: 24 September 2023).

Brodie, E., Hughes, T., Jochum, V., Miller, S., Ockenden, N. and Warburton, D. (2011) *Pathways through Participation: What Creates and Sustains Active Citizenship?* London: NCVO.

Brownlee, J.L., Walker, S., Wallace, E., Johansson, E. and Scholes, L. (2019) Doing the right thing in the early years of primary school: a longitudinal study of children's reasoning about right and wrong. *Australian Educational Researcher,* 46(5): 863–878.

Butler, P. (2023) 'Hostile, authoritarian' UK downgraded in civic freedoms index. *The Guardian*, 16 March. Available at: https://www.theguardian.com/uk-news/2023/mar/16/hostile-authoritarian-uk-downgraded-in-civic-freedoms-index (Accessed: 31 August 2023).

Butler, U.M. (2008) Children's participation in Brazil: a brief genealogy and recent innovations. *International Journal of Children's Rights*, 16(3): 301–312.

Cameron, L. (2020) *The Impact of the Linking Network: Gathering Perspectives of Schools and Linking Facilitators*. Linking Network. Available at: https://thelinkingnetwork.org.uk/about/ (Accessed: 14 October 2023).

Champine, R.B., Wang, J., Ferris, K.A., Hershberg, R.M., Erickson, K., Johnson, B.R. and Lerner, R.M. (2016) Exploring the out-of-school time program ecology of Boy Scouts. *Research in Human Development*, 13(2): 97–110.

Chang, C.T. and Lee, Y.K. (2009) Framing charity advertising: influences of message framing, image valence, and temporal framing on a charitable appeal. *Journal of Applied Social Psychology*, 39(12): 2910–2935.

Chapman, C.M., Masser, B.M. and Louis, W.R. (2020) Identity motives in charitable giving: explanations for charity preferences from a global donor survey. *Psychology & Marketing*, 37(9): 1277–1291.

Charities Aid Foundation (CAF) (2013) *Growing up Giving: Insights into How Young People Feel about Charity*. London: Charities Aid Foundation.

Ciocarlan, A., Masthoff, J. and Oren, N. (2023) Kindness makes you happy and happiness makes you healthy: actual persuasiveness and personalisation of persuasive messages in a behaviour change intervention for wellbeing. In *International Conference on Persuasive Technology*. Cham: Springer Nature Switzerland, pp 198–214.

Citizens UK (2023) About us. Available at: https://www.citizensuk.org/ (Accessed: 12 October 2023).

Civic Power Fund (2021) Growing grassroots. Available at: https://growingthegrassroots.civicpower.org.uk/chapters/background-to-this-research (Accessed: 12 October 2023).

Civicus (2023) *State of Civil Society Report 2023*. Available at: https://www.civicus.org/documents/reports-and-publications/SOCS/2023/state-of-civil-society-report-2023_en.pdf (Accessed: 31 August 2023).

Clarke, J. (2005) New Labour's citizens: activated, empowered, responsibilized, abandoned? *Critical Social Policy*, 25(4): 447–463.

Climateworks (2023) Funding trends 2023: climate change mitigation philanthropy. Available at: https://www.climateworks.org/report/funding-trends-2023/

Cloughton, I. (2021) Global youth activism on climate change. *Social Work & Policy Studies: Social Justice, Practice and Theory*, 4(1).

Coady, M. (2008) Beings and becomings: historical and philosophical considerations of the child as citizen. In G. MacNaughton, P. Hughes and K. Smith (eds) *Young Children as Active Citizens*. Newcastle: Cambridge Scholars Publishing, pp 2–14.

Coughlin, J. and Hauck, C. (2023) What kind of hero is Greta? In M. Etherington (ed) *Environmental Education: An Interdisciplinary Approach to Nature*. Eugene, OR: Wipf and Stock Publishers, p 155.

Cousteau, P. and Hopkinson, D. (2016) *Follow the Moon Home: A Tale of One Idea, Twenty Kids, and a Hundred Sea Turtles*. San Francisco: Chronicle Books.

Covell, K. and Howe, R.B. (2001) Moral education through the 3 Rs: rights, respect and responsibility. *Journal of Moral Education*, 30(1): 29–41.

Crawley, H. (2011) 'Asexual, apolitical beings': the interpretation of children's identities and experiences in the UK asylum system. *Journal of Ethnic and Migration Studies*, 37(8): 1171–1184.

Crick, B. (1998) *Education for Citizenship and the Teaching of Democracy in Schools: Final Report of the Advisory Group on Citizenship*. London: Qualifications and Curriculum Authority.

Cuevas-Parra, P. (2023) Multi-dimensional lens to Article 12 of the UNCRC: a model to enhance children's participation. *Children's Geographies*, 21(3): 363–377.

Cuevas-Parra, P. (2021) Thirty years after the UNCRC: children and young people's participation continues to struggle in a COVID-19 world. *Journal of Social Welfare and Family Law*, 43(1): 81–98.

Cultural Learning Alliance (2023) What is the National Youth Guarantee (NYG)? 26 June. Available at: https://www.culturallearningalliance.org.uk/what-is-the-national-youth-guarantee-nyg/ (Accessed: 8 January 2024).

Curry, O.S., Rowland, L.A., van Lissa, C.J., Zlotowitz, S., McAlaney, J. and Whitehouse, H. (2018) Happy to help? A systematic review and meta-analysis of the effects of performing acts of kindness on the well-being of the actor. *Journal of Experimental Social Psychology*, 76: 320–329.

Dahl, A. and Brownell, C.A. (2019) The social origins of human prosociality. *Current Directions in Psychological Science*, 28(3): 274–279.

Daly, A. (2013) Demonstrating positive obligations: children's rights and peaceful protest in international law. *George Washington International Law Review*, 45: 763.

Daly, S. (2012) Philanthropy as an essentially contested concept. *Voluntas: International Journal of Voluntary and Nonprofit Organizations*, 23: 535–557.

Danka, A. (2019) The right of children to be heard through peaceful protests. In P. Czech, L. Heschl, K. Lukas, M. Nowak and G. Oberleitner (eds) *European Yearbook on Human Rights 2019*. Cambridge: Intersentia, pp 405–416.

Davies, N. (2018) *The Day War Came*. London: Walker Books.

Davies, R. (2023) Good for ratings? MrBeast & philanthropy in the attention economy. Why philanthropy matters. Available at: https://whyphilanth ropymatters.com/article/good-for-ratings-mrbeast-philanthropy-in-the-attention-economy/

De Tocqueville, A. (1956 [1835]) *Democracy in America*. Translated by H. Reeve. New York: Vintage Books.

Dean, J. (2011) Baden-Powell's Scouting for Boys: governmentality, state power and the responsibilization of youth. Available at: https://shura.shu.ac.uk/6456/3/Dean_Scouts_paper.pdf (Accessed: 22 May 2024).

Dean, J. (2013) Manufacturing citizens: the dichotomy between policy and practice in youth volunteering in the UK. *Administrative Theory & Praxis*, 35(1): 46–62.

Dean, J. (2020) *The Good Glow: Charity and the Symbolic Power of Doing Good*. Bristol: Policy Press.

Devine-Wright, P., Devine-Wright, H. and Fleming, P. (2004) Situational influences upon children's beliefs about global warming and energy. *Environmental Education Research*, 10(4): 493–506.

Dewey, J. (1900). *The School and Society*. Chicago: University of Chicago Press.

Dewey, J. (1902) *The Educational Situation*. New York: Arno Press.

Dewey, J. (1909) *Moral Principles in Education*. New York: Arcturus Books.

Dewey, J. (1916) *Democracy and Education*. New York: The Free Press.

Dias, T. and Menezes, I. (2014) Children and adolescents as political actors: collective visions of politics and citizenship. *Journal of Moral Education*, 43(3): 250–268.

Dibben, C., Playford, C. and Mitchell, R. (2017) Be(ing) prepared: guide and Scout participation, childhood social position and mental health at age 50 – a prospective birth cohort study. *Journal of Epidemiology and Community Health*, 71(3): 275–281.

Dickson, E. (2022) Is MrBeast for real? Inside the outrageous world of YouTube's cash-happy stunt king. *Rolling Stone*, 19 April. Available at: https://www.rollingstone.com/culture/culture-features/mrbeast-yout ube-cover-story-interview-1334604/ (Accessed: 22 October 2023).

Duffy, B., Stoneman, P., Hewlett, K., May, G., Woollen, C., Norman, C., Skinner, G. and Gottfried, G. (2022) Woke, cancel culture and White privilege: the shifting terms of the UK's 'culture war'. King's College London. Available at: https://www.kcl.ac.uk/policy-institute/assets/the-shifting-terms-of-the-uks-culture-war.pdf (Accessed: 22 October 2023).

Dugmore, O. (2019) Tories confirm contempt of young people with response to climate change protests. *JOE*, 16 February. Available at: https://www.joe.co.uk/politics/tories-climate-change-protest-219964 (Accessed: 31 August 2023).

Duong, J. and Bradshaw, C.P. (2017) Links between contexts and middle to late childhood social-emotional development. *American Journal of Community Psychology*, 60(3–4): 538–554.

Durlak, J.A., Weissberg, R.P., Dymnicki, A.B., Taylor, R.D. and Schellinger, K.B. (2011) The impact of enhancing students' social and emotional learning: a meta-analysis of school-based universal interventions. *Child Development*, 82(1): 405–432.

Eidhof, B. and de Ruyter, D. (2022) Citizenship, self-efficacy and education: a conceptual review. *Theory and Research in Education*, 20(1): 64–82. doi: 10.1177/14778785221093313

Eisenberg, N. (1983) *The Socialization and Development of Empathy and Prosocial Behavior*. Tempe: Arizona State University.

Eisenberg, N. and Miller, P.A. (1987) The relation of empathy to prosocial and related behaviors. *Psychological Bulletin*, 101(1): 91.

Eisenberg, N., Fabes, R.A. and Spinrad, T.L. (2006) Prosocial Development. In N. Eisenberg, W. Damon and R.M. Lerner (eds) *Handbook of Child Psychology: Social, Emotional, and Personality Development*. Chichester: John Wiley & Sons, pp 646–718.

Eisenberg, N., Spinrad, T.L. and Knafo-Noam, A. (2015) Prosocial development. *Handbook of Child Psychology and Developmental Science*: 1–47.

Eisenberg-Berg, N. (1979) Development of children's prosocial moral judgment. *Developmental Psychology*, 15(2): 128–137.

Eskew, G. (1997) *But for Birmingham: The Local and National Movements in the Civil Rights Struggle*. Chapel Hill: University of North Carolina Press.

Fajerman, L. (2001) *Children Are Service Users, Too: A Guide to Consulting Children and Young People*. Plymouth: Save the Children Publications.

Fehr, E., Bernhard, H. and Rockenbach, B. (2008) Egalitarianism in young children. *Nature*, 454(7208): 1079–1083.

Feigin, S., Owens, G. and Goodyear-Smith, F. (2014) Theories of human altruism: a systematic review. *Journal of Psychiatry and Brain Function*, 1(5): 1–8.

Feinstein, L. and Bynner, J. (2004) The importance of cognitive development in middle childhood for adulthood socioeconomic status, mental health, and problem behavior. *Child Development*, 75(5): 1329–1339.

Fisher, R. (2008) Philosophical intelligence: what is it and how do we develop it? *Thinking: The Journal of Philosophy for Children*, 19(1): 12–19.

Fisher, R. and Ma, Y. (2014) The price of being beautiful: negative effects of attractiveness on empathy for children in need. *Journal of Consumer Research*, 41(2): 436–450.

Fitzgerald, C. (2021) Social bonding and children's collaborations as citizen-peers at primary school. *Education, Citizenship and Social Justice*, 18(1). doi:10.1177/17461979211040464

Flanagan, C. (2009) Young People's Civic Engagement and Political Development. In A. Furlong (ed) *Handbook of Youth and Young Adulthood: New Perspectives and Agendas*. Abingdon: Routledge, pp 291–300.

Fleming, C. (2003) *Boxes for Katje*. New York: Melanie Kroupa Books.

Forester, J. (2021) Our curious silence about kindness in planning: challenges of addressing vulnerability and suffering. *Planning Theory*, 20(1): 63–83.

Foster, J. (2008) Baden-Powell and the Siege of Mafeking: the enactment of Mythical place. In *Washed with Sun: Landscape and the Making of White South Africa*. Pittsburgh: University of Pittsburgh Press, pp 91–118.

Freeman, M. (2000) The future of children's rights. *Children & Society*, 14(4): 277–293.

Fretwell, N. and Barker, J. (2023) From active to activist parenting: educational struggle and the injuries of institutionalized misrecognition. In M.-P. Moreau, C. Lee and C. Okpokiri (eds) *Reinventing the Family in Uncertain Times: Education, Policy and Social Justice*. London: Bloomsbury, pp 187–208.

Galligan, A. and Miller, E.T. (2022) Justice is more important than kindness: antiracist pedagogy in a first-grade classroom. *Language Arts*, 99(5): 348–356.

Garlen, J.C. (2019) Interrogating innocence: 'childhood' as exclusionary practice. *Childhood*, 26(1): 54–67

Gasparri, G., El Omrani, O., Hinton, R., Imbago, D., Lakhani, H., Mohan, A., Yeung, W. and Bustreo, F. (2021) Children, adolescents, and youth pioneering a human rights-based approach to climate change. *Health and Human Rights*, 23(2): 95–108.

George, E., Schmidt, C., Vella, G. and McDonagh, I. (2017) Promoting the rights and responsibilities of children: a South Australian example. *Global Health Promotion*, 24(1): 53–57.

Gibbs, J. (2019) *Moral Development and Reality: Beyond the Theories of Kohlberg and Hoffman*. London: Sage.

Gibson, C. (2018) *Deciding Together: Shifting Power and Resources through Participatory Grantmaking*. Brussels: European Foundation Centre.

Gillies, V. (2014) Troubling families: parenting and the politics of early intervention. In *Thatcher's Grandchildren? Politics and Childhood in the Twenty-First Century*. London: Palgrave Macmillan, pp 204–224.

Girl Scout Research Institute (2012) *Girl Scouting Works: The Alumnae Impact Study*. Available at: https://www.girlscouts.org/content/dam/girlscouts-gsusa/forms-and-documents/about-girl-scouts/research/girl_scouting_works_the_alumnae_impact_study.pdf (Accessed: 6 November 2018).

Giroux, H.A. (1997) *Pedagogy and the Politics of Hope: Theory, Culture and Schooling – A Critical Reader*. Boulder, CO: Westview.

Gorczyca, M. and Hartman, R.L. (2017) The new face of philanthropy: the role of intrinsic motivation in millennials' attitudes and intent to donate to charitable organizations. *Journal of Nonprofit & Public Sector Marketing*, 29(4): 415–433.

Gordon, F., McAlister, S. and Scraton, P. (2015) *Behind the Headlines: Media Representation of Children and Young People in Northern Ireland: Summary of Research Findings*. Belfast: Queen's University Belfast.

Götzmann, A. (2015) *The Development of Political Knowledge in Elementary School*. Wiesbaden: Springer-Verlag.

Grylls, B. (2017) Bear Grylls on why you should follow the Scout code of conduct. *GQ*, 3 January. Available at: https://www.gq-magazine.co.uk/article/bear-grylls-scout-essentials (Accessed: 18 June 2024).

Grusec, J.E., Davidov, M. and Lundell, L. (2002) Prosocial and helping behavior. In K.S. Smith and C.H. Hart (eds) *Blackwell Handbook of Childhood Social Development*. Malden, MA: Blackwell, pp 457–474.

Hamilton, M.C., Anderson, D., Broaddus, M. and Young, K. (2006) Gender stereotyping and under-representation of female characters in 200 popular children's picture books: a twenty-first century update. *Sex Roles*, 55: 757–765.

Han, H., Kim, J., Jeong, C. and Cohen, G.L. (2017) Attainable and relevant moral exemplars are more effective than extraordinary exemplars in promoting voluntary service engagement. *Frontiers in Psychology*, 8: 283.

Hanel, P.H., Wolfradt, U., Wolf, L.J., Coelho, G.L.D.H. and Maio, G.R. (2020) Well-being as a function of person-country fit in human values. *Nature Communications*, 11(1): 5150.

Harper, P. (2016) *A People's History of the Woodcraft Folk*. London: Woodcraft Folk.

Hart, R. (1992) *Children's Participation: From Tokenism to Citizenship*. Florence: UNICEF.

Haste, H. (2004) Constructing the citizen. *Political Psychology*, 25(3): 413–439.

Haworth-Booth, A. (2021) Children on Strike. *History Workshop*, 26 July. Available at: https://www.historyworkshop.org.uk/activism-solidarity/children-on-strike (Accessed: 24 August 2023).

Hayward, B. (2020) *Children, Citizenship and Environment:#SchoolStrike Edition*. London: Routledge.

Herro, A. and Obeng-Odoom, F. (2019) Foundations of radical philanthropy. *VOLUNTAS: International Journal of Voluntary and Nonprofit Organizations*, 30: 881–890.

Hickman, C., Marks, E., Pihkala, P., Clayton, S., Lewandowski, R.E., Mayall, E.E., Wray, B., Mellor, C. and Van Susteren, L. (2021) Climate anxiety in children and young people and their beliefs about government responses to climate change: a global survey. *The Lancet Planetary Health*, 5(12): e863–e873.

Hill, A. (2022) UK children raise funds for Ukraine with haircuts, walks and bakes. *The Guardian*, 14 March. Available at: https://www.theguardian.com/money/2022/mar/14/uk-children-raise-ukraine-funds-charity (Accessed: 31 August 2023).

Hilton, A. (2022) The elite education of education secretaries. *Political Quarterly*, 93(1): 112–120.

HM Government (2018) *Civil Society Strategy: Building a Future That Works for Everyone*. London: Cabinet Office.

Hogg, E. (2016) Constant, serial and trigger volunteers: volunteering across the lifecourse and into older age. *Voluntary Sector Review*, 7(2): 169–190.

Hogg, E. and de Vries, R. (2018) *Different Class? Exploring the Relationship between Socio-economic Advantage and Volunteering during Adolescence*. Canterbury: University of Kent.

Holbert, A. and Waymer, L.D. (2022) Teaching race and cultural sensitivity in public relations: the case of Comic Relief and the Western savior ideology. *Public Relations Education*, 8(1): 116–131.

Holden, C. and Minty, S. (2011) Going global: young Europeans' aspirations and actions for the future. *Citizenship Teaching & Learning*, 6(2): 123–137.

Holgate, J. (2015) Community organising in the UK: a 'new' approach for trade unions? *Economic and Industrial Democracy*, 36(3): 431–455.

Holland, P. (2004) Picturing Childhood: The Myth of the Child in Popular Imagery. London: Bloomsbury.

Horgan, D., Forde, C., Martin, S. and Parkes, A. (2017) Children's participation: moving from the performative to the social. *Children's Geographies*, 15(3): 274–288.

Howard, F. (2023) Youth work, music making and activism. *Youth*. 3(3): 1053–1062.

Hutnyk, J. (2004) Photogenic poverty: souvenirs and infantilism. *Journal of Visual Culture*, 3(1): 77–94.

Inayatullah, N. and Blaney, D.L. (2012) The dark heart of kindness: the social construction of deflection. *International Studies Perspectives*, 13(2): 164–175.

Independent, The (2021) I'm 11 and pitched a tent by No 10 – then Dilyn came to say hello. 20 July. Available at: https://www.independent.co.uk/voices/max-woosey-camping-charity-boycott-your-bed-b1887091.html (Accessed: 31 August 2023).

Irfan, F. (2022) Young people power. *BBC Children in Need*. Available at: https://www.bbcchildreninneed.co.uk/grants/the-work-we-do/our-point-of-view/young-people-power/ (Accessed: 3 October 2023).

ITV News (2021) Marathon charity camper Max Woosey meets Prime Minister at Number 10 Downing Street. 10 July. Available at: https://www.itv.com/news/westcountry/2021-07-10/marathon-charity-camper-max-woosey-meets-prime-minister (Accessed: 31 August 2023).

Jang, S.J., Johnson, B.R., Kim, Y.I., Polson, E.C. and Smith, B.G. (2014) Structured voluntary youth activities and positive outcomes in adulthood: an exploratory study of involvement in scouting and subjective well-being. *Sociological Focus*, 47(4): 238–267.

Jefferess, D. (2008) Global citizenship and the cultural politics of benevolence. *Critical Literacy: Theories and Practices*, 2(1): 27–36.

Jefferies, S. (2016) 'We took on the Tories and won!' ... why Liverpool's striking schoolkids are back. *The Guardian*, 5 July. Available at: https://www.theguardian.com/artanddesign/2016/jul/05/we-took-on-the-tories-and-won-liverpool-striking-schoolkid (Accessed: 24 August 2023).

Jerome, L. and Kisby, B. (2019) *The Rise of Character Education in Britain: Heroes, Dragons and the Myths of Character*. London: Springer Nature.

Jerome, L. and Kisby, B. (2022) Lessons in character education: incorporating neoliberal learning in classroom resources. *Critical Studies in Education*, 63(2): 245–260.

Jerome, L. and Starkey, H. (2021) *Children's Rights Education in Diverse Classrooms: Pedagogy, Principles and Practices*. London: Bloomsbury.

Johnson, L. and Morris, P. (2010) Towards a framework for critical citizenship education. *The Curriculum Journal*, 21(1): 77–96.

Johnson, V. (2017) Moving beyond voice in children and young people's participation. *Action Research*, 15(1): 104–124.

Jones, C.A., Davison, A. and Lucas, C. (2023) Innocent heroes or self-absorbed alarmists? A thematic review of the variety and effects of storylines about young people in climate change discourses. *Wiley Interdisciplinary Reviews: Climate Change*, 14(6): e853.

Kamerāde, D. (2022) The same but different: a comparison between family volunteers, other formal volunteers and non-volunteers. *Voluntary Sector Review*: 1–12.

Kerr, D. and Cleaver, E. (2004) *Citizenship Education Longitudinal Study: Literature Review*. London: Department for Education.

Kidd, D. (2020) *A Curriculum of Hope: As Rich in Humanity as in Knowledge*. Carmarthen: Crown House Publishing.

Kidd, D. and Castano, E. (2013) Reading literary fiction improves theory of mind. *Science*, 342: 377–380.

Kim, J. and Morgül, K. (2017) Long-term consequences of youth volunteering: voluntary versus involuntary service. *Social Science Research*, 67: 160–175.

Kim, Y.I., Jang, S.J. and Johnson, B. (2016) Tying knots with communities: youth involvement in scouting and civic engagement in adulthood. *Nonprofit and Voluntary Sector Quarterly*, 45(6): 1113–1129.

King Jr., M. (2019) *Strength to Love*. Boston, MA: Beacon Press.

Kirkman, E., Sanders, M. and Emanuel, N. (2015) Evaluating youth social action, an interim report: does participating in social action boost the skills young people need to succeed in adult life. Behavioural Insights Team Report. Available at: https://www.bi.team/publications/evaluating-youth-social-action/ (Accessed: 17 June 2024).

Kisby, B. (2017) Politics is ethics done in public: exploring linkages and disjunctions between citizenship education and character education in England. *Journal of Social Science Education*, 16(3): 7–20.

Koss, M. (2015) Diversity in contemporary picturebooks: a content analysis. *Journal of Children's Literature*, 41(1): 32–42.

Kotzé, L.J. and Knappe, H. (2023) Youth movements, intergenerational justice, and climate litigation in the deep time context of the Anthropocene. *Environmental Research Communications*, 5(2): 025001.

Lai, O. (2022) 10 young climate activists leading the way on global climate action. *Earth.Org*, 12 August. Available at: https://earth.org/young-clim ate-activists-leading-the-way-on-global-climate-action/ (Accessed: 23 January 2024).

Lamarra, J., Chauhan, A. and Litts, B. (2019) Designing for impact: shifting children's perspectives of civic and social issues through making mobile games. In Proceedings of the 18th ACM International Conference on Interaction Design and Children, pp 274–279. Available at: https://www. researchgate.net/publication/333630165_Designing_for_Impact_Shifting_ Children's_Perspectives_of_Civic_and_Social_Issues_Through_Making_ Mobile_Games (Accessed: 14 June 2024).

Landin, C. (2017) When I camped with Corbyn – and what British politics can learn from the Woodcraft Folk. *iNews*, 11 June. Available at: https:// inews.co.uk/opinion/comment/woodcraftcorbyn-71903 (Accessed: 11 January 2024).

Larsen, N., Lee, K. and Ganea, P. (2018) Do storybooks with anthropomorphized animal characters promote prosocial behaviors in young children? *Developmental Science*, 21: e12590.

Lau, E. and Body, A. (2021) Community alliances and participatory action research as a mechanism for re-politicising social action for students in higher education. *Educational Action Research*, 29(5): 738–754.

LBC (2021) Charity camper, 11, meets PM after pitching up in No10 garden. 9 July. Available at: https://www.lbc.co.uk/news/charity-camper- 11-meets-boris-johnson-after-pitching-up-no10-garden/ (Accessed: 31 August 2023).

Leader, The (2023) Kind-hearted Wrexham boy's fundraisers for foodbanks now open. 20 May. Available at: https://www.leaderlive.co.uk/news/ 23534729.kind-hearted-wrexham-boys-fundraisers-foodbanks-now-open/ (Accessed: 6 September 2023).

Lecce, S., Bianco, F., Devine, R.T., Hughes, C. and Banerjee, R. (2014) Promoting theory of mind during middle childhood: a training program. *Journal of Experimental Child Psychology*, 126: 52–67.

Leimgruber, K.L., Shaw, A., Santos, L.R. and Olson, K.R. (2012) Young children are more generous when others are aware of their actions. *PloS One*, 7(10): e48292.

Liberty (2023) Liberty launches legal action against Home Secretary for overriding Parliament on protest powers. Available at: https://www.lib ertyhumanrights.org.uk/issue/liberty-launches-legal-action-against-home-secretary-for-overriding-parliament-on-protest-powers/ (Accessed: 31 August 2023).

Lim, M. and Moufahim, M. (2017) The spectacularization of suffering: an analysis of the use of celebrities in 'Comic Relief' UK's charity fundraising campaigns. In *Celebrity, Convergence and Transformation*. Abingdon: Routledge, pp 73–93.

Lister, R. (2008) Investing in children and childhood: a new welfare policy paradigm and its implications. In *Childhood: Changing Contexts*. Leeds: Emerald Publishing, pp 383–408.

Louis, W.R., Thomas, E., Chapman, C.M., Achia, T., Wibisono, S., Mirnajafi, Z. and Droogendyk, L. (2019) Emerging research on intergroup prosociality: group members' charitable giving, positive contact, allyship, and solidarity with others. *Social and Personality Psychology Compass*, 13(3): e12436.

Lynch, A.D., Ferris, K.A., Burkhard, B., Wang, J., Hershberg, R.M. and Lerner, R.M. (2016) Character development within youth development programs: exploring multiple dimensions of activity involvement. *American Journal of Community Psychology*, 57(1–2): 73–86.

MacQuillin, I. (2021) *Normative Fundraising Ethics: A Review of the Field*. Rogare – the Fundraising Think Tank.

MacQuillin, I. (2023) Normative fundraising ethics: a review of the field. *Journal of Philanthropy and Marketing*, 28(4): e1740.

Marshall, L., Rooney, K., Dunatchik, A. and Smith, N. (2017) Developing character skills in schools. Department for Education. Available at: https://assets.publishing.service.gov.uk/government/uploads/system/uploads/atta chment_data/file/674231/Developing_Character_skills_survey-report.pdf (Accessed: 1 August 2023).

Martin, M. (1994) *Virtuous Giving: Philanthropy, Voluntary Service, and Caring*. Indianapolis: Indiana University Press.

Martin, M. (2012) *Happiness and the Good Life*. Oxford: Oxford University Press.

Martzoukou, K. (2020) 'Maddie is online': an educational video cartoon series on digital literacy and resilience for children. *Journal of Research in Innovative Teaching & Learning*, 15(1): 64–82.

McArthur, L. (2023) To save democracy, fund organizing. *Stanford Social Innovation Review*. Available at: https://ssir.org/articles/entry/to_save_de mocracy_fund_organizing (Accessed: 1 September 2023).

McBrie, P. (2001) *Beatrice's Goat*. New York: Aladdin Paperbacks.

McFarland, D. and Thomas, R. (2006) Bowling young: how youth voluntary associations influence adult political participation. *American Sociological Review*, 71(3): 401–425.

McGuinness, A. (2019) Theresa May criticises pupils missing school to protest over climate change. Sky News, 15 February. Available at: https://news.sky.com/story/theresa-may-criticises-pupils-missing-school-to-prot est-over-climate-change-11638238 (Accessed: 18 June 2024).

McGoey, L. (2015) *No Such Thing as a Gift: The Gates Foundation and the Price of Philanthropy*. London: Verso.

McHarg, G., Fink, E. and Hughes, C. (2019) Crying babies, empathic toddlers, responsive mothers and fathers: exploring parent–toddler interactions in an empathy paradigm. *Journal of Experimental Child Psychology*, 179: 23–37.

McLaughlin, T.H. (1992) Citizenship, diversity and education: a philosophical perspective. *Journal of Moral Education*, 21(3): 235–250.

McMurry, N. (2019) The right for protest to be heard. *Diplomatic & International Relations*, 21: 93.

Meins, E., Fernyhough, C., Johnson, F. and Lidstone, J. (2006) Mind-mindedness in children: individual differences in internal-state talk in middle childhood. *British Journal of Developmental Psychology*, 24(1): 181–196.

Meister, K. (2019) *Call Me Maybe: An Analysis of the Effect of the Celebrity Persona on the American Telethon*. Honors Capstone Projects – All. 1073.

Mejias, S. and Banaji, S. (2020) Preaching to the choir: patterns of non-diversity in youth citizenship movements. In S. Meijas and S. Banaji (eds) *Youth Active Citizenship in Europe: Ethnographies of Participation*. Dordrecht: Springer International, pp 121–157.

Miller, S.A. (2009) Children's understanding of second-order mental states. *Psychological Bulletin*, 135(5): 749.

Miller, V. and Hogg, E. (2023) 'If you press this, I'll pay': MrBeast, YouTube, and the mobilisation of the audience commodity in the name of charity. *Convergence*: 13548565231161810.

Mills, S. (2022) *Mapping the Moral Geographies of Education: Character, Citizenship and Values*. Abingdon: Routledge.

Mohan, J. and Breeze, B. (2016) *The Logic of Charity: Great Expectations in Hard Times*. Dordrecht: Springer.

Moriarty, S. (2021) Modelling environmental heroes in literature for children: stories of youth climate activist Greta Thunberg. *The Lion and the Unicorn*, 45(2): 192–210.

Morris, C. (2020) Locals prevent removal of Baden-Powell statue from Poole Quay. *The Guardian*, 11 June. Available at: https://www.theguard ian.com/uk-news/2020/jun/11/scouts-founder-robert-baden-powell-sta tue-poole-storage-petition (Accessed: 8 January 2024).

Morton, A. (2021) Australian court finds government has duty to protect young people from climate crisis. *The Guardian*, 27 May. Available at: https://www.theguardian.com/australia-news/2021/may/27/austral ian-court-finds-government-has-duty-to-protect-young-people-from-clim ate-crisis (Accessed: 12 October 2023).

Morvaridi, B. (ed) (2015) *New Philanthropy and Social Justice: Debating the Conceptual and Policy Discourse.* Bristol: Policy Press.

Muddiman, E., Power, S. and Taylor, C. (2020) *Civil Society and the Family.* Bristol: Policy Press.

Murphy, P.D. (2021) Speaking for the youth, speaking for the planet: Greta Thunberg and the representational politics of eco-celebrity. *Popular Communication*, 19(3): 193–206.

Musick, M. and Wilson, J. (2007) *Volunteers: A Social Profile.* Bloomington: Indiana University Press.

Narvaez, D. (2002) Does reading moral stories build character? *Educational Psychology Review*, 14(2): 155–171.

Nasar, S. (2020) Remembering Edward Colston: histories of slavery, memory, and Black globality. *Women's History Review*, 29(7): 1218–1225.

Nickel, P.M. and Eikenberry, A.M. (2009) A critique of the discourse of marketized philanthropy. *American Behavioral Scientist*, 52(7): 974–989.

Nicotera, N. (2008) Building skills for civic engagement: children as agents of neighborhood change. *Journal of Community Practice*, 16(2): 221–242.

Nisbett, N. and Spaiser, V. (2023) Moral power of youth activists: transforming international climate politics? *Global Environmental Change*, 82 : 102717.

Nolas, S. (2014) Exploring young people's and youth workers' experiences of spaces for 'youth development': creating cultures of participation. *Journal of Youth Studies*, 17(1): 26–41.

Nolas, S. (2015) Children's participation, childhood publics and social change: a review. *Children & Society,* 29(2): 157–167.

Nonomura, R. (2017) Political consumerism and the participation gap: are boycotting and 'buycotting' youth-based activities? *Journal of Youth Studies*, 20(2): 234–251.

Nussbaum, M.C. (1998) *Cultivating Humanity.* Cambridge, MA: Harvard University Press.

Nussbaum, M.C. (2016) *Not for Profit: Why Democracy Needs the Humanities.* Princeton: Princeton University Press.

Oberman, R., Waldron, F. and Dillon, S. (2012) Developing a global citizenship education programme for three to six year olds. *International Journal of Development Education and Global Learning*, 4(1): 37–60.

Ockenden, N. and Stuart, J. (2014) *Review of Evidence on the Outcomes of Youth Volunteering, Social Action and Leadership.* London: Institute for Volunteering Research.

OECD (2019) *TALIS Starting Strong 2018 Technical Report.* Paris: OECD Publishing.

Office of High Commissioner of Human Rights (OHCHR) (2023) Children are agents of change. 13 July. Available at: https://www.ohchr.org/en/stories/2023/07/children-are-agents-change (Accessed: 24 August 2023).

Ofsted (2016) How social action is being applied to good effect in a selection of schools and colleges. Available at: assets.publishing.service.gov.uk/ (Accessed: 4 December 2023).

Ongley, S.F., Nola, M. and Malti, T. (2014) Children's giving: moral reasoning and moral emotions in the development of donation behaviors. *Frontiers in Psychology*, 5. doi: 10.3389/fpsyg.2014.00458

Ottoni-Wilhelm, M., Osili, U. and Han, X. (2023) Charitable giving role-modeling: parent transmission frequency and adolescent reception. *Oxford Economic Papers*, 75(4): 1053–1072.

Ottoni-Wilhelm, M., Zhang, Y., Estell, D. and Perdue, N. (2017) Raising charitable children: the effects of verbal socialization and role-modeling on children's giving. *Journal of Population Economics*, 30(1): 189–224.

Parent, D., Habibiazad, G. and Kelly, A. (2022) At least 58 Iranian children reportedly killed since anti-regime protests began. *The Guardian*, 20 November. Available at: https://www.theguardian.com/global-development/2022/nov/20/iran-protests-children-killed-reports-mahsa-amini (Accessed: 24 August 2023).

Parker, L., Mestre, J., Jodoin, S. and Wewerinke-Singh, M. (2022) When the kids put climate change on trial: youth-focused rights-based climate litigation around the world. *Journal of Human Rights and the Environment*, 13(1): 64–89.

Patuzzi, L. and Pinto, L.L. (2022) *Child and Youth Participation in Philanthropy: Stories of Transformation*. Philanthropy Europe Association.

Paulus, M. and Moore, C. (2012) Producing and understanding prosocial actions in early childhood. *Advances in Child Development and Behavior*, 42: 271–305.

Payne, K.A., Adair, J.K., Colegrove, K.S.S., Lee, S., Falkner, A., McManus, M. and Sachdeva, S. (2020) Reconceptualizing civic education for young children: Recognizing embodied civic action. *Education, Citizenship and Social Justice*, 15(1): 35–46.

Payton, R.L. and Moody, M.P. (2008) *Understanding Philanthropy: Its Meaning and Mission*. Bloomington: Indiana University Press.

People United (2017) *Changing the World through Arts and Kindness: Evidence from People United Projects 2007–2017*. Available at: https://peopleunited.org.uk/research/changing-the-world-through-arts-and-kindness/?doing_wp_cron=1716473856.8633630275726318359375 (Accessed: 22 May 2024).

Percy-Smith, B. and Burns, D. (2012) Exploring the role of children and young people as agents of change in sustainable community development. *Local Environment*, 18(3): 323–339.

Peterson, A. (2016) *Compassion and Education: Cultivating Compassionate Children, Schools and Communities*. New York: Springer.

Peterson, A., Civil, D. and Ritzenthaler, S. (2021) *Educating for Civic Virtues and Service: School Leaders Perspectives*. Jubilee Centre for Character and Virtues, University of Birmingham. Available at: https://www.jubileecentre.ac.uk/userfiles/jubileecentre/pdf/projects/CelebrationBritain/CivicVirtues/EducatingforCivicVirtuesandServiceInitialInsights.pdf (Accessed: 22 May 2024).

Picer, N. and Evans, R. (2006) Developing children and young people's participation in strategic processes: the experiences of the Children's Fund initiative. *Social Policy and Society*, 5(2): 177–188.

Pollen, A. (2016) Who are these folk all dressed in green? Reflections on the first fifty years of Woodcraft Folk costume evolution. In P. Harper, J. Helm, J. Nott, A. Pollen, M. Pover and N. Samson (eds) *A People's History of Woodcraft Folk*. London: The Woodcraft Folk, pp 40–45.

Pontes, A.I., Henn, M. and Griffiths, M.D. (2019) Youth political (dis)-engagement and the need for citizenship education: encouraging young people's civic and political participation through the curriculum. *Education, Citizenship and Social Justice*, 14(1): 3–21.

Power, S. and Smith, K. (2016) Giving, saving, spending: what would children do with £1 million? *Children & Society*, 30(3): 192–203.

Power, S. and Taylor, C. (2018) The mainstreaming of charities into schools. *Oxford Review of Education*, 44(6): 702–715.

Power, S., Muddiman, E., Moles, K. and Taylor, C. (2018) Civil society: bringing the family back in. *Journal of Civil Society*, 14(3): 193–206.

Prior, N. (2021) Llanelli school strike: the schoolboys who defied the cane. *BBC News*, 11 October Available at: https://www.bbc.co.uk/news/uk-wales-58775671 (Accessed: 24 August 2023).

Prout, A. and James, A. (1997) A new paradigm for the sociology of childhood? Provenance, promise and problems. In A. James and A. Prout (eds) *Constructing and Reconstructing Childhood: Contemporary Issues in the Sociological Study of Children*, 2nd edn. London: Falmer Press, pp 7–32.

Prynn, D. (1983) The Woodcraft Folk and the labour movement 1925–70. *Journal of Contemporary History*, 18(1): 79–95.

Ramsay, A. (2023) How police in England can now stop basically any protest. *Open Democracy*. Available at: https://www.opendemocracy.net/en/police-powers-ban-protest-laws-suella-braverman/ (Accessed: 31 August 2023).

Ramsey, P. (2008) Children's responses to differences. *NHSA Dialog*, 11(4): 225–237.

Redwood, H., Fairey, T. and Hasić, J. (2022) Hybrid peacebuilding in Bosnia and Herzegovina: participatory arts and youth activism as vehicles of social change. *Journal of Peacebuilding & Development*, 17(1): 42–57.

Reed, D. (2020) Why did the youth social action agenda fail? Part 1. *Medium*. Available at: https://ddotreed.medium.com/why-did-the-social-action-agenda-fail-fe7aa2862102 (Accessed: 28 December 2023).

Reich, R. (2018) *Just Giving: Why Philanthropy Is Failing Democracy and How It Can Do Better*. Princeton: Princeton University Press.

Richmond, T. (2020) How Captain Tom Moore restored British values. *Yorkshire Post*, 21 April. Available at: https://www.yorkshirepost.co.uk/news/opinion/columnists/how-captain-tom-moore-restored-british-values-tom-richmond-2543882 (Accessed: 7 September 2023).

Ritchie, D. and Ord, J. (2017) The experience of open access youth work: the voice of young people. *Journal of Youth Studies*, 20(3): 269–282.

Rivera, R. and Santos, D. (2016) Civic and political participation of children and adolescents: a lifestyle analysis for positive youth developmental programs. *Children and Society*, 30(1): 59–70.

Roche, J. (1999) Children: rights, participation and citizenship. *Childhood*, 6(4): 475–493.

Rodríguez-Garavito, C. (2022) Litigating the climate emergency: the global rise of human rights-based litigation for climate action. In C. Rodríguez-Garavito (ed) *Litigating the Climate Emergency: How Human Rights, Courts, and Legal Mobilization Can Bolster Climate Action*. Cambridge: Cambridge University Press.

Ross, E.W. and Vinson, K.D. (2013) Resisting neoliberal education reform: insurrectionist pedagogies and the pursuit of dangerous citizenship. *Cultural Logic: A Journal of Marxist Theory & Practice*, 20: 17–45.

Rosso, H. (1991) A philosophy of fundraising. In E.R. Temple (ed) *Hank Rosso's Achieving Excellence in Fundraising*. Chichester: John Wiley & Sons, pp 13–21.

Roughley, N. and Schramme, T. (eds) (2018) *Forms of Fellow Feeling*. Cambridge: Cambridge University Press.

Ruddock, J. and Flutter, J. (2004) *How to Improve Your School*. London: Continuum.

Sabherwal, A., Ballew, M.T., van der Linden, S., Gustafson, A., Goldberg, M.H., Maibach, E.W., Kotcher, J.E., Swim, J.K., Rosenthal, S.A. and Leiserowitz, A. (2021) The Greta Thunberg effect: familiarity with Greta Thunberg predicts intentions to engage in climate activism in the United States. *Journal of Applied Social Psychology*, 51(4): 321–333.

Sarre, S. and Tarling, R. (2010) The volunteering activities of children aged 8–15. *Voluntary Sector Review*, 1(3): 293–307.

Saunders, J., Munford, R. and Thimasarn-Anwar, T. (2016) Staying on-track despite the odds: factors that assist young people facing adversity to continue with their education. *British Educational Research Journal*, 42(1): 56–73.

Saunders-Hastings, E. (2022) *Private Virtues, Public Vices: Philanthropy and Democratic Equality*. Chicago: University of Chicago Press.

Schervish, P.G. (2014) Beyond altruism: philanthropy as moral biography and moral citizenship of care. In V. Jeffries (ed) *The Palgrave Handbook of Altruism, Morality, and Social Solidarity*. New York: Palgrave Macmillan, pp 389–405.

Schervish, P.G. (2006) The moral biography of wealth: philosophical reflections on the foundation of philanthropy. *Nonprofit and Voluntary Sector Quarterly*, 35(3): 477–492.

Schleicher, A. (2019) *PISA 2018: Insights and Interpretations*. Paris: OECD Publishing.

Scott, N. and Seglow, J. (2007) *Altruism*. London: McGraw-Hill Education (UK).

Scott, R., Reynolds, L. and Cadywould, C. (2016) *Character by Doing: Evaluation. Giving Schools and Non-formal Learning Providers the Confidence to Work in Partnership*. London: Demos.

Scouts (2023) Scouts Annual Report 2022–2023. Available at: https://www.scouts.org.uk/about-us/our-impacts-and-reports/scouts-annual-rep ort-2022-23/ (Accessed: 18 June 2024).

Šerek, J. and Umemura, T. (2015) Changes in late adolescents' voting intentions during the election campaign: disentangling the effects of political communication with parents, peers and media. *European Journal of Communication*, 30(3): 285–300.

Sheila McKechnie Foundation and Civil Exchange (2023) *Defending Our Democratic Space: A Call to Action*. Available at: https://smk.org.uk/wp-cont ent/uploads/2023/07/Defending-our-democratic-space_August-2023.pdf (Accessed: 31 August 2023).

Shier, H. (2001) Pathways to participation: openings, opportunities and obligations. *Children & Society*, 15(2): 107–117.

Sierksma, J., Thijs, J. and Verkuyten, M. (2014) Children's intergroup helping: the role of empathy and peer group norms. *Journal of Experimental Child Psychology*, 126: 369–383.

Silke, C., Brady, B., Boylan, C. and Dolan, P. (2018) Factors influencing the development of empathy and prosocial behaviour among adolescents: a systematic review. *Children and Youth Services Review*, 94(2018): 421–436.

Simpson, J. (2017) 'Learning to unlearn' the charity mentality within schools. *Policy & Practice: A Development Education Review*, 25: 88–108.

Small, D.A. and Verrochi, N.M. (2009) The face of need: facial emotion expression on charity advertisements. *Journal of Marketing Research*, 46(6): 777–787.

Smart, C. (2023) By reviewing the name of the Baden-Powell Award, Scouts Australia is grappling with its colonial past. *The Conversation*, 7 November. Available at: https://theconversation.com/by-reviewing-the-name-of-the-baden-powell-award-scouts-australia-is-grappling-with-its-colonial-past-216172 (Accessed: 8 January 2024).

Spiteri, J. (2020) Early childhood education for sustainability. In W. Leal Filho, A. Azul, L. Brandli, P. Ozuyar and T. Wall (eds) *Quality Education. Encyclopedia of the UN Sustainable Development Goals*. Cham: Springer, pp 185–196.

Spyrou, S. (2020) Children as future-makers. *Childhood*, 27(1): 3–7.

St Antony's Catholic Primary School (n.d.) Living wage week. Available at: https://www.stantonyscatholicprimary.co.uk/stantse7/news-and-eve nts/living-wage-week/#:~:text=Says%20headteacher%20Angela%20Mo ore%3A%20%E2%80%9CWhenever,wage%20has%20on%20their%20f amilies (Accessed: 18 June 2024).

Suissa, J. (2015) Character education and the disappearance of the political. *Ethics and Education*, 10(1): 105–117.

Sullivan, J. and Transue, J. (1999) The psychological underpinnings of democracy: a selective review of research on political tolerance, interpersonal trust, and social capital. *Annual Review of Psychology*, 50: 625–650.

Swalwell, K. and Payne, K.A. (2019) Critical civic education for young children. *Multicultural Perspectives*, 21(2): 127–132.

Tejani, M. and Breeze, H. (2021) *Citizens of Now: High Quality Youth Social Action in Primary Schools*. London: RSA.

The Matchgirls Memorial (n.d.) The story of the strike. Available at: https://www.matchgirls1888.org/the-story-of-the-strike (Accessed: 18 June 2024).

Thunberg, G. (2019) 'Our house is on fire': Greta Thunberg, 16, urges leaders to act on climate. *The Guardian*, 25 January. Available at: https://www.theguardian.com/environment/2019/jan/25/our-house-is-on-fire-greta-thunberg16-urges-leaders-to-act-on-climate

Thunberg, G. (2024) *The Climate Book: The Facts and the Solutions*. London: Penguin.

Tisdall, E.K.M. and Cuevas-Parra, P. (2022) Beyond the familiar challenges for children and young people's participation rights: the potential of activism. *International Journal of Human Rights,* 26(5): 792–810.

Torres-Harding, S., Baber, A., Hilvers, J., Hobbs, N. and Maly, M. (2018) Children as agents of social and community change: enhancing youth empowerment through participation in a school-based social activism project. *Education, Citizenship and Social Justice*, 13(1): 3–18.

Trott, C.D. (2021) What difference does it make? Exploring the transformative potential of everyday climate crisis activism by children and youth. *Children's Geographies*, 19(3): 300–308.

Tucker, Z. and Persico, Z. (2019) *Greta and the Giants*. London: Frances Lincoln.

Tyler-Rubinstein, I., Vallance, F., Michelmore, O. and Pye, J. (2016) *Evaluation of the Uniformed Youth Social Action Fund 2*. London: Evaluation.

UK Scouts (2023) Scouts wins 6.35m funding boost from DCMS Uniformed Youth Fund to support our growth work. Available at: https://www.scouts.org.uk/news/2023/april/scouts-wins-635m-funding-boost-from-dcms-uniformed-youth-fund-to-support-our-growth-work/ (Accessed: 12 August 2023).

UNICEF (2020) *Early Moments Matter*. New York: UNICEF. Available at: https://www.unicef.org/early-moments (Accessed: 12 August 2023).

United Nations (2023) Causes and effects of climate change. Available at: https://www.un.org/en/climatechange/science/causes-effects-climate-change (Accessed: 12 October 2023).

United Nations (1989) United Nations Convention on the Rights of the Child (UNCRC). Treaty no. 27541. Available at: https://www.unicef.org.uk/wpcontent/uploads/2010/05/UNCRC_united_nations_convention_on_the_rights_of_the_child.pdf (Accessed: 12 October 2023).

University of Bristol (2023) New survey reveals British public generally think disruptive, non-violent protesters should not be imprisoned. Available at: https://www.bristol.ac.uk/sps/news/2023/non-violent-protesters. html?fbclid=IwAR1hxhtXkZqbO1B6VTjW0SOv_GW6epB16Bcd_S o521vCEM2xD-DUp2Fh_wI (Accessed: 31 August 2023).

Urban Institute (2021) #65 Teaching kids how to give. 24 February. Available at: https://www.urban.org/critical-value/65-teaching-kids-how-give (Accessed: 12 October 2023).

Vaish, A., Carpenter, M. and Tomasello, M. (2009) Sympathy through affective perspective taking and its relation to prosocial behavior in toddlers. *Developmental Psychology*, 45(2): 534–543.

Vallely, P. (2020) *Philanthropy: From Aristotle to Zuckerberg*. London: Bloomsbury.

Van Deth, J.W., Abendschön, S. and Vollmar, M. (2011) Children and politics: an empirical reassessment of early political socialization. *Political Psychology*, 32: 147–174.

Veugelers, W. (2007) Creating critical-democratic citizenship education: empowering humanity and democracy in Dutch education. *Compare: A Journal of Comparative and International Education*, 37(1): 105–119.

Villanueva, E. (2018) *Decolonizing Wealth*. Oakland, CA: Berrett-Koehler Publishers Inc.

Wade, M. (2023) Kindness for clicks: MrBeast and the problem of philanthropy as spectacle. *ABC Religion and Ethics*, 21 June. Available at: https://www.abc.net.au/religion/mrbeast-and-the-problem-of-phila nthropy-as-spectacle/101998574 (Accessed: 22 October 2023).

Wang, J., Ferris, K.A., Hershberg, R.M. and Lerner, R.M. (2015) Developmental trajectories of youth character: a five-wave longitudinal study of Cub Scouts and non-Scout boys. *Journal of Youth and Adolescence*, 44: 2359–2373.

Warneken, F. and Tomasello, M. (2008) Extrinsic rewards undermine altruistic tendencies in 20-month-olds. *Developmental Psychology*, 44(6): 1785–1788.

Warneken, F. and Tomasello, M. (2009) Varieties of altruism in children and chimpanzees. *Trends in Cognitive Sciences*, 13(9): 397–402.

Weinberg, J. and Flinders, M. (2018) Learning for democracy: the politics and practice of citizenship education. *British Educational Research Journal*, 44(4): 573–592.

Weller, D. and Lagattuta, K. (2013) Helping the in-group feels better: children's judgments and emotion attributions in response to prosocial dilemmas. *Child Development*, 84(1): 253–268.

Wells, N.M. and Lekies, K.S. (2006) Nature and the life course: pathways from childhood nature experiences to adult environmentalism. *Children, Youth and Environments*, 16(1): 1–24.

Westheimer, J. and Kahne, J. (2004) What kind of citizen? The politics of educating for democracy. *American Educational Research Journal*, 41(2): 237–269.

Westheimer, J. (2015) *What Kind of Citizen? Educating Our Children for the Common Good.* New York: Teachers College Press.

White, E.S. (2021) Parent values, civic participation, and children's volunteering. *Children and Youth Services Review*, 127: 106115.

White, E.S. and Mistry, R.S. (2016) Parent civic beliefs, civic participation, socialization practices, and child civic engagement. *Applied Developmental Science*, 20(1): 44–60.

White, E.S. and Mistry, R.S. (2019) Teachers' civic socialization practices and children's civic engagement. *Applied Developmental Science*, 23(2): 183–202.

Wildeboer, A., Thijssen, S., Bakermans-Kranenburg, M.J., Jaddoe, V.W., White, T., Tiemeier, H. and van IJzendoorn, M.H. (2017) Anxiety and social responsiveness moderate the effect of situational demands on children's donating behavior. *Merrill-Palmer Quarterly*, 63(3): 340–366.

Wilhelm, M.O., Brown, E., Rooney, P.M. and Steinberg, R. (2008) The intergenerational transmission of generosity. *Journal of Public Economics*, 92(10–11): 2146–2156.

Williams, Q., Haupt, A., Alim, H.S. and Jansen, E. (2020) *Neva Again: Hip Hop Art, Activism and Education in Post-apartheid South Africa. Ethnomusicology Review*, 22(2).

Wörle, M. and Paulus, M. (2018) Normative expectations about fairness: the development of a charity norm in preschoolers. *Journal of Experimental Child Psychology*, 165: 66–84.

Wright, J.C., Warren, M.T. and Snow, N.E. (2020) *Understanding Virtue: Theory and Measurement.* Oxford: Oxford University Press.

Wuthnow, R. (1995) *Learning to Care: Elementary Kindness in an Age of Indifference.* Oxford: Oxford University Press.

Yeom, M., Caraballo, L., Tsang, G., Larkin, J. and Comrie, J. (2020) Reimagining impact: storying youth research, arts, and activism. *Review of Education, Pedagogy, and Cultural Studies*, 42(5): 482–503.

YMCA (2022) *Out of Service.* London: YMCA. Available at: https://www.ymca.org.uk/wp-content/uploads/2020/01/YMCA-Out-of-Service-report.pdf (Accessed: 6 January 2024).

Youth Climate Justice Fund (2023) *Youth Climate Justice Study.* Available at: https://ycjf.org/ (Accessed: 12 December 2023).

Zahn-Waxler, C., Schoen, A. and Decety, J. (2018) An interdisciplinary perspective on the origins of concern for others. In N. Roughley and T. Schramme (eds) *Forms of Fellow Feeling: Empathy, Sympathy, Concern and Moral Agency.* Cambridge: Cambridge University Press, pp 184–215.

Index

In the text, *child/children* and *youth* were often used interchangeably. In the index, references for *child* and *children* include *youth* as well.

References to tables appear in **bold** type.